PSYCHO HERESY

HERESY

The Psychological Seduction of Christianity

PSYCHO HERESY

The Psychological Seduction of Christianity

Martin and Deidre Bobgan

EAS GATE
Publishers
Santa Barbara, CA 93110

All Scripture quotations in this book, unless noted otherwise, are from the *New American Standard Bible*, © 1960, 1962, 1963, 1968, 1971, 1973, 1975, and 1977 by The Lockman Foundation, and are used by permission.

Verses marked KJV are taken from the King James Version of the Bible.

First Printing April 1987
Second Printing November 1987

PSYCHOHERESY: THE PSYCHOLOGICAL SEDUCTION OF CHRISTIANITY

Copyright © 1987 Martin and Deidre Bobgan
Published by EastGate Publishers
Santa Barbara, California

Library of Congress Catalog Card Number 87-080001
Trade edition ISBN 0-941717-00-3
Cloth edition ISBN 0-941717-01-1

Printed in the United States of America

To
Jay E. Adams
who has continually promoted and counseled
the truth of Scripture
rather than
the psychological opinions of men.

ACKNOWLEDGEMENTS

We wish to thank Reed Jolley and T. A. McMahon for their very helpful comments. We particularly thank Dave and Ruth Hunt for their careful, detailed and intelligent evaluation. Their strong suggestions led to many changes just when we thought the manuscript was done. They knew it needed more work and provided the specific direction that it finally took. "Faithful are the wounds of a friend."

About this book . . .

"Some people will say the Bobgans are hitting too hard—naming names and all that—but I don't think so. Whenever someone writes for the Christian public he sets forth his views to the scrutiny of others, but if others think what he says is dangerous to the church they, like Paul (who named names too), have an obligation to say so. The chapter "Amalgamania" is the best. Indeed, it should be enlarged and made into an entire book!"

> Dr. Jay E. Adams, Professor of Practical Theology, Westminster Theological Seminary, and Dean of the Institute of Pastoral Studies, Christian Counseling and Educational Foundation.

"The modern church is being inundated with human philosophy. It has been deluded into believing that psychology and psychiatry can be used to replace the eternal verities of God's Word in the redemption of mankind, Martin and Deidre Bobgan warn God's people of this great peril."

> W. Phillip Keller, author of more than thirty-five books, including *A Shepherd Looks at Psalm 23*.

"This is a book that should have been written ten years ago, and the message should be gotten to every conservative pastor in this nation today. It has a very important message for this hour."

> Dr. J. Vernon McGee, pastor and Bible teacher, Thru the Bible Radio.

"This book is devastating to those who would choose the 'psychological way.' Its research is extensive, thorough and well-documented. There are many insightful, often profound statements that point out the discrepancy between biblical counseling and psychotherapy. If Christians who practice psychotherapy read this book, they will have to increase the complexity of their mental gymnastics to justify their position. It is difficult to see how they can refute the precise biblical analysis contained in this book."

Ed Payne, M.D., Professor of Family Medicine, Medical College of Georgia, and author of *Biblical/Medical Ethics*.

"This psychoheresy is a menace and threatening to become a plague in the pulpit. Your trumpet voice is needed against what I think is nothing less than heresy."

Leonard Ravenhill, evangelist, conference speaker, and author.

"Traditionally, people sought counsel for problems in living in religion. Today, for the most part, they seek it in psychiatry and psychology. We are in grave danger of ignoring the competition and conflict between these two approaches; or worse, declaring the religious approach unscientific and therefore illegitimate. Deidre and Martin Bobgan are exceptionally able and wise protagonists and protectors of the religious—explicitly Christian—approach to counseling. Their work is important and I recommend it highly."

Thomas Szasz, M. D., Professor of Psychiatry, State University of New York, and author of numerous books.

Foreword

Experts in the secular world are increasingly expressing their disillusionment with psychotherapy and exposing both its impotence to help and its power to harm. At the same time growing numbers of Christians are awakening to the staggering fact that many church leaders, though well intentioned, are feeding psychotherapy's deadly poison to the Body of Christ. Alarmed by the accelerating psychologizing of Christianity, a larger segment of the church than most leaders realize is looking for definite answers to specific questions.

In my travels I am repeatedly confronted by those who want to know exactly where and why the teachings and practices of specified Christian psychologists are not Biblical. No one is better qualified to provide such answers than Martin and Deidre Bobgan, and this is exactly what they have done in the following pages. In so doing, they have rendered a great service to the church.

The careful and scholarly yet readable critique the Bobgans have provided is not intended to judge the hearts of the individuals they name nor to destroy their reputations. The only purpose is to examine popular and influential teachings in the light of science, logic and Scripture. Issues, not personalities, are dealt with. Christian leaders should be held accountable for what they say in books, magazines and pulpit or on radio and television. Certainly no one can object if what he has stated publicly is quoted or questioned publicly. If any church leader is granted immunity from challenge or correction, then the Reformation was in vain and we are back under the unscriptural authoritarianism of a Protestant popery.

Those who intend to influence the Body of Christ by what they say can hardly complain when others who disagree check their teachings against the Bible. Issues vital to the church and daily Christian living must be dealt with openly. For too long the false claims of Christian psychology have gone unchallenged. If its teachings are valid and Biblical, then its proponents have nothing to fear from a factual and Scriptural analysis of its tenets; and if its precepts are in fact false and dangerous, then lovers of God and truth will be grateful when error is exposed.

In this their fourth book the Bobgans have provided a valuable service for us all. The wealth of research material they have gathered makes fascinating and at times shocking reading. A vivid and important picture is presented of both secular and Christian psychology that will be informative and challenging even to students of the subject. The following pages will not only hold the interest of but intrigue and broaden the horizons of the average reader, and will serve as a valuable reference handbook for everyone. I heartily recommend this important volume.

Dave Hunt, author of numerous books including *Beyond Seduction* and coauthor of *The Seduction of Christianity*.

TABLE OF CONTENTS

Part One
PSYCHOSEDUCTION

> The seduction of Christianity is definitely not confined to fringe elements. The Freudian/Jungian myths of psychic determinism and the unconscious have been so universally accepted that these unfounded assumptions now exert a major influence upon Christian thinking throughout the church. . . . As a major vehicle of the seduction that unites most of its elements, psychology is a Trojan horse par excellence that has slipped past every barrier.
>
> Dave Hunt and T. A. McMahon
> *The Seduction of Christianity*[1]

Multitudes of Christians view psychology with respect and awe. It is paradoxical that at a time when more and more secular psychological researchers are demonstrating less and less confidence in psychological counseling, more and more Christians are pursuing it in one way or another. Christian counseling centers are springing up all over the nation offering what many believe to be the perfect combination: Christianity plus psychology. Furthermore, Christians who are not even in counseling look to what psychologists say about how to live, how to relate to others, and how to meet the challenges of life. But what are the roots of all of this psychological advice? Is psychological counseling, with all of its variations and combinations, part of the seduction of Christianity?

1
Leaven in the Loaf

See to it that no one takes you captive through philosophy
and empty deception, according to the tradition of men,
according to the elementary principles of the world, rather
than according to Christ. (Colossians 2:8)

The world offers all kinds of ideas that clearly stand in opposition to the Bible. However, the greatest problems for Christians are
not those of clear contradiction, such as direct denial of God or
blatant atheism. Jesus warned:

Watch out and beware of the leaven of the Pharisees and
Sadducees. (Matthew 16:6)

Do you not know that a little leaven leavens the whole lump
of dough? (1 Corinthians 5:6)

One of the most subtle and dangerous deceptions today is a slow-
acting poisonous leaven which is permeating the church. The
leaven easily entered the liberal branches of Christendom under the
guise of science and medicine. It gave people something to hang
onto as their faith in the inspired Word of God flagged. The leaven

then spread to conservative churches, Bible colleges, and semi-naries.

In their desire to help the sheep and expand church growth, many pastors have been adding that same leaven to the Word of God. They have been taking what appears to be good for the bleeding sheep and feeding it to the entire flock in one form or another. The leaven has been like a food additive which seems to have positive benefits, but which eventually weakens the flock.

WHAT IS THE LEAVEN?

What is this insidious leaven and why would seminaries and pastors who truly care for their flocks be promoting this leaven in the church? The leaven is psychology. Psychological leaven con-sists of secular theories and techniques which are "according to the tradition of men." They are man-made ideas which offer sub-stitutes for salvation and sanctification.

When we speak of the leaven of psychology we are not referring to the entire field of psychological study. Instead, we are referring to that part of psychology which deals with the nature of man, how he should live, and how he can change. It involves values, attitudes, and behavior. We will be using the words *psychology*, *psychological counseling*, *the psychological way*, and *psycho-therapy* interchangeably when referring to such man-made sys-tems of understanding and treatment.

Because testimonials of success and happiness abound, many eagerly follow the promises of the psychological way. However, we will be taking a hard look at what psychological systems for understanding and helping people really have to offer. We all hear and read about testimonials that claim marvelous help from psy-chology. However, few hear or read about the failures. The research that will be cited later in this book will illustrate the fact that psychological explanations about life and psychological solutions to life's problems are questionable at best, detrimental at worst, and spiritual counterfeits at least.

Although some have recognized the contradictions, failures, and false promises, many continue to think in psychological terms and turn to psychology for answers to life. Our twentieth-century culture is steeped in psychological theories and ideas. In fact, most people do not even think twice about the origin of some of the psychological ideas they take for granted.

WHAT ABOUT "CHRISTIAN PSYCHOLOGY"?

But, how does all of this relate to the church? Just because secular psychologies out in the world reek of anti-Christian bias, contradictions, and failures, does it follow that psychology in the church is also contaminated? Unfortunately what has been labeled "Christian psychology" is made up of the very same confusion of contradictory theories and techniques. Well-meaning psychologists who profess Christianity have merely borrowed the theories and techniques from secular psychology. They dispense what they believe to be the perfect blend of psychology and Christianity. Nevertheless, the psychology they use is the same as that used by non-Christian psychologists and psychiatrists. They use the theories and techniques devised by such men as Freud, Jung, Rogers, Janov, Ellis, Adler, Berne, Fromm, Maslow, and others, none of whom embraced Christianity or developed a psychological system from the Word of God.

The Christian Association for Psychological Studies (CAPS) is a group of psychologists and psychological counselors who are professing Christians. At one of their meetings the following was said:

> We are often asked if we are "Christian psychologists" and find it difficult to answer since we don't know what the question implies. We are Christians who are psychologists but at the present time there is no acceptable Christian psychology that is markedly different from non-Christian psychology. It is difficult to imply that we function in a manner that is fundamentally distinct from our non-Christian colleagues . . . as yet there is not an acceptable theory, mode of research or treatment methodology that is distinctly Christian.[1]

Although Christian psychological counselors claim to have taken only those elements of psychology that fit with Christianity, anything can be made to fit the Bible, no matter how silly or even satanic it is. Each Christian therapist brings his own individual psychology borrowed from the world to the Bible and modifies the Word to make it fit. What they use comes from the bankrupt systems of ungodly and unscientific theories and techniques.

Christians who seek to integrate psychology with Christianity have actually turned to secular, ungodly sources for help. And, because these unbiblical, unsubstantiated theories and techniques have been blended into the dough, they are well hidden in the loaf. Thus many Christians honestly believe that they are using only a purified, Christianized psychology. Instead, we are left with a contaminated loaf, not with the unleavened bread of the Word of God. A. W. Tozer declares:

> At the heart of the Christian system lies the cross of Christ with its divine paradox. The power of Christianity appears in its antipathy toward, never in its agreement with, the ways of fallen men. . . . The cross stands in bold opposition to the natural man. Its philosophy runs contrary to the processes of the unregenerate mind, so that Paul could say bluntly that the preaching of the cross is to them that perish foolishness. To try to find a common ground between the message of the cross and man's fallen reason is to try the impossible, and if persisted in must result in an impaired reason, a meaningless cross and a powerless Christianity.[2]

PSYCHOLOGICAL SEDUCTION.

The psychological seduction of Christianity is the most subtle and widespread leaven in the church. It has permeated the entire loaf and is stealthily starving the sheep. It promises far more than it can deliver and what it does deliver is not the food that nourishes Christians. Jesus said, "I am the bread of life; he who comes to Me shall not hunger, and he who believes in Me shall never thirst." (John 6:35) Jesus is "the way, the truth, and the life," not Freud, Jung, Adler, Rogers, Maslow, or Ellis or any other such men. Jesus, the apostles, and the early church did not send the sheep out to feed in other pastures. They did not turn to man-made systems either to understand the nature of man or to discover answers to the problems of living. Jesus offered Himself as the bread of life. He gives the pure water of the Word of God which springs up into eternal life.

Pastors have been called to feed the sheep the "unleavened bread of sincerity and truth." (1 Corinthians 5:8) Yet, shepherds who have been influenced by the psychological way are ministering the leaven of psychology and subjecting suffering sheep to professional psychological counseling. We are not suggesting that all pastors or all Christian leaders or all college and seminary professors or all lay people are psychologically seduced. However, we are saying that the overwhelming weight of pronouncements and practices and recommendations and referrals favors the psychological way.

The psychological seduction of Christianity is not simply a future event that may occur. It has already happened. It is not something that is about to take place or merely in the process of taking place. The leaven is already in the loaf and is spreading at incredible speed. The leaven of the psychological way has already spread beyond the pastor's office, beyond the vast referral system, and right down into the sermons. It permeates Christian media and floods the literature.

In attempting to be relevant, many preachers, teachers, counselors, and writers promote a psychological perspective of life rather than a theological one. The church has joined *The Psychological Society*[3] and has become the PSYCHOLOGICAL CHURCH. The symbol of psychology overshadows the cross of Christ, and psychological jargon contaminates the Word of God.

We have chosen the term *psychoheresy* because what we describe is a psychological heresy. It is a heresy because it is a departure from the fundamental truth of the Gospel. The departure is the use of the unproven and unscientific psychological opinions of men instead of absolute confidence in the biblical truth of God. What William Law wrote two centuries ago is even more evident today: "Man needs to be saved from his own wisdom as much as from his own righteousness, for they produce one and the same corruption."[4] Besides offering only the dregs of the broken cisterns of man-made ideas rather than the fresh springs of living water, the theories of psychological counseling poison the soul. They draw a person away from the True Bread and the Living Water. Furthermore, once a person has embraced the psychological way he becomes vulnerable to greater and greater deceptions.

The Bible is the true food for the church, but it is also an excellent hiding place for deceptive ideas. A lie placed in the midst of truth often goes unnoticed and may be as fully accepted as the Gospel Truth. In fact, the shepherds are often unaware of the deceptive nature of the leaven they are adding to the loaf. If the leaven were obviously evil, the shepherds entrusted with the care of God's flock would avoid it altogether. Those who use the psychological way of assisting people and who preach psychologized sermons have faith in psychology. They generally believe four major myths about the psychological way which we will examine in detail throughout this book.

FOUR MYTHS ABOUT PSYCHOLOGY.

① The first major myth is that psychotherapy (psychological counseling along with its theories and techniques) is science rather than religion. The supposition is that since psychotherapy is science it is truthful and objective—simply another acceptable means of understanding and helping humanity. If the shepherds thought that psychotherapy might be a competing religion, they would surely guard their sheep.

② The second major myth is that the best kind of counseling utilizes both psychology and the Bible. Those psychologists who are also Christians generally claim that they are more qualified to help people understand themselves and change than persons untrained in psychology. They also believe that they are better able to help people than those persons who are trained in psychology but are not Christians. The ranks of this group have multiplied rapidly as Christians have adopted faith in the psychological way.

③ The third major myth is that people who are experiencing mental-emotional-behavioral problems are mentally ill. They are supposedly psychologically sick and therefore need psychological therapy. The common argument is that the doctor treats the body, the psychologist treats the mind and emotions, and the minister deals strictly with spiritual things. Ministers are then supposedly unqualified to help people suffering from serious problems of living, unless they are psychologically trained.

④ The fourth major myth is that psychotherapy has a high record of success. The myth is that professional psychological counseling produces greater results than other forms of help, such as self-help or that provided by family, friends. or pastors. This promotes a further belief, that psychological counseling can be more effective in helping Christians than biblical counseling. The assumption is that because psychotherapists are trained in counseling, they are better able to serve the needs of Christians who need help with problems of living. And, that is one of the main reasons why so many Christians are training to become psychotherapists.

In examining the four major myths about the psychological way, we will uncover a great deal of research, much of which lies hidden in professional journals. Whether these myths are based upon truth or deception is of great consequence to each individual's walk with the Lord. Evaluating these beliefs is extremely important to the future condition of the church of Jesus Christ.

In this book we name people in reference to what they have taught or written. However, we want to make it clear that while we are critical of their promotion and use of psychological theories and techniques, we are not questioning their faith. We have not used as many names as possible, since the number is legion. The few examples in this book give only a small glimpse of an almost endless list. However, we hope that this brief sampling will demonstrate that there is a tremendous amount of psychologizing in and of Christianity. And, by psychologizing we mean teaching, trusting, and promoting unscientific and unproven psychological opinions in areas where the Bible has already spoken.

The rise of psychological solutions to life's problems within the church is symptomatic of the failing and falling of Christianity. It is doubly unfortunate, but Christianity's attachment to the psychological way is both umbilical and unbiblical. The attachment is umbilical in that the church has become tied to psychology and believes that it needs the nurturance of psychology to survive. And, the attachment is unbiblical because psychological ideas have displaced, replaced or unnecessarily augmented long-held biblical understandings and solutions to the problems of living. It is our desire to cut the psychological cord so that the church might once again seek only the Lord and follow His Word in confronting the issues of life.

It is the responsibility of every Christian to discern the leaven and remove it from the household of faith.

Clean out the old leaven, that you may be a new lump, just as you are in fact unleavened. For Christ our Passover also has been sacrificed. Let us therefore celebrate the feast, not with old leaven, nor with the leaven of malice and wickedness, but with the unleavened bread of sincerity and truth. (1 Corinthians 5:7-8)

The Lord Himself is the Christian's source for living and for dealing with problems of living. The Bible gives the only accurate understanding of why man is the way he is and how he is to change. The concerns of how Christians are to live and change are spiritual, not psychological matters.

2

Psychology as Religion

The Bible is full of explanations of why people behave the way they do and how they change. Beginning with Genesis, God demonstrated the basic problem of mankind: separation from God through sin. And, God provided the only lasting remedy for change: a restored relationship with God by faith in the death and resurrection of Jesus. A person's separation from God or his active relationship with God will affect every attitude, every choice, and every action. The study of mankind from any other perspective will bring about a distorted view. Although we can observe, record and report external aspects of human nature, we must turn to Scripture for explanations of why people behave the way they do and how they can change. Every other explanation must be fully in agreement with Scripture to be accurate.

Psychology deals with the very same areas of concern already dealt with in Scripture. Explanations of why people behave the way they do and how they change have concerned philosophers, theologians, cultists, and occultists throughout the centuries. Since God has given an Instruction Book on how to live, all ideas about the why's of behavior and the how's of change must be viewed as religious in nature. Whereas the Bible claims divine revelation, psychotherapy claims scientific substantiation. Nevertheless, when it comes to behavior and attitudes and morals and values, we are

11

dealing with religion, either the Christian faith or any one of a number of other religions including that of secular humanism.

Psychotherapy fits more reasonably into the category of religion than into the field of science. Those who look at psychotherapy from an analytical, research point of view have long suspected the religious nature of psychotherapy. Psychiatrist Jerome Frank says that "psychotherapy is not primarily an applied science. In some ways it more resembles a religion."[1]

Many who practice psychotherapy embrace its religious aspects. According to Victor Von Weizsaecker, "C. G. Jung was the first to understand that psychoanalysis belonged in the sphere of religion."[2] Jung himself wrote:

> Religions are systems of healing for psychic illness. . . . That is why patients force the psychotherapist into the role of a priest, and expect and demand of him that he shall free them from their distress. That is why we psychotherapists must occupy ourselves with problems which, strictly speaking, belong to the theologian.[3]

Note that Jung used the word *religions* rather than *Christianity*. Jung himself had repudiated Christianity and explored other forms of religious experience, including the occult. Without throwing out the religious nature of man, Jung dispensed with the God of the Bible and assumed his own role as priest.

ROOTS OF RELIGIOUS ALTERNATIVES.

From its very beginning psychological theories and methods of counseling created doubt about Christianity. Each great innovator of psychological theories sought an understanding about mankind apart from the revealed Word of God. Each created an unbiblical system to explain the nature of man and to bring about change. Men like Sigmund Freud (1856-1939) and Carl Jung (1875-1961) eroded confidence in Christianity and established systems in direct opposition to the Word of God. Occultism, atheism, and antagonism towards Christianity were disguised by psychological, scientific sounding language.

Sigmund Freud reduced religious beliefs to illusions and called religion "the obsessional neurosis of humanity."[4] Jung, an early follower of Freud, however, viewed all religions as collective mythologies. He did not believe they were real in essence, but that they could affect the human personality. While Freud viewed religion as the source of mental problems, Jung believed that religion was a solution. Freud argued that religions are delusionary and therefore evil. Jung, on the other hand contended that all religions are imaginary but good. Both positions are anti-Christian. One denies Christianity and the other mythologizes it.

Religious bias colored the psychological systems of both Freud and Jung. They were not dealing with science, but with values, attitudes, and behavior. And because they were working in areas about which the Bible gives the authoritative Word of God, they were developing antibiblical religions. Jay Adams says:

> Because of the teaching of the Scriptures, one is forced to conclude that much of clinical and counseling psychology, as well as most of psychiatry, has been carried on without license from God and in autonomous rebellion against Him. This was inevitable because the Word of the sovereign God of creation has been ignored.

> In that Word are "all things pertaining to life and godliness." By it the man of God "may be fully equipped for every good work." And it is that Word—and only that Word—that can tell a poor sinner how to love God with all of the heart, and mind, and soul, and how to love a neighbor with the same depth of concern that he exhibits toward himself. [5]

Professor of psychiatry and author Thomas Szasz contends, "The popular image of Freud as an enlightened, emancipated, irreligious person who, with the aid of psychoanalysis, 'discovered' that religion is a mental illness is pure fiction."[6] He says, "One of Freud's most powerful motives in life was the desire to inflict vengeance on Christianity for its traditional anti-Semitism."[7] Freud used scientific-sounding language to disguise his hostility towards religion. However, Szasz declares, "There is, in short, nothing scientific about Freud's hostility to established religion, though he tries hard to pretend that there is." Freud was not an objective observer of humanity, nor was he an objective observer of religion.

While Freud grew up in a Jewish home, Jung's father was a protestant minister. Jung's description of his early experience with Holy Communion reveals his disappointment with Christianity. He wrote:

> Slowly I came to understand that this communion had been a fatal experience for me. It had proved hollow; more than that it had proved to be a total loss. I knew that I would never again be able to participate in this ceremony. "Why, that is not religion at all," I thought. "It is an absence of God; the church is a place I should not go to. It is not life which is there, but death."[8]

This significant experience could have led Jung to deny all religions as Freud did, but he did not. For him all religions were myths which contained some truth about the human psyche. For him, psychoanalysis was a religious activity. And, since all religions held some elements about truth, he denied the authority of Scripture and the exclusive claim of Jesus Christ to be the only way of salvation.

Carl Jung repudiated Christianity and became involved in idolatry. He renamed and replaced everything Christian and everything biblical with his own mythology of archetypes. And as he moved in his own sphere of idolatry, the archetypes took form and served him as familiar spirits. He even had his own personal familiar spirit by the name of Philemon. He also participated in the occultic practice of necromancy.[9] Jung's teachings serve to mythologize Scripture and reduce the basic doctrines of the faith into esoteric gnosticism.

Rather than objective observation and scientific discovery, Freud and Jung each turned his own experience into a new belief system and called it psychoanalysis. Freud attempted to destroy the spirituality of man by reducing religion to illusion and neurosis. Jung attempted to debase the spirituality of man by presenting all religion as mythology and fantasy. Repudiating the God of the Bible, both Freud and Jung led their followers in the quest for alternative understandings of mankind and alternative solutions to problems of living. They turned inward to their own limited imaginations and viewed their subjects from their own anti-Christian subjectivity.

Because they rest on different foundations, move in contrasting directions, and rely on opposing belief systems, psychotherapy and Christianity are not now, nor were they ever, natural companions in helping individuals. The faith once delivered to the saints was displaced by a substitute faith, often disguised as medicine or science, but based upon foundations which are in direct contradiction to the Bible.

Mary Stewart Van Leeuwen indicates the impetus psychology received from those who sought to repudiate Christianity by saying, "It appears that certain of the most influential pioneers in American psychology found in it an ideal vehicle for renouncing their own Christian upbringing in the name of science."[10]

Carl Rogers is another example of one of those influential pioneers. While attending Union Theological Seminary, he and some of his fellow classmates "thought themselves right out of religious work."[11] He did not find what he was looking for in Christianity and thus turned away from his Christian upbringing and Christian calling.[12] Carl Rogers renounced Christianity and became one of the most respected leaders of humanistic psychology. He confessed, "I could not work in a field where I would be required to believe in some specified religious doctrine."[13] Psychology was attractive to him since he was interested in the "questions as to the meaning of life," but did not want to be restricted by the doctrines of Christianity.[14] Not only did Carl Rogers embrace another religion, secular humanism; he later turned to the occult. Rogers engaged in the forbidden practice of necromancy, which is communication with the dead through a medium.[15] What does a man who has repudiated Christianity have to offer the church about how to live?

From its inception, psychotherapy was developed as an alternative means of healing and help, not as an addition or complement to Christianity. It is not only a substitute method of helping troubled souls, it is a surrogate religion. Szasz contends:

> Contrition, confession, prayer, faith, inner resolution, and countless other elements are expropriated and renamed as psychotherapy; whereas certain observances, rituals, taboos, and other elements of religion are demeaned and destroyed as symptoms of neurotic or psychotic "illness."[16]

RELIGIOUS ROOTS OF MESMERISM.

The religious nature of psychological theories and methods of counseling reaches back beyond Freud to Franz Anton Mesmer. Mesmer believed that he had discovered the great universal cure of both physical and emotional problems. In 1779 he announced, "There is only one illness and one healing."[17] Mesmer presented the idea that an invisible fluid was distributed throughout the body. He called the fluid "animal magnetism" and believed that it influenced illness or health in both the mental-emotional and the physical aspects of life. He considered this fluid to be an energy existing throughout nature. He taught that proper health and mental well-being came from the proper distribution and balance of the animal magnetism throughout the body.

Mesmer's ideas may sound rather foolish from a scientific point of view. However, they were well received. Furthermore, as they were modified they formed much of the basis for present-day psychotherapy. The most important modification of mesmerism was getting rid of the magnets. Through a series of progressions, the animal magnetism theory moved from the place of the physical affect of magnets to the psychological affects of mind over matter. Thus the awkward passing of magnets across the body of a person sitting in a tub of water was eliminated.

Mesmerism became psychological rather than physical with patients moving into trance-like states of hypnosis. Furthermore, some of the subjects of mesmerism moved into deeper states of consciousness and spontaneously engaged in telepathy, precognition, and clairvoyance.[18] Gradually mesmerism evolved into an entire view of life. Mesmerism presented a new way of healing people through conversation with an intense rapport between a practitioner and his subject. Those involved in medicine used mesmerism in their investigation of supposed unseen reservoirs of potential for healing within the mind.

The theories and practices of mesmerism greatly influenced the up-and-coming field of psychiatry with such early men as Jean-Martin Charcot, Pierre Janet, and Sigmund Freud. These men used information gleaned from patients in the hypnotic state.[19] The followers of Mesmer promoted the ideas of hypnotic suggestion, healing through talking, and mind-over-matter. Thus, the three main thrusts of Mesmer's influence were hypnosis, psychotherapy, and positive thinking.

Although hypnosis had been used for centuries in various occultic activities, including medium trances, Mesmer and his followers brought it into the respectable realm of Western medicine. And, with the shift in emphasis from the physical manipulation of magnets to so-called psychological powers hidden in the depths of the mind, mesmerism moved from the physical to the psychological and spiritual.

Mesmerism incited much interest in America as a Frenchman by the name of Charles Poyen lectured and conducted exhibitions during the 1830's. Audiences were impressed with the feats of mesmerism because hypnotized subjects would spontaneously exercise clairvoyance and mental telepathy. While under the spell, subjects could also experience and report deeper levels of consciousness in which they could feel utter unity with the universe—beyond the confines of space and time. Furthermore, they could give apparent supernatural information and diagnose diseases telepathically. This led people to believe that great untapped powers of the mind were available to them.[20]

The thrust of mesmerism also changed directions in America.[21] In his book *Mesmerism and the American Cure of Souls*, Robert Fuller describes how it promised great psychological and spiritual advantages. Its promises for self-improvement, spiritual experience, and personal fulfillment were especially welcomed by unchurched individuals. Fuller says that mesmerism offered "an entirely new and eminently attractive arena for self-discovery—their own psychological depths." He says that "its theories and methods promised to restore individuals, even unchurched ones, into harmony with the cosmic scheme."[22] Fuller's description of mesmerism in America is an accurate portrayal of twentieth-century psychotherapy as well as of so-called mind-science religions.

The users of mesmerism did not suspect the occultic connections of hypnosis. Both the practitioners and subjects believed that hypnosis revealed untapped reservoirs of human possibility and powers. They believed that these powers could be used to understand the self, to attain perfect health, to develop supernatural gifts, and to reach spiritual heights. Thus, the goal and impetus for discovering and developing human potential grew out of mesmerism and stimulated the growth and expansion of psychotherapy, positive thinking, the human potential movement, and the mind-science religions.

Mesmer's far reaching influence gave an early impetus to scientific-sounding religious alternatives to Christianity. And he started the trend of medicalizing religion into treatment and therapy. Nevertheless, he only gave the world false religion and false hope. Professor of psychiatry Thomas Szasz describes Mesmer's influence this way:

> Insofar as psychotherapy as a modern "medical technique" can be said to have a discoverer, Mesmer was that person. Mesmer stands in the same sort of relation to Freud and Jung as Columbus stands in relation to Thomas Jefferson and John Adams. Columbus stumbled onto a continent that the founding fathers subsequently transformed into the political entity known as the United States of America. Mesmer stumbled onto the literalized use of the leading scientific metaphor of his age for explaining and exorcising all manner of human problems and passions, a rhetorical device that the founders of modern depth psychology subsequently transformed into the pseudomedical entity known as psychotherapy.[23]

PSYCHOLOGY OR RELIGION?

Critics of the scientific facade of psychotherapy have especially noted its religious nature. Nobelist Richard Feynman, in considering the scientific status of psychotherapy, says that "psychoanalysis is not a science" and that it is "perhaps even more like witch-doctoring."[24] Lance Lee refers to "psychoanalysis as a religion hidden beneath scientific verbiage," and as a "substitute religion for both practitioner and patient."[25]

Professor Perry London, in his book *The Modes and Morals of Psychotherapy*, points out that psychotherapists constitute a priesthood.[26] Psychiatrist Jerome Frank says that the psychiatrist "cannot avoid infringing on the territory of religion."[27] One writer refers to "the 'Jehovah effect' in which the therapist recreates patients into his own image."[28]

Psychiatrist Thomas Szasz, in his book *The Myth of Psychotherapy*, says, "The basic ingredients of psychotherapy are religion, rhetoric, and repression.,"[29] He points out that while psychotherapy does not always involve repression, it does always involve religion and rhetoric. By "rhetoric" Szasz means "conversation." Just as conversation is always present in psychotherapy, so too is religion. Szasz says very strongly that "the human relations we now call 'psychotherapy,' are, in fact, matters of religion—and that we mislabel them as 'therapeutic' at great risk to our spiritual well-being."[30] Elsewhere Szasz refers to psychotherapy as religion:

> It is not merely a religion that pretends to be a science, it is actually a fake religion that seeks to destroy true religion.[31]

He warns us of "the implacable resolve of psychotherapy to rob religion of as much as it can, and to destroy what it cannot."[32] Christopher Lasch, author of *The Culture of Narcissism* would probably agree since he says, "Therapy constitutes an anti-religion."[33] It is a fake religion that is "anti" the true religion of the Bible.

CURE OF SOULS OR CURE OF MINDS?

There was a cure of souls ministry which existed in the early church and was practiced up to the present century. In this ministry there was a dependence on the Bible for understanding the human condition and for relieving troubled minds. Prayer and healing in the early church were not limited to small problems, but covered all personal disturbances. The cure of souls ministry dealt with all nonorganic mental-emotional-personal problems of living.

With the rise of psychological counseling in the twentieth century, biblical counseling waned until presently it is almost nonexistent. The cure of souls, which once was a vital ministry of the church, has now in this century been displaced by a cure of minds called "psychotherapy." The authors of *Cults and Cons* note this shift:

> For many, traditional religion no longer offers relevant answers and more and more people are seeking answers in strange, new packages. Thousands, if not millions, are turning to that part of psychology which promises *the*

answer and an effortless, painless ride into the Promised
Land, perfectly meeting our present and prevailing need
for quick solutions to hard problems.[34] (Emphasis theirs).

Martin Gross observes:

When educated man lost faith in formal religion, he
required a substitute belief that would be as reputable in
the last half of the twentieth century as Christianity was in
the first. Psychology and psychiatry have now assumed
that role.[35]

Carl Rogers confesses, "Yes, it is true, psychotherapy is subver-
sive. . . . Therapy, theories and techniques promote a new model of
man contrary to that which has been traditionally acceptable."[36]
    Bernie Zilbergeld, in his book *The Shrinking of America: Myths
of Psychological Change*, says:

Psychology has become something of a substitute for old
belief systems. Different schools of therapy offer visions
of the good life and how to live it, and those whose
ancestors took comfort from the words of God and wor-
shipped at the altars of Christ and Yahweh now take solace
from and worship at the altars of Freud, Jung, Carl Rogers,
Albert Ellis, Werner Erhard, and a host of similar
authorities. While in the past the common reference point
was the Bible and its commentaries and commentators, the
common reference today is a therapeutic language and the
success stories of mostly secular people changers.[37]

Christopher Lasch charges that the "contemporary climate is
therapeutic, not religious," and says, "People today hunger not for
personal salvation . . . but for the feeling, the momentary illusion of
personal well-being, health and psychic security."[38]
    Lasch says, "The medicalization of religion facilitated the rap-
prochement between religion and psychiatry."[39] As soon as
religious problems were medicalized (made into diseases), they
became psychiatric problems. Problems of thought and behavior,
once considered to be the concern of clergymen, were transformed
into medical, and therefore supposedly scientific problems. They

were then transferred from the church to the couch. In referring to this change from the spiritual to the psychological and from religion to science, Szasz says:

> Educated in the classics, Freud and the early Freudians remolded these images into, and renamed them as, medical diseases and treatments. This metamorphosis has been widely acclaimed in the modern world as an epoch-making scientific discovery. Alas, it is, in fact, only the clever and cynical destruction of the spirituality of man, and its replacement by a positivistic "science of mind."[40]

As we have noted elsewhere:

> The recipe was simple. Replace the cure of souls with the cure of minds by confusing an abstraction (mind) with a biological organ (brain), and thus convince people that mental healing and medical healing are the same. Stir in a dash of theory disguised as fact. Call it all science and put it into medicine and the rest is history. With the rise in psychotherapy, there was a decline in the pastoral cure of souls until it is now almost nonexistent.[41]

Szasz also says that "psychotherapy is a modern, scientific-sounding name for what used to be called the 'cure of souls.'"[42] One of his primary purposes for writing *The Myth of Psychotherapy* was:

> ... to show how, with the decline of religion and the growth of science in the eighteenth century, the cure of (sinful) souls, which had been an integral part of the Christian religions, was recast as the cure of (sick) minds, and became an integral part of medicine.[43]

The words *sinful* and *sick* in parentheses are his. By replacing the word *sinful* with the word *sick* and by replacing the word *soul* with the word *mind*, psychological practitioners have supplanted spiritual ministers in matters that have more to do with religion and values than with science and medicine.

Of course the central aspect of the cure of souls was to bring a person into a right relationship with God. Souls were "cured" through confession, repentance, and forgiveness. By following the biblical patterns set forth by Jesus and the Apostles, individuals will learn to live abundant lives. They will find comfort and strength in the midst of problems and wisdom to know what to do. Furthermore, as ordinary human beings receive the life of God into their own being through the Holy Spirit they have an inward Guide as well as the written Word.

PSYCHOTHERAPY AS RELIGION.

Although all forms of psychotherapy are religious, the fourth branch of psychology—the transpersonal—is more blatantly religious than the others. Transpersonal psychologies involve faith in the supernatural. They include the belief that there is something beyond the natural, physical universe. However, the spirituality they have to offer includes mystical experiences of both the occult and Eastern religions. Although they are very religious and attempt to meet the spiritual needs of individuals, they are in direct contradiction to the Bible. Any religion that claims to be the only way is anathema to transpersonal psychologies. According to them, it's alright to believe anything, no matter how ridiculous, as long as one does not contend that there is only one way.

Through such transpersonal psychotherapies various forms of Eastern religion are creeping into Western life. Psychologist Daniel Goleman quotes Chogyam Trungpa as saying, "Buddhism will come to the West as psychology." Goleman points out how Oriental religions "seem to be making gradual headway as psychologies, not as religions."[44] Jacob Needleman says:

> A large and growing number of psychotherapists are now convinced that the Eastern religions offer an understanding of the mind far more complete than anything yet envisaged by Western science. At the same time, the leaders of the new religions themselves—the numerous gurus and spiritual teachers now in the West—are reformulating and adapting the traditional systems according to the language and atmosphere of modern psychology.

He further notes:

> With all these disparate movements, it is no wonder that

thousands of troubled men and women throughout America no longer know whether they need psychological or spiritual help. The line is blurred that divides the therapist from the spiritual guide.[45]

Karl Kraus, a Viennese journalist, wrote,

Despite its deceptive terminology, psychoanalysis is not a science but a religion—the faith of a generation incapable of any other.[46]

The same could be said of the various psychotherapies which have followed psychoanalysis. The tragedy is that few in the church recognize that psychotherapy, though attiring itself in the garb of science, is as naked as the emperor in "The Emperor's New Clothes." And sadder yet is the great admiration for this pseudogarment.

Because psychotherapy deals with meaning in life, values, and behavior, it is religion in theory and in practice. Every branch of psychotherapy is religious. Therefore, combining Christianity with psychotherapy is joining two or more religious systems. Psychotherapy cannot be performed and people cannot be transformed without affecting a person's beliefs. Because psychotherapy involves morals and values, it is religion.

Psychological theories and methods continue to subvert Christianity. Rather than being directly antagonistic, however, promoters of psychology have covertly weakened the faith. By offering a substitute for the cross of Christ, purveyors of the psychological way encourage the pseudo faith described by A. W. Tozer:

Many of us Christians have become extremely skillful in arranging our lives so as to admit the truth of Christianity without being embarrassed by its implications. We arrange things so that we can get on well enough without divine aid, while at the same time ostensibly seeking it. We boast in the Lord but watch carefully that we never get caught depending on Him. "The heart is deceitful above all things, and desperately wicked: who can know it?"

Pseudo faith always arranges a way out to serve in case

God fails it. Real faith knows only one way and gladly
allows itself to be stripped of any second way or makeshift
substitutes. For true faith, it is either God or total collapse.
And not since Adam first stood up on the earth has God
failed a single man or woman who trusted Him.

The man of pseudo faith will fight for his verbal creed but
refuse flatly to allow himself to get into a predicament
where his future must depend upon that creed being true.
He always provides himself with secondary ways of escape
so he will have a way out if the roof caves in.

What we need very badly these days is a company of
Christians who are prepared to trust God as completely
now as they know they must do at the last day. [47]

Christianity is more than a religion. It is relationship with the
Creator of the universe. It is relationship with God the Father
through the costly price of the cross of Christ. It is the indwelling
presence of the Holy Spirit. Christians are called to live by the very
life of God. Paul prayed for believers to live by faith:

For this reason also, since the day we heard of it, we have
not ceased to pray for you and to ask that you may be filled
with the knowledge of His will in all spiritual wisdom and
understanding, so that you may walk in a manner worthy
of the Lord, to please Him in all respects, bearing fruit in
every good work, and increasing in the knowledge of God;
strengthened with all power, according to His glorious
might, for the attaining of all steadfastness and patience;
joyously giving thanks to the Father, who has qualified us
to share in the inheritance of the saints in light. For He
delivered us from the domain of darkness, and transferred
us to the kingdom of His beloved Son, in whom we have
redemption, the forgiveness of sins. (Colossians 1:9-14)

Paul then admonished:

As you therefore have received Christ Jesus the Lord, so
walk in Him, having been firmly rooted and now being

built up in Him and established in your faith, just as you were instructed, and overflowing with gratitude.

See to it that no one takes you captive through philosophy and empty deception, according to the tradition of men, according to the elementary principles of the world, rather than according to Christ. For in Him all the fulness of Deity dwells in bodily form, and in Him you have been made complete, and He is the head over all rule and authority. (Colossians 2:6-10)

3

Science or Pseudoscience?

Men and women of God seek wisdom and knowledge both from the written revelation of Scripture and from the physical world. Paul contends that everyone is accountable before God because of God's evidence of Himself in creation:

> For since the creation of the world His invisible attributes, His eternal power and divine nature, have been clearly seen, being understood through what has been made, so that they are without excuse. (Romans 1:20)

And David sang:

> The heavens are telling of the glory of God;
> And their expanse is declaring the work of His hands.
> (Psalms 19:1)

As Christians examine the universe, their faith in a God who is both creator and sustainer will cause them to see regularities and consistent patterns. Therefore, scientific study and discovery can be very useful in many walks of life.

Scientists develop theories based on what they observe. Then they examine each theory with rigorous tests to see if it accurately describes reality. The scientific method works well in observing and recording physical data and in reaching conclusions which form the theories. Therefore, scholars who desired to study human nature hoped to be able to apply the scientific method to observe, record, and treat human behavior. They figured that if people could be studied in a scientific manner there would be more accuracy in understanding present behavior, in predicting future behavior, and in altering behavior through some kind of scientific intervention.

AN ELUSIVE DREAM.

The dream of a scientific study of human nature and a scientific method of treating unacceptable behavior was most alluring. The hoped-for science of behavior promised much to those who had been struggling to unravel the vast complexities of individual personalities in equally complex circumstances. Thus, through study and imagination, psychologists pursued the dream of discovering scientific methods of observing, explaining, and transforming human behavior.

Psychology and its active arm of psychotherapy have indeed adopted the scientific posture. However, from a strictly scientific point of view they have not been able to meet the requirements. In attempting to evaluate the status of psychology, the American Psychological Association appointed Sigmund Koch to plan and direct a study which was subsidized by the National Science Foundation. This study involved eighty eminent scholars in assessing the facts, theories, and methods of psychology. The results of this extensive endeavor were then published in a seven volume series entitled *Psychology: A Study of a Science*.[1] Koch describes the delusion from which we have been suffering in thinking about psychology as a science:

> The *hope* of a psychological science became indistinguishable from the *fact* of psychological science. The entire subsequent history of psychology can be seen as a ritualistic endeavor to emulate the forms of science in order to sustain the delusion that it already *is* a science.[2] (Emphasis his.)

Koch also says: "Throughout psychology's history as 'science,'

the *hard* knowledge it has deposited has been uniformly negative."[3] (Emphasis his.)

SCIENCE OR OPINION?

Psychological statements which describe human behavior or
which report results of research can be scientific. However, when
we move from describing human behavior to explaining it and
particularly changing it, we move from science to opinion. An
example of this difference is found in the phenomenon called the
Stockholm syndrome.

The Stockholm syndrome sometimes occurs when persons are
taken hostage in bank robberies. Under these circumstances, some
captives identify with and desire to protect their captors. Captives
sometimes fear the police more than they fear the robbers and have
been known to become voluntary shields for their captors to protect
them from being shot by the police. SWAT teams are aware that
certain captives cannot be counted on for help and that some
hostages will oppose the police who are trying to save them.

Such a description of human behavior under adverse circumstances may be factual. Captives sometimes do behave in ways just
described.[4] However, the explanations of this behavior are opinions
and vary from one "expert" to another. An FBI report explains the
behavior in this way:

> The Stockholm syndrome is viewed by this author as
> regression to a more elementary level of development than
> is seen in the five-year-old who identifies with a parent.
> The five-year old is able to feed himself, speak for himself
> and has locomotion. The hostage is more like the infant
> who must cry for food, cannot speak and may be bound.
>
> The infant is blessed with a mother figure who sees to his
> needs. As these needs are satisfactorily met by the mother
> figure, the child begins to love this person who is protect-
> ing him from the outside world. So it is with the hostage—
> his extreme dependence, his every breath a gift from the
> subject. He is now as dependent as he was as an infant; the
> controlling, all-powerful adult is again present; the outside
> world is threatening once again. . . . So the behavior that

worked for the dependent infant surfaces again as a coping device, a defense mechanism, to lead the way to survival.[5]

The writer of the FBI report presents only one of many possible explanations of the phenomenon. The *description* of this syndrome to the extent that it is accurate is factual, but the *explanation* is merely opinion. Whenever we move from *what* happened in human behavior to *why* it happened, and especially how to change human behavior, we move from science to conjecture.

The move from description to prescription is a move from objectivity to opinion. And such opinion about human behavior presented as truth or scientific fact is merely pseudoscience. It rests upon false premises (opinions, guesses, subjective explanations) and leads to false conclusions.

PSEUDOSCIENCE.

One part of the total discipline of psychology which is riddled with pseudoscience is that of psychotherapy. The dictionary defines *pseudoscience* as "a system of theories, assumptions, and methods erroneously regarded as scientific."[6] Pseudoscience or pseudoscientism includes the use of the scientific label to protect and promote opinions which are neither provable nor refutable.

If psychotherapy had succeeded as a science, then we would have some concensus in the field regarding mental-emotional-behavioral problems and how to treat them. Instead, the field is filled with many contradictory theories and techniques, all of which communicate confusion rather than anything approximating scientific order.

In a book titled *The Sorcerer's Apprentice*, Mary Stewart Van Leeuwen, a professor of psychology, reveals "that the apprenticeship of psychology to natural science . . . does not work."[7] Psychiatrist Lee Coleman titled his book about psychiatry *The Reign of Error*. In this book he demonstrates that "psychiatry does not deserve the legal power it has been given" and that "psychiatry is not a science."[8] He says:

> I have testified in over one hundred and thirty criminal and civil trials around the country, countering the authority of psychiatrists or psychologists hired by one side or the

other. In each case I try to educate the judge or jury about why the opinions produced by these professionals have no scientific merit.[9]

Now as never before, the status of psychotherapy as science has been questioned. However, psychotherapists persistently claim to operate under scientific principles and consider themselves solidly scientific. Research psychiatrist Jerome Frank says that most psychotherapists "share the American faith in science. They appeal to science to validate their methods just as religious healers appeal to God."[10]

TRUTH OR CONFUSION?

Psychotherapy proliferates with many conflicting explanations of man and his behavior. Psychologist Roger Mills, in his article "Psychology Goes Insane, Botches Role as Science," says:

> The field of psychology today is literally a mess. There are as many techniques, methods and theories around as there are researchers and therapists. I have personally seen therapists convince their clients that all of their problems come from their mothers, the stars, their bio-chemical make-up, their diet, their life-style and even the "kharma" from their past lives.[11]

Rather than knowledge being added to knowledge with more recent discoveries resting on a body of solid information, one system contradicts or disenfranchises another, one set of opinions is exchanged for another, and one set of techniques is replaced by another.

As culture and life styles change, so does psychotherapy. With over 250 separate systems, each claiming superiority over the rest, it is hard to view so many diverse opinions as being scientific or even factual. The entire field is amassed in confusion and crowded with pseudo-knowledge and pseudo-theories resulting in pseudo-science.

"ALL TRUTH IS GOD'S TRUTH"?

In spite of this hodge-podge of unscientific opinions and contradictions, those who call themselves "Christian psychologists" proclaim, "All truth is God's truth." They use this statement to support their use of psychology, but they are not clear about what God's truth is. Is God's truth Freudian pronouncements of obsessive neurosis? Or is God's truth Jung's structure of arche- types? Or is God's truth Rogers's ideas on human love? Or is God's truth the behaviorism of B. F. Skinner? Or is God's truth "I'm OK; You're OK"?

Psychology, as well as many other religions, will include ele- ments of truth. Even Satan's temptation of Eve included both truth and lie. The enticement of the "All truth is God's truth" fallacy is that there is some similarity between the Biblical teachings and the psychological ideas. Similarities do not make psychology com- patible with Christianity. They merely indicate that the systems of psychological counseling are indeed religious. There are just as many similarities between Christianity and other world religions as between Christianity and psychology. The scriptures of the Hindu, Buddhist, and Moslem faiths contain statements about attitudes and behavior which may be similar to some Bible verses. Chris- tians should no more turn to psychologists than to leaders of non- Christian faiths to find wisdom and help with problems of living.

Since there is not one standardized Christian psychology, each so-called Christian psychologist decides for himself which of the many psychological opinions and methods constitute his ideas of "God's truth." In so doing, the subjective observations and biased opinions of mere mortals are placed on the same level as the inspired Word of God. Perhaps they think that what has been observed in nature by the limited minds of men equals God's truth. The Bible contains the only pure truth of God. All else is distorted by the limitations of human perception. Whatever else one can discover about God's creation is only partial knowledge and partial understanding. It cannot be equal to God's truth.

The statement "All truth is God's truth" is discussed in the popular *Baker Encyclopedia of Psychology*. The book claims that its contributors are "among the finest evangelical scholars in the field."[12] In the section on "Christian Psychology," natural revela- tion (e.g. the physical world and how it functions) is touted as supporting special revelation as if God's Word needs substantia- tion, confirmation, expansion, or any other kind of support. In his review of this book, Dr. Ed Payne, Associate Professor of Medicine at Medical College of Georgia, says, "Almost certainly the message of the book and its authors is that the Bible and psychological literature stand on the same authoritative level."[13] This book merely reflects what the church has come to accept. Unscientific, unsubstantiated, unproven psychological opinions of men have now been leavened into the church through the semantic sorcery of "All truth is God's truth." The equating of psychology and theology reveals that the leaven has now come to full loaf.

The terms used for the hoped for hybridizing of the psychological way and the biblical way are *integration* or *amalgamation*. The goal is to integrate or amalgamate the truth of Scripture with the so-called truth of psychology to produce a hybrid that is superior to the truth of each. However, there is an assumption that psychological "truth" is scientific truth. The faulty foundation of this amalgamation is "All truth is God's truth." This slogan seems to be the alpha and omega of the amalgamationists.

Dr. Gary Collins, a popular psychologist and psychologizer of Christianity, is professor and chairman of the Division of Pastoral Counseling and Psychology at Trinity Evangelical Divinity School. He is the author and editor of more than twenty books. In his book *Psychology and Theology: Prospects for Integration*, Collins says:

> . . . there will be no conflict or contradiction between truth as revealed in the Bible (studied by Bible scholars and theologians), and truth as revealed in nature (studied by scientists, including psychologists and other scholars).[14]

He uses this as a basis for integrating psychology and theology. However he does not define integration or what brands of psychology and theology he hopes to integrate.

Dr. John Carter and Dr. Bruce Narramore, both of Rosemead Graduate School of Psychology, have written a book titled *The Integration of Psychology and Theology*.[15] Carter and Narramore refer to and repeat, "All truth is God's truth." This has obviously become the abracadabra of integrationists. The incantation is sprinkled throughout their book as it is in the writings of others who espouse the amalgamationists' position. Such books repeatedly state, but cannot support, the "all truth is God's truth" platitude. They talk about it but cannot demonstrate the connection between "all truth is God's truth" and so-called psychological truth. The lack of uniformity in psychological theories and practices among those who preach integration should prove that theological-psychological amalgamania is in a sad state of confusion.

After looking at the over 250 competing and often contradictory therapies and over 10,000 not-always-compatible techniques, and after surveying Christian therapists and finding how little consistency there is among them in what they practice and in how great the variety of their approaches, one has to conclude that the integrationists make what they call "God's truth" look more than just a little confused. As we shall show later, when one reviews all of the research and considers all of the researchers one can also conclude that if the integrationists are referring to psychotherapy as science (truth), one gets the impression that God's truth is very unscientific. The use of psychotherapy in Christianity is not a testimony to science. It is a testimony to how much the church can be deceived.

Biblical theology did without psychology for almost two thousand years. The prophets of the Old Testament, the disciples and apostles of the New Testament, and the saints right up to the present century did very well without psychology. Why would the church need the modern-day psychologizers now? We shudder to think of what a twentieth-century psychologist would have said to Ezekiel seeing "a wheel in the middle of a wheel," or to Elijah hearing "a still small voice," or Isaiah seeing "the Lord sitting upon a throne, high and lifted up," or Peter and his vision of unclean things, or the man who was caught up to the third heaven.

To even hint that the often-conflicting discoveries of such unredeemed men as Freud, Jung, Rogers, etc. are God's truth is to undermine the very Word of God. The revealed Word of God does not need the support or the help of psychological pronouncements. The Word alone stands as the truth of God. That psychologists who call themselves Christian would even use such a phrase to justify their use of psychology indicates the direction of their faith. William Law's concern about adding the wisdom of men to the Word of God in matters of who we are and how we are to live are perhaps more applicable today than when he wrote them. He warned:

What is the source of all this spiritual blindness which

from age to age thus mistakes and defeats all the gracious designs of God towards fallen mankind? Look at the origin of the first sin, and you have it all. Had Eve desired no knowledge but that which came from God, Paradise had still been the habitation of her and of all her offspring. . . .

But now corruption, sin, death, and every evil of the world have entered into the Church, the spouse of Christ, just as they entered into Eve, the spouse of Adam, in Paradise. And in the very same way, and from the same cause: namely, a desire for knowledge other than that which comes from the inspiration of the Spirit of God alone. This desire is the serpent's voice in every man, doing everything to him and in him which Satanic deception did to Eve in the garden. It carries on the first deceit, it shows and recommends to him that same beautiful tree of human wisdom, self-will, and self-esteem springing up within him, which Eve saw in the garden.[16]

Psychotherapy is not science. It is not scientific theory. Psychotherapy rests upon the erroneous assumption that problems of thinking and living constitute illnesses or pathologies and therefore require cures by psychologically trained professionals. One writer very wisely pointed out that the prevailing popular psychotherapeutic systems merely reflect the current culture.[17] We know that the truths of Scripture are eternal. But, which psychological "truths" are eternal? It is unfortunate that Christians have followed the psychological way and its pseudosolutions to real problems.

Because of psychotherapy's nonstatus as a science and because it is nonsense as medicine, people who choose psychotherapy do so by faith. They believe the claims of psychotherapy rather than the research evidence. Psychotherapy falls short of the objectivity and testability of science. As we have said elsewhere, "Psychotherapy is not a coherent science in principle or in theory, diagnosis, or treatment."[18]

SCIENTIFIC FACADE.

Many critics in the field recognize the pseudo-scientific nature of psychotherapy. Psychiatrist-lawyer Jonas Robitscher, in his book *The Powers of Psychiatry*, says regarding the scientific status of psychiatric advice:

> His advice is followed because he is a psychiatrist, even though the scientific validity of his advice and recommendations has never been firmly established.[19]

Robitscher also says, "The infuriating quality of psychiatrists is . . . their insistence that they are scientific and correct and that their detractors, therefore, must be wrong."[20] Research psychiatrist E. Fuller Torrey is even more blunt when he says:

> The techniques used by Western psychiatrists are, with few exceptions, on exactly the same scientific plane as the techniques used by witch doctors.[21]

Torrey also says, "If anything, psychiatric training may confer greater ability to rationalize subjective conviction as scientific fact."[22]

Walter Reich refers to "the sudden recognition among psychiatrists that, even as a *clinical* enterprise, psychoanalysis and the approaches derived from it are neither scientific nor effective."[23] Reich mentions "the dangers of ideological zeal in psychiatry, the profession's preference for wishful thinking to scientific knowledge, and the backlash that is provoked, perhaps inevitably, when the zeal devours the ideology and the wish banishes the science."[24]

Linda Riebel, in an article titled "Theory as Self-Portrait and the Ideal of Objectivity," points out clearly that "theories of human nature reflect the theorist's personality as he or she externalizes it or projects it onto humanity at large." She says, " . . . the theory of human nature is a self-portrait of the theorist . . . emphasizing what the theorist needs."[25] Her main point is that theorizing in psychotherapy "cannot transcend the individual personality engaged in that act."[26]

Karl Popper, who is considered to be one of the most influential thinkers today and considered by many to be the greatest twentieth-century philosopher of science, has examined psychological theories having to do with the why of human behavior and the what to do about it. He says that these theories, "though posing as sciences, had in fact more in common with primitive myths than with science; that they resembled astrology rather than astronomy." He also says, "These theories describe some facts but in the manner of myths. They contain most interesting psychological suggestions, but not in testable form."[27]

Psychologist Carol Tavris compares astrology and psychological determinism. She says:

> Now the irony is that many people who are not fooled by astrology for one minute subject themselves to therapy for years, where the same errors of logic and interpretation often occur.[28]

Jerome Frank also refers to psychotherapies as myths because "they are not subject to disproof."[29] One can devise a system of explaining all human behavior and then interpret all behavior in the light of that explanation. This is just as true of psychotherapeutic theories as it is true of graphology, astrology, and other such "ologies."

Crucial to a science is the possibility of not only refuting theories but also predicting future events, reproducing results obtained, and controlling what is observed. Lewis Thomas says, "Science requires, among other things, a statistically significant number of reproducible observations and, above all, controls."[30]

As we move from the natural sciences to the so-called behavioral sciences, we move away from refutability, predictability, reproducibility, and controllability. In addition, the cause and effect relationship, so evident in the natural sciences, is ambiguous or absent in the behavioral "sciences." Instead of causation (cause and effect), psychotherapy rests heavily upon covariation (events which appear together which may not necessarily be related.) From cause and effect, where there is a direct relationship, psychotherapy utilizes covariation even though the events which seem to be related may in fact have nothing to do with each other.

There is a great temptation to assume that when two events occur together (covariation) one must have caused the other. This is the basis of much superstition. For example, if one walks under a ladder and then has "bad luck," a cause and effect relationship is assumed and one then avoids walking under ladders for fear of "bad luck." This type of superstitious relationship occurs often in the behavioral "sciences." The superstitious nonscientific illusions of psychotherapy are many.

Psychotherapy escapes the rigors of science because the mind is not equal to the brain and man is not a machine. Psychotherapy deals with individuals who are unique and possess a will. Interaction in a therapeutic setting involves the individuality and volition of both the therapist and the person being counseled. Additionally, there are variables of time and changing circumstances in the lives of both therapist and counselee and in their values, which are an inevitable part of therapy. Science is at a loss because the deep thoughts and motivations of humanity escape the scientific method. Instead, the study is more the business of philosophers and theologians.

Dave Hunt addresses this issue in his book *Beyond Seduction*:

> True faith and true science are not rivals, but deal with different realms. . . . To mix faith with science is to destroy both. . . . The God who created us in His image exists beyond the scope of scientific laws. Therefore, human personality and experience, which come from God and not from nature, must forever defy scientific analysis. No wonder psychotherapy, which pretends to deal "scientifically" with human behavior and personality, has failed so miserably! No human being has the power to define from within himself, much less dictate to others, what constitutes right or wrong behavior. Only God can set such standards, and if there is no Creator God, then morality is nonexistent. This is why psychology's "scientific" standards for "normal" behavior are arbitrary, changeable, meaningless, and inevitably amoral.[31]

The authors of a prestigious book about human behavior admit after reporting 1,045 scientific findings on the subject:

> Indeed, as one reviews this set of findings, he may well be impressed by striking omission. As one lives life or observes it around him (or within himself) or finds it in a work of art, he sees a richness that has somehow fallen through the present screen of the behavioral sciences. This book, for example, has rather little to say about the central human concerns: nobility, moral courage, ethical tor-

ments, the delicate relation of father and son or of the marriage state, life's way of corrupting innocence, the rightness and wrongness of acts, evil, happiness, love and hate, death, even sex.[32]

The actual foundations of psychotherapy are not science, but rather various philosophical world views, especially those of determinism, secular humanism, behaviorism, existentialism, and even evolutionism. With its *isms* within *isms* psychotherapy penetrates every area of modern thought. Its influence has not been confined to the therapist's office, for its varied explanations of human behavior and contradictory ideas for change have permeated society. One of the authors of a national study titled "The Inner America: Americans View Their Jobs and Marital Health" reveals that individuals were much more likely to view problems psychologically than they were twenty years earlier.[33]

PSYCHOLOGICAL ENTRENCHMENT.

The labyrinth of psychotherapeutic theories leads to far reaching influences, not only in thought but in behavior. It is said of Sigmund Freud:

His ideas about dreams, religion, creativity and the unconscious motivations underlying all human behavior are so pervasive that it would be difficult to imagine twentieth-century thought without them.[34]

The Christian community has not escaped the all-pervasive influence of psychotherapy. The church has unwittingly and even eagerly embraced the pseudoscientisms of psychotherapy and has intimately incorporated this spectre into the very sinew of its life. Not only does the church include the concepts and teachings of psychotherapists in sermons and seminaries, it steps aside and entrusts the mentally and emotionally halt and lame to the "high altar" of psychotherapy.

Many church leaders contend that the church does not have the ability to meet the needs of people suffering from depression, anxiety, fear, and other problems of living. They therefore trust the paid practitioners of the pseudoscientisms of psychotherapy more than they trust the Word of God and the work of the Holy Spirit. Because of the confusion between science and pseudoscience, church leaders have elevated the psychotherapist to a position of authority in the modern church. Thus, any attack on the amalgamation of psychotherapy and Christianity is considered to be an attack on the church itself.

Although the church has quite universally accepted and endorsed the psychological way, there are others who have not. Jay Adams says:

> In my opinion, advocating, allowing and practicing psychiatric and psychoanalytical dogmas within the church is every bit as pagan and heretical (and therefore perilous) as propagating the teachings of some of the most bizarre cults. The only vital difference is that the cults are less dangerous because their errors are more identifiable.[35]

Dave Hunt, in his book *The Cult Explosion*, says:

> Today the church is being destroyed from within by "Christian psychology" that interprets Scripture on the basis of a bankrupt, atheistic philosophy, which at best turns Christ into a heavenly psychiatrist. Months and even years of "Christian psychiatry" are now attempting to do what was once accomplished in a moment by coming to the cross.[36]

Paul exhorts Timothy to avoid "profane and vain babblings" and refers to "science falsely so-called." (1 Timothy 6:20) Scofield comments,

> If theories that rest upon mere speculation or insufficient evidence are presented as fact, in any area of knowledge, e.g. in religion, philosophy, science, etc., they deserve the description that the apostle gives here: "knowledge [*science*, KJV] falsely so-called."[37]

Psychotherapy is a most subtle and devious spectre haunting the church, because it is perceived and received as a scientific salve for the sick soul rather than for what it truly is: a pseudoscientific substitute system of religious relief.

The early church faced and ministered to mental-emotional-behavioral problems which were as complex as the ones that exist today. If anything, the conditions of the early church were more difficult than those we currently face. The early Christians suffered persecution, poverty, and various afflictions which are foreign to most of twentieth-century Christendom (especially in the West). The catacombs in Rome are a testimony to the extent of the problems faced by the early church.

If we suffer at all, it is from affluence and ease, which have propelled us toward a greater fixation on self than would likely have occurred in less affluent times. However, the cure for the sins of self-preoccupation existed in the early church and is just as available today. In fact, biblical cures used by the early church are just as potent if used today. The Word of God and the work of the Holy Spirit are applicable to all problems of living and therefore do not need to be superceded by talk therapies and talk therapists.

Has the modern church given up its call and obligation to minister to suffering individuals? If so, it is because Christians believe the myth that psychological counseling is science. However, psychological counseling is not science,[38] but rather another religion and another gospel. (Galatians 1:6) The conflict between the psychological way of counseling and the biblical way is not between true science and true religion. The conflict is strictly religious—a conflict between many religions grouped under the name of psychotherapy (psychological counseling) and the one true religion of the Bible.

Part Two
PSYCHOTHEOLOGY

The old conventional sources of explaining the mysteries of human existence, such as religion and science, no longer hold much water for a lot of people. So people have turned largely to psychology as one field which attempts to answer questions about the meaning of life

George Albee, Past President, American Psychological Association.[1]

Promises of both psychological and spiritual transformation entice the sheep to the professional Christian counselors' quarters. And glowing testimonies assure the sheep that the pastures are safe, that the grass is green and the water is pure. What are the promises? Is there a truly Christian blend of psychology and the Bible? Has a psychological salvation somehow joined itself to the cross of Christ?

4

Promises, Promises, Promises

> The appeal of human-potential programs has always been the promise they offered of quick, dramatic improvements in our lives. And over the last twenty years the claims made for these approaches have grown increasingly extravagant.[1]
>
> Art Levine

Promises abound in psychological counseling. Most are direct but some are implied. Nonetheless, the psychological landscape is littered with them. Promises entice the needy, yet unwary person to sample the wares of the psychic merchants. The false promises of some psychotherapies range from the advertised 95 percent cure rate for Primal Therapy[2] to the mere ten minutes supposedly needed to cure phobias in Neuro Linguistic Programming.[3] Implied or direct promises of health, happiness, and self transformation abound. Byram Karasu, director of the Department of Psychiatry at the Bronx Municipal Hospital Center says:

> Underneath the melodrama of who's right or wrong, all therapies have one thing in common. Much is promised and little is delivered, as with everything else in life.[4]

Psychologist Bernie Zilbergeld reports that "changes made in counseling rarely live up to what is claimed by many therapists and believed by many clients."[5] To put it simply, there is a huge discrepancy between promise and product in the psychological shopping center.

The psychological marketplace is glutted with promises but rarely produces the promised results. There are endless examples. One appeared as an ad in our local newspaper just as we were writing this section. It was an ad for an "anger exploration workshop" which promised the following: "You will be able to *immediately* implement anger management activities, which are under your *control*." (Emphasis ours.)[6] Many people have struggled for years with anger and now this workshop promises *immediate* results and *control*. The promise is open ended. It literally includes everyone, no matter how many years the problem has persisted or the number of workshops or seminars one has already attended. The message is that this one WILL work.

Well, it's wonderful if such a workshop does work and if the change is long lasting. However, any change is usually just a temporary quick fix. Research does not support such promises and rarely reveals long term successes in anger management. Certain difficult areas, such as anger and various forms of addictive behavior, have extremely high relapse rates. This means that even though there may appear to be immediate improvement, it is generally followed by deterioration. The seeming improvement is short lived. Can you imagine how a person might attend such a workshop with high hopes only to find out a day later, a week later, or a month later that the problem still persists?

CAMBRIDGE-SOMERVILLE YOUTH STUDY.

The Cambridge-Somerville Youth Study is well known to researchers but little known to the public. If the promises of the project had been fulfilled it would have become a household word, but the results of follow-up research were too embarrassing. The goal of the project was the prevention of delinquency. The methods were highly touted and expensive. However, the project turned out to be a clear demonstration of how research results can contradict promises of success.

The study began by selecting 650 underprivileged boys between the ages of six and ten who were high risk with respect to becoming delinquents. Two groups were formed by matching the boys on a number of variables, such as age, IQ, and background. Then by a flip of a coin the boys were assigned to either a treatment group or a control group (no treatment). Those who were treated received, on the average, five years of psychotherapy in addition to academic tutoring, summer camp, and other involvement with organizations such as the Boy Scouts and the Y.M.C.A. The boys in the control group were provided no services by the project.

At the end of the project the counselors believed that they had greatly helped the boys they had treated. Furthermore, a large majority of the treated boys claimed great benefit. Based upon testimonies of counselors and counselees, the project seemed to be a great success. It was a classic "they lived happily ever after" ending that was told over and over again as a testimony to the success of psychology in the remedy of human problems and the rehabilitation of human beings.

Imagine the bragging about salvation from a life of delinquency! Consider the financial benefits gained through the prevention of future crime! The psychological pats on the back were hard and loud. The profuse puffery promulgated as a result of this project was pathetic. It was pathetic because it was premature. No follow up studies had yet been done. No acid test of future delinquency had yet been made.

Imagine the surprise when the first follow up study was conducted and revealed slightly more delinquent behavior among the boys who had received the special treatment than among the boys who had received no treatment at all. Surprise turned to downright embarrassment when both groups were looked at thirty years after all the fuss. In looking at both groups in terms of criminal behavior, mental problems, and alcoholism, the researchers discovered that the ones who had received treatment (on the average of five years of psychotherapy, academic tutoring, and participation in summer camp, etc.) were doing worse than those who had been left alone. Joan McCord, who conducted the follow-up study, concludes:

> The objective evidence presents a disturbing picture. The program seems not only to have failed to prevent its clients from committing crimes—thus corroborating studies of

other projects— but also to have produced negative side effects.[7]

Without the control (untreated) group and without the later follow-up research to check out the promises, the Cambridge-Somerville project would have been deemed a huge success when in actuality it was a great failure.

This seeming-success-but-actually-a-failure pattern predominates throughout psychotherapy. Promises of success undergirded by testimonies of success do not equal true success. People want to believe that such efforts as the Cambridge-Somerville project produce positive benefits. When research indicates the reverse of expectations built on promises, it is often ignored. After all, in a society that wants a quick fix, there is little interest in follow-up studies and scientific proof even among Christians.

Unfulfilled promises not only exist in the secular world. Similar promises are made by Christians. The Christian therapist is often just a reflection of his secular counterpart. The promises are almost as prolific in Christianity as in society. One sees and hears them in abundance. We have chosen three examples.

PROMISES IN CHRISTIAN BOOKS.

Numerous examples could be given of exaggerated, unfulfilled promises in Christian books. The popular Christian book *Telling Yourself the Truth* by Dr. William Backus, a clinical psychologist, and Marie Chapian, a psychotherapist, is one of the many examples. The book utilizes cognitive therapy and biblical ideas. It promises that you will: "Find your way out of depression, anxiety, fear, anger and other common problems by applying the principles of misbelief therapy."[8] The authors state:

> Misbelief therapy *will* work for you. It will work for you even if nothing else has because its effectiveness depends upon very explicit psychological laws which are as universal as the law of gravity.[9]

This is a universal promise that supposedly empowers the process (Misbelief Therapy) as if it were omnipotent over "depression, anxiety, fear, anger and other common problems." Like the "law of gravity" it will supposedly cause cure no matter what. Common sense would dictate that if such promises were true everyone would be using Misbelief Therapy. Whereas it is only one of a myriad of approaches used by therapists (and, as a matter of fact, hardly used at all). In addition, no independent research or follow up studies exist to prove the phenomenal promises of that system to the other practitioners of other psychological approaches.

The promises of *Telling Yourself the Truth* are erroneously supported by misunderstanding and misapplying Scripture. Backus and Chapian use Proverbs 23:7, "For as he thinketh in his heart, so is he" (KJV) to promote their inflated promises and prescriptions "to help you possess the happiness you desire and to be the person you'd like to be" so that "You can live happily ever after with the person you are and make a profound affect on those around you because of it."[10] However, the full context of that verse says that one should not go solely on outward appearances.

> Do not eat the bread of a selfish man,
> Or desire his delicacies;
> For as he thinks within himself, so is he.
> He says to you, "Eat and drink!"
> But his heart is not with you.
> You will vomit up the morsel you have eaten,
> And waste your compliments. (Proverbs 23:6-8)

The "he" referred to in Proverbs 23:7 is a person not to be trusted. The proverb is a warning to watch out for duplicity. Proverbs 23:7 cannot be used to teach that if a person changes his thoughts he will possess the happiness he desires or will become the person he would like to be. Nor can it be used to support the idea that one will "live happily ever after" if he practices Misbelief Therapy. When anyone begins with psychology and attempts to use Scripture to support an idea, he is likely to end up both misunderstanding and misapplying Scripture.

PROMISES IN CHRISTIAN MAGAZINES.

Our second example is that of Dr. Martha Rogers, a Christian clinical psychologist. In her article "A Family In Crisis," printed in a popular Christian magazine, she describes how four counselors might approach the problems. The four approaches include one solely biblical approach (Nouthetic Counseling) and three psychological approaches (behavioral therapy, psychoanalytic therapy, and family systems therapy). The family systems approach is described in the most favorable light of the four. That was the therapy used to treat the family discussed in the article. Rogers says that the husband's "depression was completely alleviated and he launched another business which is proving successful. His problem drinking was resolved." Rogers then says that the wife's "long-term migraine headaches were virtually eliminated."[11]

Talk about a happy ending? Rogers claims, "The couple grew much closer and were enjoying much more time together . . . became more open with other people and were able to share their experiences as well as to extend help to others in their church body as a result of therapy."[12] And, all of this was accomplished in five months! Sounds easy, doesn't it? Research aside, family systems therapy is made to look like it provides a real bonanza of benefit to families and individuals that is rarely achieved.

PROMISES IN CHRISTIAN MEDIA.

Our third example is Dr. Paul Meier, who is a well-known Christian psychiatrist at a large clinic. In an interview on a radio station, Dr. Meier made a number of statements about a variety of mental problems and some supposed cures. Two of the promises caught our attention. First, in discussing schizophrenia he said that it results "from severe inferiority feelings and genetic predisposition and a bunch of different factors and *it's curable if you catch it early*." Then he said, *"If you don't get medical help for about six months it becomes incurable. The biochemical pathways become permanent."* Second, in discussing sleep problems, this psychiatrist said, "Insomnia is a *one-hundred-per-cent curable problem*."[13] Those sound like two wonderful promises, one for schizophrenia (if caught within the first six months) and the other for insomnia. Aside from Meier's claims about the two conditions, no literature or authorities we contacted could be found to support the promises. In fact, just the opposite. The authorities repudiated Meier's promises about those two problems.

Unfortunately Meier has specifically used the dubious "curable if you catch it early" promise to criticize certain biblical counselors. Both at Dallas Theological Seminary and in the Christian media, Meier has specifically said that thousands of Christians have been sentenced to a life of insanity because certain biblical counselors have not referred them for proper medication during this so-called critical period. Our purpose in mentioning this is to show that false promises and misinformation abound from all levels of the Christian professional counseling community.

LET THE BUYER BEWARE.

In discussing the outcomes of therapy, Zilbergeld quotes therapist/researcher Hans Strupp:

> I believe we are entering an era in which the claims and aspirations of psychotherapy will become more circumscribed and more focused. It may also spell a return to greater modesty, from which we should never have departed. [14]

Zilbergeld comments on the promises of psychotherapy: "It is close to impossible, for example, to turn a chronically depressed person into a happy-go-lucky type."[15] He further notes that "cures in therapy are not common" and that "symptoms or presenting complaints rarely disappear."[16]

After thirty years of practicing psychotherapy, Anthony Storr concludes that there is no "convincing evidence that even years of analysis in the most expert hands, radically alter a person's fundamental 'psychopathology.'"[17]

Psychiatrist Jerome Frank, after commenting about research on brainwashing, says:

> These findings raise some doubts about the claims of certain schools of psychotherapy to produce fundamental personality change. From this perspective, such changes may be analogous to false confessions. That is, the person has not changed fundamentally, but rather has learned to couch his problems and report improvement in the therapist's terms.[18]

We are not saying that change does not occur in or out of therapy.

We are only stating that the research on psychological improvement in therapy does not warrant the promises that are extant in the
books, workshops, talks, tapes, and ads of the various therapists
and therapies and the pronouncements of the practitioners and
promoters whether in or out of the church. Zilbergeld says,

> Changes made by the presumably sophisticated methods
> of therapy are usually modest and not much different from
> what people achieve on their own or with the help of their
> friends. [19]

It is rather obvious that the more severe the problem, the more
long term the problem; the more complex the problem, the less
likelihood of cure. Promises often produce hope and hope can
sometimes encourage cure. But, hope unfulfilled can also lead to
despair, depression, and even divorce, or worse yet, suicide. False
promises usually produce a false hope which usually leads to
failure. Realistic promises usually produce a realistic hope which
usually leads to realistic possibilities for success.

The worst of the primrose promises of Christian psychology is
the promise that the Bible plus psychotherapy can provide better
help than just the Bible alone. This possibility is referred to as
integration or amalgamation. We confront this issue further in the
next chapter. Suffice it to say that while this idea has been promulgated and promoted by many Christian psychotherapists, there is
no research evidence to support it. No one has ever shown that the
Bible needs psychological augmentation to be more effective in
dealing with life's problems. No one has proven that a Christianized cure of minds (psychotherapy) is any more beneficial than
the original unadulterated simple cure of souls (biblical counseling).

The research we quote in this book should certainly be a warning
against the siren song of psychological promises. Promises, direct
or implied, are usually unwarranted and unsubstantiated and
should serve as danger signals whenever and wherever discerned.
That the blatant and grandiose promises of psychotherapy should
be viewed with the greatest suspicion is obvious. But even the
subtle, implied and indirect promises should be viewed with the
same alarm.

5

Amalgamania

Do not be bound together with unbelievers; for what partnership have righteousness and lawlessness, or what fellowship has light with darkness? Or what harmony has Christ with Belial, or what has a believer in common with an unbeliever? Or what agreement has the temple of God with idols? For we are the temple of the living God; just as God said, "I will dwell in them and walk among them; and I will be their God, and they shall be My people. Therefore, come out from their midst and be ye separate. . . ." (2 Corinthians 6:14-17)

The psychologizing of the church has reached epidemic proportions. By psychologizing we mean treating problems of living by the use of psychological rather than or in addition to biblical means. This psychologizing occurs in almost every important facet of Christianity.

First, we hear it in psychologized sermons. Psychologists are quoted as authorities and psychological ideas are presented and even promoted.

Second, church counseling has become psychologized. The Bible is supposedly not enough. Thus, psychological understanding is sought and psychological techniques are applied.

Third, those who want to help people in the church who have problems of living become psychologically rather than biblically trained. We have found this to be true in even some of the remotest areas of our land.

Fourth, there is promiscuous referral. When people with problems of living seek help from their pastor, they are often referred to a professional psychological counselor. This happens with even the most basic of problems.

Fifth, there is evidence that reveals the rising number of churches providing psychological counseling with psychologically trained and licensed individuals within the church itself. The increase includes even the most conservative churches and conservative denominations.

Sixth, Christian schools, colleges, and seminaries rely either partially or even entirely upon teaching psychological rather than biblical solutions to life's problems.

Seventh, it is almost mandated that marriage and family counselors or psychologists be present at conferences whether in or out of the church and especially at the favorite camp or conference locations. Having conferences now necessitates some psychological presence like the necessity of having a pastor present at a wedding. This thought-to-be-ideal combination of psychology and theology is just another insidious dilution of Scripture and diminution of the influence of the Holy Spirit. The inclusion of such trained professionals is one additional testimony to the psychologizing of Christianity and the secularizing of the church. It demonstrates a lack of faith in what God has provided and a misplaced faith in what man has invented.

Last, but not least, nearly all of the people who are selected to review books about helping individuals with problems of living are tilted towards the psychological. Their bias is almost as automatic as their belief that the earth is round. John Sanderson, in reviewing a book that integrates Scripture and psychological insights, compares the content of the integrationism of the book with a purely biblical position. Sanderson confesses his own lack of expertise on the matter but confirms the integrationist's position. That this particular book was reviewed in a conservative Christian magazine by a conservative Christian who concluded by supporting the integrationist position is tragic but typical of the extent of the psychologizing of the church.[1]

It would be possible to extend this list by including books, tapes, workshops, and seminars that are psychologized in one way or another. Paul Bartz says that "well-intentioned, but ignorant, Christian leaders have widely adopted psychological models to deal with everything from counseling to church growth."[2] One does not need a well trained ear, eye, nose, hand or tongue to hear, see, smell, touch or taste the evidences of the psychologizing of Christianity. It is so all pervasive that, if anything, our senses have been dulled to it. The psychologizing is rampant to say the least.

THE PSYCHOLOGIZERS.

After studying the 1223 page *Baker Encyclopedia of Psychology*,[3] Dr. Ed Payne, Associate Professor of Family Medicine, says:

> Many pastors and laymen may be deceived by the Christian label of this book. Such psychology presented by Christians is a plague on the modern church, distorting the Christian's relationship with God, retarding his sanctification, and severely weakening the church. No other area of knowledge seems to have such a stranglehold on the church. This book strengthens that hold both individually and corporately.[4]

This is a dramatically different view from the one that has enveloped the church. However, this strong statement is made by one who has the academic authority to do so. Unfortunately, these remarks made by Dr. Payne about that book, which was written by 163 of the finest evangelical scholars, also apply to other psychological activities that are being promoted in the name of Christianity. Psychology does have "a stranglehold on the church"!

Dr. J. Vernon McGee, in an article titled "Psycho-Religion— The New Pied Piper," complains about the psychologizing of Christianity. He says:

> If the present trend continues, Bible teaching will be totally eliminated from Christian radio stations as well as from TV and the pulpit. This is not a wild statement made in an emotional moment of concern. Bible teaching is

being moved to the back burner of broadcasting, while so-called Christian psychology is put up front as Bible solutions to life's problems.

He also refers to "so-called Christian psychology" in magazines and books and says, "So-called Christian psychology is secular psychology clothed in pious platitudes and religious rhetoric."[5] Elsewhere he says, "I see that this matter of psychologizing Christianity will absolutely destroy Bible teaching and Bible churches."[6]

We criticize the work of a number of individuals in this book because they have been a part of the unnecessary psychologizing of Christianity. They serve as examples of what is happening in the church today. We mention them in order to give specific examples and encourage discussion of this very important issue. We have always been open to public discussion of these matters and believe that the end result will be a stronger church and a purer theology. Church history, from its early beginnings through the Protestant Reformation, reveals that such discussion has always existed and can be beneficial. Open dialogue is an indication of strength in the church. Whereas avoidance of such discussion is a sign of fear and weakness. Open discussion of crucial matters occurred in the New Testament.

This book is an effort to bring to the level of serious discussion the reasons for a dramatic change in the church from the nineteenth to the twentieth century: a change from the way problems of living were biblically addressed in contrast to how they are psychologically therapized today. The research offered throughout this book presents a rationale for restoring the cure of souls ministry (biblical counseling). The research results also call for an elimination of the cure of minds (psychological counseling) in all of its forms, no matter where it exists in the church and no matter how popular and talented the psychologizers.

THE SELF-CENTERED GOSPEL OF PSYCHOLOGY.

One of the most popular themes in psychology is that of self-fulfillment. Although this is an extremely popular theme, it is a theme of recent origin having arisen only within the past forty years outside of the church and in the past twenty years within the church itself. Daniel Yankelovich, who is a pollster and analyst of social trends and public attitudes, in his book entitled *New Rules: Searching for Self-Fulfillment in a World Turned Upside Down*, documents the changes that have occurred and describes "the struggle for self-fulfillment" as "the leading edge of a genuine cultural revolution." He claims, "It is moving our industrial civilization toward a new phase of human experience."[7] Yankelovich describes the new rules in society throughout his book. He says:

> In their extreme form, the new rules simply turn the old ones on their head, and in place of the old self-denial ethic we find people who refuse to deny *anything* to themselves.[8] (Emphasis his.)

The description of the book states:

> *New Rules* is about 80 percent of Americans now committed to one degree or another to the search for self-fulfillment, at the expense of the older, self-denying ethic of earlier years.[9]

As society moved from self denial to self-fulfillment, a new vocabulary emerged which revealed a new inner attitude and a different view of life. The new vocabulary became the very fabric of a new psychology. This new psychological force is known as humanistic psychology. Humanistic psychology's great emphasis is on self. Self-actualization is its major focus and self-fulfillment its clarion call. And, self-fulfillment, with all its accompanying self-hyphenated and self-fixated variations such as self-love, self-acceptance, self-esteem, and self-worth, has become the new promised land. Then as the church became psychologized, the emphasis shifted from God to self.

The new formula for society has become a cause and effect relationship between a high amount of self-love, self-esteem, etc., leading to health, wealth, and happiness and a low amount to just the opposite. That idea, once having permeated society, penetrated the church. Christian books began to reflect what was accepted in society. Some examples are *Love Yourself*, *The Art of Learning to Love Yourself*, *Loving Yourselves*, *Celebrate Yourself*, *You're Some-*

one Special, *Self Esteem: You're Better than You Think*, and probably best known, Robert Schuler's *Self Esteem: The New
Reformation*. The list of books and examples of the psychological
self-stroking mentality are numerous.

One of the major themes of James Dobson is that of self-esteem.
In his popular book *Hide and Seek*, he talks about the prevalence of
low self-esteem and claims that women are particularly afflicted
with it. He says:

> If I could write a prescription for the women of the world,
> it would provide each one of them with a healthy dose of
> self-esteem and personal worth (taken three times a day
> until the symptoms disappear). *I have no doubt that this is
> their greatest need.*[10] (Emphasis added.)

In his book *What Wives Wish Their Husbands Knew About Women*,
Dobson describes low self-esteem:

> It is sitting alone in a house during the quiet afternoon
> hours, wondering why the phone doesn't ring . . . wonder-
> ing why you have no "real" friends. It is longing for
> someone to talk to, soul to soul, but knowing there is no
> such person worthy of your trust. . . . It is wondering why
> other people have so much more talent and ability than you
> do. It is feeling incredibly ugly and sexually unattractive.
> It is admitting that you have become a failure as a wife and
> mother. It is disliking everything about yourself and wish-
> ing, constantly wishing, you could be someone else. It is
> feeling unloved and unlovable and lonely and sad. It is
> lying in bed after the family is asleep, pondering the vast
> emptiness inside and longing for unconditional love. It is
> intense self-pity. It is reaching up in the darkness to
> remove a tear from the corner of your eye. *It is depres-
> sion!*[11] (Emphasis his.)

Is that low self-esteem or is it a collection of self-centered
thoughts? Low self-esteem is popular because it's much easier to
accept the idea of having "low self-esteem" than confessing evil,
ungodly, self-centered thoughts and then repenting through believing what God has said in His Word. Low self-esteem calls for

psychological treatment to raise the self-esteem. Sinful thinking calls for confession, repentance, restoration, and walking by faith in a love relationship with God provided by the cross of Christ. We would suggest that one look to Scripture to discover one's greatest need and to find an antidote to life's problems, rather than to attempt to scripturalize some psychological fad. Mankind's greatest need is for Jesus Christ, not self-esteem.

Psychological research reveals that low self-esteem is not the number one mental health problem. Social psychologist Carol Tavris reports:

> Preliminary results from a comprehensive study by the National Institute of Mental Health (NIMH), designed to assess the prevalence of mental disorders in the United States, suggests that anxiety disorders are the number one mental health problem for women.[12]

So, contrary to what Dobson reports, it is anxiety disorders, not low self-esteem, that afflicts women. Of course one could argue that anxiety is due to low self-esteem. However, other psychologists could equally argue that anxiety is due to rejection or rage or early psychosexual stages of development or the primal pool of pain or whatever they choose.

Nevertheless, Dobson warns about the enormous possible national consequences of low self-esteem. He says:

> The matter of personal worth is not only the concern of those who lack it. In a real sense, the health of an entire society depends on the ease with which the individual members gain personal acceptance. *Thus, whenever the keys to self-esteem are seemingly out of reach for a large percentage of the people, as in twentieth-century America, then widespread "mental illness," neuroticism, hatred, alcoholism, drug abuse, violence, and social disorder will certainly occur.*[13] (Emphasis his.)

In response to Dobson's statement, Dave Hunt and T. A. McMahon say in their book *The Seduction of Christianity*:

> This idea that low self-esteem is rampant and the root of almost all problems is confidently stated as though it were

proven fact. Yet many other psychologists would strongly disagree. Although the author sincerely desires to be biblical, he has based his ministry upon a belief that was not derived from Scripture, but is only one of many conflicting psychological theories.[14]

Dobson's psychological self-esteem prescription echoes the world. And, aside from his personal opinion about the matter, there is no research to prove conclusively the above quote. In fact many authorities would greatly disagree with Dobson and some would state just the opposite. Dr. Edward Stainbrook, a nationally-known expert on human behavior, believes that "self-preoccupation is jeopardizing America's future."[15]

One research study supported by the National Institute of Mental Health attempted to find a relationship between self-esteem and delinquent children. The researchers concluded that "the effect of self-esteem on delinquent behavior is negligible."[16] The researchers confess, "Given the extensive speculation and debate about self-esteem and delinquency, we find these results something of an embarrassment."[17]

David Myers, in his book *The Inflated Self*, points out how research has revealed a self-serving bias in man. Although many in the church now claim that people need ego boosting and self-esteem raising, Myers's research led him to conclude:

> Preachers who deliver ego-boosting pep talks to audiences who are supposedly plagued with miserable self images are preaching to a problem that seldom exists.[18]

A research project at Purdue University compared two groups of individuals, one with low self-esteem and the other with high self-esteem, in regard to problem solving. The results of the study once more explodes the myth that high self-esteem is a must for mankind. The results of the study were reported by one of the two researchers assigned to the project. He says, "Self-esteem is generally considered an across-the-board important attitude, but this study showed self-esteem to correlate negatively with performance." He concludes by stating that in that particular study, "The higher the self-esteem, the poorer the performance."[19]

In a research study seeking to find underlying causes for coronary heart disease it was found that frequent self-references on the part of the subjects was definitely implicated in coronary heart disease. Self-references were measured by the subjects' use of "I," "me," "my," and "mine." In contrast, the researchers mention that "it is interesting to note that the Japanese, with the lowest rate of coronary heart disease of any industrialized nation, do not have prominent self-references in their language."[20] The researchers conclude by saying:

> Our central thesis, stated in a sentence, is that self-involve-ment, which arises from one's self-identity and one's attachment to that identity and its extensions, forms the substrate for all the recognized psychosocial risk factors of coronary heart disease.[21]

Paul Vitz notes the danger of self-actualization:

> The relentless and single-minded search for and glorifica-tion of the self is at direct cross purposes with the Christian injunction to lose thyself. Certainly Jesus Christ neither lived nor advocated a life that would qualify by today's standards as "self-actualized." For the Christian the self is the problem, not the potential paradise. Understanding this problem involves an awareness of sin, especially the sin of pride; correcting this condition requires the practice of such un-self-actualized states as contrition and peni-tence, humility, obedience, and trust in God.[22]

John Piper says sadly, "Today the first and greatest commandment is 'Thou shalt love thyself.'" He rightly complains that today the "ultimate sin is no longer the failure to honor God and thank Him but the failure to esteem oneself."[23]

Unless Scripture is molded to conform to the self-promoting teachings, the Bible teaches one to be Christ-centered and other-oriented. Loving God above all else and with one's entire being and loving neighbor as much as one ALREADY loves oneself are the primary injunctions of the Bible. The admonition to love oneself or to esteem oneself is missing.

The teachings of self-love, self-esteem, and self-worth have been brought in from the world rather than gleaned from Scripture.

They are products of humanistic psychologists rather than the truth from the Word of God. Jay Adams warns about this serious encroachment:

> Any system that proposes to solve human problems apart from the Bible and the power of the Holy Spirit (as all of these pagan systems, including the self-worth system, do) is automatically condemned by Scripture itself. Neither Adler nor Maslow [humanistic psychologists] professed Christian faith. Nor does their system in any way depend upon the message of salvation. Love, joy, peace, etc., are discussed as if they were not the fruit of the Spirit but merely the fruit of right views of one's self which anyone can attain without the Bible or the work of the Spirit in his heart. [24]

Adams continues:

> For these reasons the self-worth system with its claimed biblical correspondence must be rejected. It does not come from the Bible; Christians called the Bible into service long after the system was developed by others who had no intention of basing their system on God's Word. Any resemblance between biblical teaching and the teaching of the self-worth originators is either contrived or coincidental. [25]

Rather than self-love being taught as a virtue in Scripture, it is placed among the diabolical works of the flesh. Paul addresses the issue of self-love from just the opposite perspective from the present-day promoters:

> But realize this, that in the last days difficult times will come. For men will be lovers of self, lovers of money, boastful, arrogant, revilers, disobedient to parents, ungrateful, unholy, unloving, irreconcilable, malicious gossips, without self-control, brutal, haters of good, treacherous, reckless, conceited, lovers of pleasure rather than lovers of God; holding to a form of godliness, although they have denied its power; and avoid such men as these. (2 Timothy 3:1-5)

Detail by detail Paul's prophecy of the last days describes the twentieth-century Western culture. Anyone from a third-world country watching Western television could more easily equate our culture with that verse than with any biblical description of Christianity.

Worse than that, what Paul has described floods over into the church when Christians compromise their faith with the enticement of the world. J. I. Packer notes the trend of Christians to love self and pleasure more than God:

> Modern Christians tend to make satisfaction their religion. We show much more concern for self-fulfillment than for pleasing our God. Typical of Christianity today, at any rate in the English-speaking world, is its massive rash of how-to books for believers, directing us to more successful relationships, more joy in sex, becoming more of a person, realizing our possibilities, getting more excitement each day, reducing our weight, improving our diet, managing our money, licking our families into happier shape, and whatnot. For people whose prime passion is to glorify God, these are doubtless legitimate concerns; but the how-to books regularly explore them in a self-absorbed way that treats our enjoyment of life rather than the glory of God as the center of interest. Granted, they spread a thin layer of Bible teaching over the mixture of popular psychology and common sense they offer, but their overall approach clearly reflects the narcissism—"selfism" or "me-ism" as it is sometimes called—that is the way of the world in the modern West.[26]

Dave Hunt reminds us:

> Those who grow up under totalitarian regimes hostile to the gospel expect to be rejected, despised, ridiculed, and even imprisoned or killed for their faith, and would not understand the importance that Christians in the West place upon self-esteem, self-acceptance, and self-fulfillment.[27]

The clear teaching of Scripture is not self-esteem, but rather denying the self. Jesus says:

> If anyone wishes to come after Me, let him deny himself,
> and take up his cross, and follow Me. For whoever wishes
> to save his life shall lose it; but whoever loses his life for
> My sake and the gospel's shall save it. (Mark 8:34-35)

John Wesley has said:

> Denying ourselves and taking up our cross isn't a little side
> issue—it is absolutely necessary to becoming or continu-
> ing to become a disciple of Jesus. . . . All of the things that
> hold us back from being right with God or growing in the
> Lord can be boiled down to this: either we won't deny
> ourselves or we won't take up our cross.[28]

Over 200 years ago William Law wrote:

> Self is all the evil that he [man] has, and God is all the
> goodness that he can ever have; but self and God are
> always with him. Death to self is the only entrance into the
> Church of the living God; and nothing but God can give
> this death, and that alone through the inward work of the
> cross of Christ by His Spirit made real in the soul.[29]

Ruth Graham says it concisely: "Self is spiritual BO."[30]

In an article in *Moody* magazine, Elwood McQuaid says, "A
new, hybrid faith is infiltrating evangelicalism. Self is at its center.
While in most quarters its creed is still orthodox, its conclusions
are humanistic."[31]

Psychiatrist E. Fuller Torrey says:

> When *The Scarlet Letter* was written, in 1850, adultery
> was explained by a minister as the product of evil inside the
> woman. If the same book were written today the author
> would have a psychiatrist explain the woman's behavior as
> due to her low self-esteem and difficulty in getting close to
> people.[32]

Psychologist William Kirk Kilpatrick says:

> . . . the most shameful incidents of my life—things I now

wince to think about—were the product of a happy self-acceptance, the period during which I was most smitten with self-esteem, "innocently" following what I had convinced myself were good or at least neutral impulses. My self-esteem simply wouldn't allow any honest self-awareness: that only came later.[33]

Furthermore the Bible admonishes believers to esteem others better than self.

Paul Brownback, in his excellent book *The Dangers of Self-Love*, addresses the subject of self-love and self-esteem. His chapters "The Evidence from Scripture," Parts One and Two, are particularly important when evaluating the matter.[34] Seminary professor Dr. Jay Adams's recent book, *The Biblical View of Self-Esteem, Self-Love, and Self-Image*, reveals the unbiblical basis of self-esteem.[35]

Two books on the subject of self-actualization describe it as a great detriment rather than an asset. They are *Habits of the Heart*[36] and *Psychology's Sanction for Selfishness*. The authors of the first book speak of the Americans' cult of the individual and its effects on society. One of the authors points out how therapy, in focusing on the self, often leads to a discarding of tradition and can possibly lead to a weakening of the larger moral fabric on which to base decisions. The second book is "about selfishness and psychology's role in promoting it."[37] Wallach and Wallach introduce their well reasoned and documented investigation by saying:

> Our analysis suggests that the roots of psychology's ubiquitous sanction for selfishness lie in fundamental assumptions about motivation that almost all psychologists have come to take for granted. . . . The directions taken by psychological theorizing that serve to support and encourage selfishness do not, we find, seem justified in the light of current knowledge and evidence.[38]

T. A. McMahon, coauthor of *The Seduction of Christianity*, wrote to Dobson after McMahon and his coauthor Dave Hunt visited him. McMahon says, "Self-esteem has become a new doctrine in the church today . . . it is a false doctrine." McMahon also says,

> I've read most of the secular and Christian (C.A.P.S., Trobish, Narramore, Wagner, Osborne, Hoekema, et al) psychological self theories along with your [Dobson] own and have found them to be only superficially different from each other while basically at odds with the Word of God.[39]

Christians should not use such terms as self-esteem, self-worth, or self-image, because these terms originate from a secular human-istic society. They have been picked up and popularized by human-istic psychologists. And, they have been used as a distortion of biblical truth. These terms have already been defined by a flesh-oriented society and are often fatal even in small doses.

The California Legislature passed a bill promoting self-esteem teachings throughout the state in both the public and private sector. The legislature has funded the bill with $245,000 with a possibility of another $500,000 from other sources. It is certain that this is going to be the beginning of a nation-wide surge in self-esteem teaching. Unfortunately, self-esteem teachings are already offered as popular remedies for individuals with problems at even the most conservative churches and educational institutions.

John Vasconcellos (author of the bill to promote self-esteem) and Mitch Saunders wrote about this issue in the Association for Humanistic Psychology Newsletter:

> The issue is *always* whether or not we believe that we humans are inherently good, trustworthy and responsible. This issue is becoming *the* central social and political challenge of our times.[40] (Emphasis theirs.)

It is also becoming *the* spiritual issue of our times. The issue is whether Christians are going to contend for the faith once delivered to the saints or if they are going to slip into the faith of secular humanism through the cracks of psychology and self-esteem.

The self-esteem leaven turned loose and fueled by the finances of state monies will fool many more in Christian churches, schools, colleges, and seminaries. These institutions have already been introduced to such teachings by influential psychologists who are Christians, or by those pastors, teachers, and writers who have been influenced by their teachings. Christians do not realize that underlying much of what these people teach is a psychological, not biblical message.

In summary, a high-self-esteem-will-help-you-low-self-esteem-will-hurt-you formula is not biblical. Nor is it proven in the research. It is unfortunate that many Christian leaders and psychologists have chosen to promote self-esteem. Self-fulfillment, self-actualization, self-love, and the other combinations and permutations of self-enlarging words are just various facets of the desire to be like God which originated in the Garden of Eden. Amalgamating Scripture with psychology only baptizes the flesh with the Holy Water of the Word, but it is a false message.

PSYCHOLOGICAL PASTORS.

Numerous are the examples of Christian psychologists who are ordained ministers. They begin with a desire to Christianize psychology and end up psychologizing Christianity. Dr. Richard Dobbins is an example of the many ministers who have turned to psychology with the inevitable result of their theology conforming to psychology. Dobbins is founder and director of Emerge Ministries. He is very popular within his own denomination and has done a great amount of teaching, speaking, and writing. One of his teaching films epitomizes the well-intentioned desire to wed psychology and theology, which results in elevating humanistic psychology and corrupting biblical theology. In Dobbins's teaching film *The Believer and His Self Concept* he leads the viewers through a series of steps to end up chanting, "I am a lovable person. I am a valuable person. I am a forgivable person."[41] The confusion that occurs is between the biblical fact that God loves, values and forgives us and the humanistic psychological lie that we are intrinsically lovable, valuable and forgivable. If we have one iota of loveliness or one iota of value or one iota of forgivability, then it makes no sense that Christ should have to die for us.

God has chosen to set his love upon us because of His essence, not because of ours, even after we are believers. His love, His choice to place value upon us, and His choice to forgive us is by grace alone. It is fully undeserved. It is not because of who we are by some intrinsic value of our own or by our own righteousness.

The paradoxical, profound and powerful truth of Scripture is that though we are not intrinsically lovable, valuable, or forgivable, God loves, values and forgives us. That is the pure theology of

Scripture and the overpowering message of Christ's death and resurrection. The hymn writer states it much better than the psychologist. "Nothing in my hand I bring. Simply to Thy cross I cling." Nothing? Nothing! The biblical truth is better presented as: "I am not a lovable person. I am not a valuable person. I am not a forgivable person. But, Christ died for me!"

The focus of the Christian should be directed at Christ as the lovable person, the valuable person, and the forgiving person. In his book *Man: The Dwelling Place of God*, A. W. Tozer declares:

> The victorious Christian neither exalts nor downgrades himself. His interests have shifted from self to Christ. What he is or is not no longer concerns him. He believes that he has been crucified with Christ and he is not willing either to praise or deprecate such a man. [42]

The alternative to self-love is not self-hate, but rather love in relationship with God and others. The alternative to self-esteem is not self-denigration, but rather an understanding of the greatness of God dwelling in a weak vessel of flesh. The alternative to self-fulfillment is not a life of emptiness or meaninglessness. It is God's invitation to be so completely involved with His will and His purposes that fulfillment comes through relationship rather than through self. The awesome realization that the God and Creator of this universe has chosen to set His love upon human beings should engender love and esteem for God rather than for self. The amazing truth that He has called us in relationship with Him to do His will far surpasses the puny dreams of self-fulfillment.

Dobbins wrote a four-part series on "Anger: Master or Servant," which appeared in the *Pentecostal Evangel*. [43] The series was based on a chapter from his book *Your Spiritual and Emotional Power*. [44] His writings on anger need to be examined from both a scientific and a biblical perspective to see whether or not they contain truth or error.

Prior to the last 25 years self-control was encouraged and was the model for behavior. If one were angry the advice and the encouragement was for internalizing it rather than externalizing. Now, however, everyone seems bent on self-expression rather than self restraint and many reasons are given to do so. We have moved from an era of restraint to one of release.

It is easy to see where Dr. Dobbins is on the matter. He says, "People who attempt to control anger by clamming up risk damaging themselves." He adds, "Psychosomatic illnesses feed on unexpressed anger."[45] To explain his theory, Dobbins says, "...energy cannot be destroyed; it can only be transformed. Once you are angry you are in possession of energy which cannot be destroyed."[46] Dobbins warns, "If you don't develop ways of getting that energy out of you in nondestructive activities, sooner or later it will find symptomatic expression among the weakest of your organic systems. So don't clam up and run the risk of damaging your physical health."[47] To release this energy Dobbins recommends tackling dummies, pounding mattresses, and punching bags as well as other activities.

Dobbins's first error is to take a physical law about energy (energy cannot be destroyed) and to apply it to the mental world (anger is energy which cannot be destroyed). As any philosopher of science would tell him, it is a grave error to equate the physical world and the mental world. There is as much difference between physics and emotions as between nerves and nervousness. The idea that the energy associated with anger is like the energy in the natural world and must therefore be expended outwardly to prevent internal damage is without academic support.

Researchers refer to this particular model as the hydraulic model of emotions. The model says simply that if emotional energy is blocked in one place it must be released elsewhere. Researcher Carol Tavris says, "Today the hydraulic model of energy has been scientifically discredited."[48] She goes on to tell how psychologists expand the hydraulic idea to all emotions *contrary to research*. She says that in spite of the research evidence against the idea, "These therapists still argue that any feeling that is 'dammed up' is dangerously likely to 'spill over' and possibly 'flood' the system." Tavris declares, "There's little evidence that supressing anger is dangerous to health."[49]

Leonard Berkowitz, who has extensively studied violence and aggression, disagrees with the idea that it is desirable to let out one's aggressive feelings. Those therapists that encourage such active expressions of negative emotions are called "ventilationists." Their therapies, according to Berkowitz, stimulate and reward aggression and "heighten the likelihood of subsequent violence." He declares, "The evidence dictates now that it is unintelligent to encourage persons to be aggressive, even if, with the best of intentions, we want to limit such behavior to the confines of psychotherapy."[50] Berkowitz finds that ventilation-by-yelling has no effect on the reduction of anger.[51] This is also true of tackling dummies, pounding mattresses, punching bags and other such activities recommended by Dobbins.

Studies on both adults and children do not support the idea of hold-it-in-and-it-will-hurt-you and let-it-out-and-it-will-help-you. Research on heart disease and anger does not suggest supressed anger as a contributor to heart disease. If anything, the men at highest risk are over-expressing anger.[52] Dobbins directs parents to encourage aggressive play for children and to reward them for it. However, studies show that children who are permitted or encour- aged to play aggressively do not become less aggressive. They become more aggressive![53] Tavris says, "Expressing anger makes you angrier, solidifies an angry attitude, and establishes a hostile habit."[54]

There is a middle ground between repression and expression. And that middle ground is suppression. The Japanese suppress such feelings as anger. They are aware that such feelings exist. However, they do not act upon them. We know for certain that the Japanese physical health rate is far better than the American. Could it be that emotion suppressed is one factor that causes the Japanese to be so healthy?

In addition to his hydraulic-ventilationist position, which is contradicted by research, psychologist Dobbins also holds other unsubstantiated notions about anger. He relates anger and hurt in a way that may reveal more about himself and how he experiences hurt than about others and how they might experience it. Dobbins says, "We won't permit people who come to Emerge Ministries to say they hurt unless they are willing to acknowledge at the same time they are angry." Dobbins insists that all people who are hurt are automatically angry. He says, "After all, how can someone hurt you without making you angry?"[55]

It may be that every time Dr. Dobbins has been hurt he has responded in anger, but it does not follow that others respond in the same way. We have seen many individuals in our own biblical counseling ministry over the years who were hurt in a variety of ways completely without anger. And almost everyone can think of situations of hurt that have not resulted in anger. Hurt is sometimes, not always as Dobbins contends, accompanied by anger. The problem of insisting on the relationship as Dobbins does is that it eventually forces an individual to be convinced about a condition which may not be true.

Dobbins relates anger and depression in a way that reveals his own love of Freudian ideas rather than any knowledge about research. He says, "Depression is another hiding place for anger. More frequently than not, situational depression is aggravated if not initially caused by anger which the person unconsciously turns inward as a form of temporary self hatred." He adds, "In most depressed people there is a large amount of disguised anger."[56]

The Freudian unconscious turns out to be a good hiding place for all kinds of unproven ideas and can be used to support almost any idea one wishes. Freud and others have used it most effectively to hide unproven ideas. Researcher Judy Eidelson says, "The traditional approach to depression has been psychoanalytic [Freudian], which is based on the concept of 'anger turned inward.'" She goes on to say, "There are different causes of anger and different causes of depression; neither necessarily 'causes' the other."[57]

Psychologist Dobbins also strikes out from a biblical perspective. Is it okay to be angry? Dobbins says, "If God is angry with the wicked every day, and Jesus experienced anger, then maybe our fear of our own anger and subsequent guilt are exaggerated reactions to a normal human emotion."[58] Dobbins's reasoning is based upon his erroneous idea that if God and Jesus became angry then maybe we shouldn't be too hard on ourselves for becoming angry. While it is true that not all anger is sin or results in sin, much of it is and does. Dobbins, through some interesting verbal gymnastics, assures his readers that anger is merely unexpressed energy. However, the Bible makes it clear that much anger is wrong because the reason and/or the expression are sinful.

Dobbins even goes so far as to encourage individuals to express anger at God. He says, "If you're angry with God, tell Him you're angry with Him. Go ahead and tell Him. He's big enough to take it."[59] Where in Scripture do we have an example of it's okay to be mad at God? Jonah was mad at God to his own detriment, but no example can be found in Scripture where anger at God is condoned.

Even Michael the archangel "did not dare pronounce against [Satan] a railing judgment, but said, "The Lord rebuke you." (Jude

9) How much more serious to vent anger on God, who is our righteous, just, and loving Creator! We know that the fear of God is the beginning of wisdom. It would follow that to be angry at God is the beginning of foolishness. King Solomon warns, "Do not be hasty in word or impulsive in thought to bring up a matter in the presence of God." (Ecclesiastes 5:2)

In Scripture we are instructed to hate sin. Therefore we may be angry over sin and evil. One may certainly speak to God about anger over sin and evil, but it is wrong to be angry at God. If a person is indeed angry at God, he must admit his anger and confess his sin. One should also be encouraged to confess all ungodly anger just as one should always admit and confess sin to God according to the promise in 1 John 1:9. "If we confess our sins, He is faithful and righteous to forgive us our sins and to cleanse us from all unrighteousness." Denying the existence of angry thoughts and feelings prevents confession and cleansing and thus leaves the person in his sin.

Knowing and acting according to the truth of God enables individuals to overcome explosive expressions and internally prolonged anger which may lead to wrath, bitterness, and depression. Changed thinking is a great help for those who have problems with anger. Emotions are not independent. They have to be nursed and expressed and encouraged to remain by thinking the kinds of thoughts that will fuel them. Proverbs 14:29 gives wisdom concerning anger: "He who is slow to anger has great understanding, but he who is quick-tempered exalts folly." Even when things go wrong, Psalms 37:8 urges: "Cease from anger, and forsake wrath; fret not yourself, it leads only to evildoing."

A Christian can use an initial emotion of anger as a signal to quickly turn to God for guidance. Looking at a situation from God's perspective may lead people who have formerly been destructive in their anger to solve problems God's way. Each incident which stimulates a feeling of anger may provide another opportunity to put away the anger and to choose a new way of acting so that problem solving with the wisdom and strength of God will replace the expression of wrath or the internal nurturing of bitterness and resentment.

Chronic anger may be due to bitterness about circumstances, resentment against God, and unforgiveness of people. Anger may stem from wanting one's own way and not getting it. A habitual attitude of anger affects every thought, emotion, and action. Only choosing to believe the goodness of God, choosing to relinquish one's will to Him, and choosing to forgive others will bring the needed change.

Whenever psychology is intermingled with Scripture it dilutes the Word and deludes the church. Anger is more complex than the dangerous simplicity that Dobbins portrays. His biblical basis for expressing anger is weak at best and misleading at least. Dobbins's articles and his book are based upon his own personal, unproven psychological opinions. Unfortunately for him, his opinions and conclusions do not square with the research. Apparently Dobbins would like us to believe what he says because he says so. However, to subscribe to the defunct hydraulic-ventilationist theory and to prescribe tackling dummies, pounding mattresses, punching a bag, etc. and to recommend getting mad at God without research or biblical proof is scientifically inexcusable and biblically unreliable.

PSYCHOLOGICAL SMORGASBORD.

H. Norman Wright is another pastor turned psychologist. Christian Marriage Enrichment (CME), headed by Wright, is an excellent example of the naive and unnecessary amalgamation of biblical and psychological ideas. The CME conferences, workshops and seminars gather together an array of individuals from somewhat biblical to very psychological.[60] The mainline CME workshopper is one who blends and brews psychological and biblical concoctions that are exemplary of the psychologizing of Christianity.

The CME conferences present much psychological advice. The psychological advice covers topics from communication to crisis counseling and from teenagers to testing. However, the conferences promote psychological opinions more than the promises of God. CME conferences are one example of amalgamania run rampant. The conferences are a perfect picture of what has happened in the church. The change from the cure of souls to the cure of minds or a mixture thereof is clearly seen. The promotion of psychological solutions ahead of theological solutions and of psychologists ahead of pastors is transparent.

The CME conferences also include the unnecessary promotion

of psychological testing. The test most touted by CME is the Taylor-Johnson Temperament Analysis (TJTA). The CME announcement refers to the TJTA as producing a profile that is "extremely useful in premarital, marital and individual counseling." The come-on litany is as follows:

> Have you ever been "stuck" in counseling?
> Have you wondered whether to work with a person yourself or refer?
> Have you wanted a way to discover a person's problems immediately without taking ten hours of counseling time?
> Would you like to be able to use a personality indicator both for counseling & group Bible studies?
> Would you like to know "What to do" in counseling sessions?
> Have you ever wanted to know how to help someone struggling with worry, anger, depression or negative self-talk?
> If you have any "yes" answers, the TJTA seminar is for you.[61]

The promises associated with the above are many, but entirely without the proper scientific support.

The most important factor related to a test is its validity. Validity tells to what extent a test does what it claims to do. Psychological Publications, which prints and distributes the TJTA, claims an empirical validity for the test, the evidence of which does not exist.[62] The TJTA is only one example of a variety of tests naively used by many Christian counselors and pastors to supposedly understand people in order to help them. People take the tests and view the numerical results as if they give an objective and meaningful representation of the person. However, they have been intellectually numbed by the numbers and do not realize how little is returned for the effort given. To compound the lack of integrity, the tests often give a sense of confidence of knowing that is not statistically warranted.

It is a well-known statistical fact that the deeper the human quality being measured, the less likely that one can meaningfully measure it. One can generally rely upon the results of a typing test because it measures a very discreet human ability to produce words, sentences and paragraphs with a degree of accuracy using a specific device. But, when one moves from a test of ability (such as a typing test) to tests of achievement, aptitude, intelligence and finally to personality tests, there is a significant loss of test integrity.

Psychologist Dr. David Myers, in his book *The Inflated Self*, makes a very sobering remark about personality tests:

> People's believing horoscope data about themselves in the same way as personality test data, and their being most receptive to personality test feedback on tests that have the lowest actual validity, raises some disconcerting implications for psychiatry and clinical psychology. Regardless of whether a particular diagnosis has any validity, the recipient is likely to stand in awe of it, especially after expending effort and money to receive it.[63]

Many who are propelled by the promises of psychological revelation based upon the use of the TJTA and other such tests are flocking in to be trained, but unaware of the lack of usefulness of those instruments. Worse yet, they leave with a naive confidence that they will know or learn something of value about the individuals who take the tests.

TOSSED SALAD.

Effective Biblical Counseling by Dr. Lawrence Crabb, Jr., is another excellent example of the amalgamation of biblical truths and psychological opinions. Crabb states:

> Again, let me insist that psychology does offer real help to the Christian endeavoring to understand and solve personal problems.[64]

Crabb believes that he, unlike some integrationists, is "spoiling the Egyptians" by taking only the best and only the biblically sound ideas from psychology. He calls other attempts at integration the "tossed salad" approach. And, he criticizes those who would use solely the Scripture as "nothing buttery."

Crabb claims that his form of integration is the result of having accurately evaluated everything from "secular psychology in the light of Scripture." Thus we wonder how Anna Freud's writings on ego-defense mechanisms survived his careful examination. Anna Freud was Sigmund Freud's daughter who not only embraced her father's theories but expanded them. Of course all of this is from the perspective that a person is an autonomous creature without responsibility to a real God and without the possibility of relationship with the God who has revealed Himself in the Bible. Her observations are not only from an unbiblical point of view. They are biased from a subjective perspective rather than from scientific investigation. Nevertheless, Crabb recommends her writings in that area.[65]

Crabb also refers to Erich Fromm's "helpful" insights on people's need for love.[66] And much of what Fromm says may seem very appealing. However, once again one wonders what a person divorced from the God of love truly knows about love. In his book *Man for Himself* Fromm says, "Love is not a higher power which descends upon man nor a duty which is imposed upon him; *it is his own power* by which he relates himself to the world and makes it truly his."[67] (Emphasis added.) He thus denies that God is love and that He is the source of love. Fromm, along with the other humanistic psychologists, believes that man is intrinsically good. He refutes God's diagnosis of sin as the basic problem with mankind. Fromm's underlying philosophy and system of understanding of the human condition is in opposition to the Bible.

Besides extolling the contributions of Anna Freud and Erich Fromm, Crabb highly regards Carl Rogers's contributions to the importance of relationship in counseling[68] (even though Rogers repudiated Christianity and turned to the occult).[69] Crabb says, "Christians would do well to read Carl Rogers on the need for profoundly accepting the client as a worthwhile human being." Then he quotes Rogers:

> I launch myself into the therapeutic relationship, having a hypothesis, or faith, that MY liking, MY confidence, MY understanding of the other person's inner world will lead to a significant process of becoming . . . I enter the relationship as a person.[70] (Emphasis added.)

Rogers's approach clearly leaves the God of the Bible out of the picture. Having repudiated the God of the Bible as the one who can enable a person to grow and develop, Rogers sets himself up as the one who will enable another person to grow and develop through his own wonderful ways. He offers another god—the therapist— and he offers another salvation and another standard for living.

The Bible speaks of love and relationship, and God is the source of love. He calls individuals into a profound relationship with Himself. His love enables them to love and to live according to His design. Yet Christians whose profession is to help people live more productive lives have turned to ungodly men to discover the meaning of love. Problems of living are not outside of God's revelation. He is the one who has given humanity the Manual for living. Nevertheless integrationists evidently do not find enough truth in Scripture. Instead, they encourage counselors to wade through a long list of psychological theories to find what is needed for counseling.[71]

When we look at what Crabb has "spoiled the Egyptians" for, we find that he has taken the need structures of such people as Abraham Maslow. Maslow's hierarchy of needs (including self-actualization) is an unbiblical way of trying to understand people. Such systems place man and his needs at the center of the universe rather than God. Furthermore, they operate as though God does not exist. They represent one of the misunderstandings about life which Jesus addressed in the Sermon on the Mount:

> Do not be anxious then, saying, "What shall we eat?" or "What shall we drink?" or "With what shall we clothe ourselves?" For all these things the Gentiles eagerly seek; for your heavenly Father knows that you need all these things. But seek first His kingdom and His righteousness; and all these things shall be added to you. (Matthew 6:31-33)

Psychological need structures are based on what the "Gentiles seek." They go beyond physical needs to so-called psychological needs, but they are still what the "Gentiles seek." They are not based upon an understanding of Scripture. Although the physical needs for food, shelter, and clothing are the same for all, the approach to meeting the needs is quite different. Furthermore, when one goes into the other so-called needs there is distortion.

Two of the primary so-called needs are security and significance. Crabb has picked from the tree of so-called needs and
decided that a need for security (female's so-called main need) and
significance (male's so-called main need) are basic to all problems.[72] The need for significance and security seem to supercede a
person's other needs. Furthermore, Crabb encourages psychological acceptance as voiced by unredeemed minds.

It is understandable why people who do not know God think that
man's greatest needs (apart from food, clothing, and shelter) are
security and significance. Relationship with God is man's greatest
need and everything else comes from that relationship. Security
and significance are miniscule aspects of relationship with God.
The psychological emphasis on security and significance tend to
focus a person's attention on himself and his own desires rather
than on God and His will and supply.

Rather than focusing on a person's need for security the Bible
emphasizes the need to trust God. Instead of emphasizing significance, which can easily lead to a prideful sense of importance, the
Bible calls for obedience to God's will and involvement in His
work. How can man's so-called need for security and significance
explain the martyrs of the first century or a mother who risks her
life by running in front of a car to save her child, or a missionary
who leaves father, mother, sister, brother and worldly security to
serve the Lord? Only love can explain such self-giving acts. Trust
and obedience to God which come from a love relationship with
Him will provide what a person may call "security and significance." However, such words tend to place the focus on self rather
than on God and a person's active relationship with Him.

Crabb also proclaims that Christians "need" to have personal
worth and that such self-worth comes from the "needs" of security
and significance being met. Then, much is said about self-acceptance. He says,

> Self-acceptance for so many people depends upon perfor-
> mance. What a tragedy in light of the fact that Christ's
> death provided God with a basis for accepting us in spite of
> our performance.[73]

There is a confusion between self-acceptance and God's acceptance. Again it is the psychological shift from God to self. If God

accepts us, shouldn't our response be love for Him rather than love and acceptance for ourselves? When there is love between two persons the gaze is not upon the self, but on the other. God accepts us because He loves us and provided the costly means to make us acceptable in Jesus. Such acceptance is received by faith that looks to Him rather than to self. A. W. Tozer emphasizes the direction of the soul that believes God:

> Faith is the least self-regarding of the virtues. It is by its very nature scarcely conscious of its own existence. Like the eye which sees everything in front of it and never sees itself, faith is occupied with the Object upon which it rests and pays no attention to itself at all. While we are looking at God we do not see ourselves—blessed riddance. . . . Sin has twisted our vision inward and made it self-regarding. Unbelief has put self where God should be, and is perilously close to the sin of Lucifer who said, "I will set my throne above the throne of God." Faith looks *out* instead of *in* and the whole life falls into line. [74]

Rather than a Christ-centered gospel, Crabb seems to be offering a self-centered gospel. He says:

> My thesis is that problems develop when the basic needs for significance and security are threatened. People pursue irresponsible ways of living as a means of defending against feelings of insignificance and insecurity. In most cases these folks have arrived at a wrong idea as to what constitutes significance and security. And these false beliefs are at the core of their problems. Wrong patterns of living develop from wrong philosophies of living. "As [a man] thinketh in his heart, so is he" (Proverbs 23:7). [75] (Emphasis his.)

As we have shown in the previous chapters, misunderstanding and misusing Proverbs 23:7 comes in very handy when one is trying to mix psychological theories with the Word of God.

With Crabb, guilt is also related to lack of significance and security. He seems to think that people continue in self-defense patterns so that they won't have to feel guilty about failure and that the church needs to show bases for significance and security. If the church busies itself with relieving guilt through making people feel significant and secure, what happens to God's old remedy of confession, forgiveness, and restoration as the means of relieving guilt?

We have looked at just a few of Crabb's ingredients in what he would never label a "tossed salad." The distinction that Crabb makes between the "tossed salad" ingredients and his own brand of "spoiling the Egyptians" is a false one. In fact, no integrationist would identify himself as a "tossed salad" type. All would insist that they are "spoiling the Egyptians." However, it is impossible to make sense of the fact that all Christian psychotherapists hope they are spoiling the Egyptians (that is, taking only the best that's out there) while their often conflicting myriad of approaches creates the opposite impression.

The variety of psychological approaches used by the variety of Christian integrationists should raise a question. Who is being spoiled? The Egyptians or the Christians? If all Christian psychotherapists are "spoiling the Egyptians," taking only the best and only that which seems to fit with Scripture, why is it that there is such a mixed bag, such a variety of salads? Every psychotherapist is eclectic. Each one picks and chooses what he wants from multitudes of man-made theories and techniques. Christian psychological counselors follow such a wide variety of conflicting approaches while all claiming to be consistent with Scripture. Thus the Bible has been made to conform not only to one psychological approach, but to many conflicting approaches. Rather than being used as a standard of measure for truth, it is twisted and bent to fit whatever psychological theories appeal to the therapists.

The concept of "spoiling the Egyptians" is a good one because what is being taken is truly from Egypt, which represents the ways of the world in contrast to the ways of God. And, indeed every Christian who has attempted to integrate the psychological way with the biblical way has "spoiled the Egyptians." However, they have spoiled the Egyptians of the very things that God warned against. When God directed the Israelites to spoil the Egyptians, He was referring to material wealth. He did not direct them to take along Egyptian ideology or idolatry into the Wilderness. When they did, they were in direct disobedience to God. The Golden Calf and the serious consequences that followed came from hearts that had given up on God and turned to man-made solutions.

MORE PSYCHOLOGICAL SPOIL.

One of the most highly regarded promoters of psychology in Christendom is Dr. Paul Tournier. He has probably had the greatest influence in making psychotherapeutic theories attractive to Christian intellectuals. Even though he points out shortcomings of the different theorists, he gives them great credibility in the search for self understanding.

In reference to the contributions of Freud, Jung, Adler, and other theorists, Tournier says, "I am fully persuaded that they all have something interesting, true and useful to contribute to the understanding of people. But they explain only mechanisms of the mind." He attributes scientific status to psychological theories and naively says, "It is precisely because objective scientific disciplines are involved that we are able to form a picture."[76]

Tournier admitted that neither psychotherapy or medicine could give a full understanding of a human being. Nevertheless, he saw psychotherapeutic theories as contributing to that understanding. Tournier himself relied heavily upon his own intuition and experience. That is not unusual. Since psychotherapy is not science, one can use whatever pleases him— personal intuition, ideas from others, a bit of the Bible. Thus, Tournier could freely pick and choose among the theorists and then form his own interpretation based upon his own intuition and life experience. He says:

> There are then two routes to be followed in the knowledge of man: one is objective and scientific, the other is subjective and intuitive. . . . One proceeds by logical analysis and precise assessment; the other by a total understanding.[77]

That kind of thinking is erroneous on two counts: (1) Psychology and psychotherapy in particular are not "objective and scientific," nor do they proceed by "logical analysis and precise assessment." They are loaded with subjectivity. (2) Subjective and intuitive approaches do not lead to "total understanding." There is only one person who has total understanding and that is God Himself, and He has revealed His understanding of the condition of humanity in

His Holy Word. To elevate intuition to such a high status contradicts the Word of God which says:

> The heart is deceitful above all things, and desperately
> wicked; who can know it? I the Lord search the heart, I try
> the reins, even to give every man according to his ways and
> according to the fruit of his doings. (Jeremiah 17:9-10,
> KJV)

God does not give the same kinds of "self understanding" that
Tournier does. Tournier's ideas on self-understanding resemble
Carl Jung's more than the Bible. In fact, Tournier's book *The
Meaning of Persons* relies heavily upon Jung's theories about the
self.[78] Tournier adopts and adapts what he wants from Freud, Jung,
and others. In his discussion of Freud, he supports Freud's understanding of the unconscious. In discussing a particular patient, he
confesses:

> I sent her of course to a Freudian colleague of mine, in
> whose hands patients like her recognize themselves to be
> quite different from what they believed. It is the Freudians
> also who have shown us how many infantile attitudes and
> reactions persist into what we fondly call adulthood.[79]

He has replaced the sinful condition of humanity with "infantile
attitudes and reactions." Why did he need Freud or anyone else to
show this to him? Why did he need to see sin as "infantile attitudes
and reactions"? One very possible reason is that if sin is seen as a
psychological problem, psychological solutions seem necessary.
Of course Tournier, as all amalgamators, attempts to bring that so-
called perfect combination of counseling: the Bible plus psychology. Or is it psychology plus the Bible?

Christians feel safe with Tournier and other amalgamists
because they do reveal the shortcomings and inadequacies of psychotherapy that they do not happen to agree with. For instance,
Tournier says,

> Psychoanalysis, of course, does nothing to remove the
> contradictions of the human heart. Psychoanalysts would
> be the first to admit this. Their methods are only a way of
> treating inhibitions and serious psychical disturbances, a

means of giving back to their patients some capacity for happiness, for normal activity and social life.[80]

Notice how he praises psychoanalysis at the same time he criticizes it. He must not have been in touch with the research done by Hans Eysenck (which we cover more completely elsewhere) which revealed that psychoanalysis, on the average, does slightly worse than no treatment at all, as current research also indicates. He both criticizes and praises psychotherapeutic theories in order to demonstrate that psychology needs Christianity and Christianity needs psychology.

As we have shown throughout this book, we do not agree that Christianity needs psychological theories to understand man, to comprehend why he acts the way he does, or to know how to help him change. The entire Bible is written to reveal God to man and to help man see himself from God's perspective. Such disclosure of the self is for the purpose of correction according to God's standard and means. Paul wrote these crucial words to Timothy:

> All Scripture is inspired by God and profitable for teaching, for reproof, for correction, for training in righteousness; that the man of God may be adequate, equipped for every good work. (2 Timothy 3:16-17)

Psychology attempts to help us know ourselves apart from knowing God. The focus is reversed. We can only become what He wants us to become by knowing Him and in knowing Him we will know ourselves—as Job came to know himself when he saw God, as Peter did when he looked at Jesus after he had denied Him three times, as Paul who refused to put confidence in the flesh. Peter was changed by knowing Jesus and by receiving His love and forgiveness by faith. Paul was changed by knowing Jesus so much that one of his greatest goals was to know Him even more. Knowing God does nothing for the old self, which is counted dead. The old self likes the search for self, the attention to the self, the understanding of self, and especially feeling good about the self. But, if we truly knew ourselves from God's perspective without truly knowing Him we would be devastated. In His love He reveals His mercy, grace, righteousness, power to restore and save while He allows us to see ourselves from His perspective. And, then there is the confidence that He will complete His work of transforming us into the image of Christ through our response of faith, hope, and love.

THE ROAD MORE TRAVELED.

Psychiatrist M. Scott Peck has become an extremely popular speaker and writer. His books *People of the Lie*[81] and *The Road Less Traveled*[82] have appeared on a leading evangelical magazine's Book of the Year list. The list is a result of votes cast by a group of evangelical writers, leaders, and theologians selected by the magazine. A *New York Times* book reviewer reveals, "The book's main audience is in the vast Bible Belt." The reviewer describes *The Road Less Traveled* as "an ambitious attempt to wed Christian theology to the 20th-century discoveries of Freud and Jung."[83]

In an interview which appeared in *Christianity Today*, Peck was asked "what he meant when he called Christ 'Savior.'" The reviewer writes,

> Peck likes Jesus the Savior as fairy godmother (a term I'm sure he does not use flippantly) and as exemplar, or one who shows us how to live and die. But he does not like the idea of Jesus the Atoner.[84]

The reviewer goes on to say,

> Peck's view of God is even more disturbing. He ends up looking suspiciously like a psychotherapist. Peck declares that God does not punish evil.[85]

The writer accurately sums up Peck's major problem and main weakness by saying, "He lets what he deems to be psychological necessity dictate theological truth."[86]

Peck's understanding of the nature of God and the nature of man comes from a blend of Jungian psychology and Eastern mysticism rather than from the Bible. In *The Road Less Traveled* he says of God and man:

> God wants us to become Himself (or Herself or Itself). We are growing toward godhood. God is the goal of evolution. It is God who is the source of the evolutionary force and

God who is the destination. This is what we mean when we
say that He is the Alpha and the Omega, the beginning and
the end. [87]

The Bible says quite the opposite:

> Thus says the Lord, the King of Israel
> And his Redeemer, the Lord of hosts:
> "I am the first and I am the last,
> And there is no God besides Me."
> (Isaiah 44:6)

Peck continues:

> It is one thing to believe in a nice old God who will take
> good care of us from a lofty position of power which we
> ourselves could never begin to attain. It is quite another to
> believe in a God who has it in mind for us precisely that we
> should attain His position, His power, His wisdom, His
> identity. [88]

The only words that approach this description are those describing
the thoughts of Lucifer.

> But you said in your heart,
> 'I will ascend to heaven;
> I will raise my throne above the stars of God,
> And I will sit on the mount of assembly
> In the recesses of the north.
> I will ascend above the heights of the clouds;
> I will make myself like the Most High.'
> (Isaiah 14:13-14)

And indeed Peck claims godhood for those who will take the
responsibility for attaining it.

> Nonetheless, as soon as we believe it is possible for man to
> become God, we can really never rest for long, never say,
> "OK, my job is finished, my work is done." We must
> constantly push ourselves to greater and greater wisdom,
> greater and greater effectiveness. By this belief we will

have trapped ourselves, at least until death, on an effortful treadmill of self-improvement and spiritual growth. God's responsibility must be our own.[89]

What a contrast to Jesus' words!

> At that time Jesus answered and said, "I praise Thee, O Father, Lord of heaven and earth, that Thou didst hide these things from the wise and intelligent and didst reveal them to babes. Yes, Father, for thus it was well-pleasing in Thy sight. All things have been handed over to Me by My Father; and no one knows the Son, except the Father; nor does anyone know the Father, except the Son, and anyone to whom the Son wills to reveal Him. Come to Me, all who are weary and heavy-laden, and I will give you rest. Take My yoke upon you, and learn from Me, for I am gentle and humble in heart; and you shall find rest for your souls. For My yoke is easy, and My load is light." (Matthew 11:25-30)

Peck defines original sin as human laziness. He proposes that it is laziness that prevents people from listening to "the God within them" which is "the knowledge of rightness which inherently resides within the minds of all mankind."[90] The prophet Jeremiah would not have agreed with Peck.

> I know, O Lord, that a man's way is not in himself; Nor is it in a man who walks to direct his steps. (Jeremiah 10:23-24)

Thus, from Peck's perspective, God resides in every single person and every single person knows what is right. He goes even further into the morass of Eastern mysticism and Jungian occultism when he says: "To put it plainly, our unconscious is God. God within us. We were part of God all the time. God has been with us all along, is now, and always will be."[91] The Bible reveals that the only way a person comes into relationship is through faith. Until a person is born of the Spirit he resides in the kingdom of darkness and is under the dominion of Satan.

> And you were dead in your trespasses and sins, in which you formerly walked according to the course of this world,

according to the prince of the power of the air, of the spirit that is now working in the sons of disobedience. Among them we too all formerly lived in the lusts of our flesh, indulging the desires of the flesh and of the mind and were by nature children of wrath, even as the rest. But God, being rich in mercy, because of His great love with which He loved us, even when we were dead in our transgressions, made us alive together with Christ (by grace you have been saved). (Ephesians 2:1-5)

Paul states very clearly that every person is alienated from God until he is saved by Christ Jesus:

Remember that you were at that time [before salvation by faith in Jesus] separate from Christ, excluded from the commonwealth of Israel, and strangers to the covenants of promise, having no hope and without God in the world. (Ephesians 2:12)

Peck's theology as well as his psychology has been greatly influenced by Jung. However he takes Jung's concepts of the unconscious a step further than Jung was willing to go. Peck says: "In my vision the collective unconscious is God; the conscious is man as individual; and the personal unconscious is the interface between them."[92] First he says that a person's unconscious is God; then he says that the collective unconscious (the unconscious of everyone who has ever lived somehow rolled together into one) is God. Then he reduces God's will to "the individual's own unconscious will,"[93] whatever that might be.

Christians seeking a deeper and closer walk with God have turned to *The Road Less Traveled*. In hopes of venturing on their own spiritual quest, many college students have read the book for their own spiritual development. However, according to Peck spiritual growth is to realize one's own godhood:

Since the unconscious is God all along, we may further define the goal of spiritual growth to be the attainment of godhood by the conscious self. It is for the individual to become totally, wholly God.[94]

Thus Satan's lie in the Garden of Eden has been recast into a blend of Eastern mysticism and western psychology.

Since writing *The Road Less Traveled* Peck says he has become a Christian. However, to date he has not repudiated anything he has written in that book. Peck, in an interview with *New Age Journal*, referred to *The Road Less Traveled* as a "gift from God" that was "dropped" on him. The interviewer describes the book as "a distinctly '80's blend of up-to-date psychology and down-to-earth religion." The interviewer then says, "Peck, in fact, insists that there is no difference between the two."[95]

Peck describes his twenty-five years of Zen Buddhism as "the ideal training ground for spiritual paradox." He says, "Without that, I don't think there was any way that I would have been able to swallow the god-awful paradoxes of Christianity."[96] Aside from his continual unabashed amalgamation of psychology and theology since his conversion, there is no way to tell whether his Christianity is based upon the Jesus of the Bible or of the Jungian collective unconscious.

CHRISTIANITY IN T.A. TERMS.

Dr. H. Newton Malony, a professor of psychology and a practicing psychotherapist, uses Transactional Analysis in his therapeutic practice. Transactional Analysis (TA), a therapeutic approach developed by Dr. Eric Berne and popularized by Dr. Thomas Harris in his book *I'm OK, You're OK*,[97] reached its crest of popularity some years ago and is now on the decline. The study of the history of psychotherapy reveals the rise and decline of one psychotherapy after another with none seeming to disappear because a newer model, newer version or newer idea comes along.

Dr. Thomas Harris discusses such biblical concepts as sin, being born again, absolutes, and grace. However, in each case his opinion on the matter is contrary to biblical Christianity. Harris does not believe that a child is born into a condition of sin. He contends that a child chooses that condition. Thus, for Harris sin is a decision that a child makes about himself (I'M NOT OK) rather than a condition in which a child finds himself. The Bible teaches that man is fallen by his inherited condition rather than by his own decision. There is a subtle, but gigantic theological difference between TA and the Bible.

As one can imagine, with a massive misconception of sin,

Harris's resulting teachings about the born-again condition are not biblical. According to Harris, it is the civilizing process that forces a person into the position of sin, and one is born again by deciding to change from I'M NOT OK to I'M OK. Thus, just as the condition of sin is a decision of man, so is the born-again experience. Here again there is a subtle, but powerful difference between the TA "truth" and biblical truth. It is the difference between the work of man to save himself and the work of God. The idea that I decide to be OK and then I am OK without the cross of Christ is a new theology.

Harris declares, "There are no doctrinal absolutes."[98] Furthermore he contends:

> The truth is not something which has been brought to finality at an ecclesiastical summit meeting or bound in a black book. *The truth is a growing body of data of what we observe to be true.*[99] (Emphasis his.)

This is Harris's way of saying that the basis for truth resides in man, not the Bible.

Besides distorting the biblical concept of sin, being born again, and absolutes, Harris mutilates the concept of grace. He has misshapen it to fit his own gospel of self-forgiveness and self-salvation. He says:

> The concept of grace . . . is a theological way of saying I'M OK—YOU'RE OK. It is not YOU CAN BE OK, IF or YOU WILL BE ACCEPTED, IF, but rather YOU ARE ACCEPTED, unconditionally.[100] (Emphasis his.)

Man is not accepted by God unconditionally as Harris believes. According to the Bible, man is saved (accepted) through faith in God, not faith in self. And, that salvation (acceptance) is not given willy nilly to everyone, but rather offered. There is only one way to receive and that is through God's Son. That is a clear teaching of the Bible. Harris probably deplores that teaching the same way he deplores other absolutes.

Harris's concept of sin, born-again, absolutes, and grace are all distortions of biblical truth. Nevertheless, at one time TA was one of the most popular therapies used by Christians. Can you imagine

how the use of TA could open a person up to all kinds of possibilities for biblical distortions and theological aberrations?

We use the example of Malony for two reasons. First, as an
illustration that there is a rise and decline of various therapeutic
approaches and, more importantly, to demonstrate how adopting a
particular approach can cause a theological change. In describing
how he uses TA, Malony says:

> In Transactional Analysis terms, I stay as close to my Free
> Child as possible. I am confident, as was Berne, that there
> is within the child part of me an area of primitive intuition
> (often termed the Little Professor) that can be trusted. I
> implicitly count on this part of my own psyche to guide me
> in making judgments and in making interventions.[101]

Please notice the words used by Malony and particularly the power
given to the Free Child. It is trusted and it is counted on to guide.
This raises the question: Where is the Holy Spirit? Malony says that
"this [free child/little professor] may be one of the ways God's Holy
Spirit works in my life."[102] Here is a prime example of how
psychology influences theology. Without these TA terms we are
certain that Malony would speak directly of the Holy Spirit as
guide. With the use of TA, Malony's theology has now become
mostly psychology, and the Holy Spirit "may" now work through
his "Free Child" or "Little Professor," though Malony can't say
for sure.

HYPNO-PSYCHO-RELIGIOUS SYNTHESIS.

Dr. Joseph Palotta, a Christian who is also a psychiatrist and
hypnotherapist, combines the worst of two evils into a practice that
he calls "hypnoanalysis." His system is an amalgamation of hypnosis and the Freudian psychosexual stages of development. His
book *The Robot Psychiatrist* is filled with unproven Freudian
concepts such as the subconscious determinants, abreaction and
the supposed determinism of early life experiences. He says that his
book contains "extremely rapid systems of treatment for emotional
disorders." He promises, "These methods bring about definite
therapeutic change of the underlying emotional problem."[103]

Palotta is completely sold on the Oedipus complex. He, like

Freud, claims that this is "a universal experience in the emotional development of every person."[104] The Oedipus Complex states that every child is filled with a desire for incest and homicide, every child desires sexual intercourse with the parent of the opposite sex, every child wants the like-sex parent to die, and every child is confronted with castration anxiety. Palotta says:

> The universal conclusion that little boys and little girls make is that somehow the little girls have lost their penises and have nothing.[105]

He goes on to describe how "little girls feel that they have been castrated, that their penises have somehow been cut off" and that little boys "fear that they will lose their penises." He says, "The little girls develop what is termed penis envy." According to Freud, every girl is merely a mutilated male who resolves her castration anxiety by wishing for the male sex organ. As Freud's theories are unveiled, we see lust, incest, castration anxiety, and for a woman, penis envy. Freud was convinced that all of these are psychologically determined by age five or six. Can you think of a more macabre, twisted and demonic explanation for human disorder?

The Oedipus Complex is based upon the Greek play entitled *Oedipus Rex* by Sophocles. Thomas Szasz, a psychiatrist who is well trained in Freudian ideas and well aware of their origins says, "By dint of his rhetorical skill and persistence, Freud managed to transform an Anthenian myth into an Austrian madness." He calls this "Freud's transformation of the saga of Oedipus from legend to lunacy."[106]

So the first evil is Freudian psychology at its worst. And, the second evil is the use of hypnosis. In our book *Hypnosis and the Christian* we consider the various problems with the use of hypnosis and show that even though it may now be used by medical doctors it originated from and is still practiced by witch doctors.[107] Research psychiatrist E. Fuller Torrey aligns hypnotic techniques with witchcraft.[108] Such techniques have been used for thousands of years by witches and shamans. After considering research on results, the occult origins, and the biblical prohibitions, we say that "Hypnotism is demonic at its worst and potentially dangerous at its best."[109] We conclude by saying:

> Because there are so many unanswered questions about its

usefulness and so many potential dangers about its usage, Christians would be wise to shun hypnosis.[110]

Palotta promises much from his hypno-psycho-analytical merger. However, recent writings from both in and out of the psychiatric profession indicate that the Freudian concepts are in question because of their tainted origins and because their tarnished history predicts a tenuous future for them. The major Freudian ideas have not stood the test of time nor have they withstood the scrutiny of research. Palotta provides a prime example of one who has combined the fallacies of Freud with the hypocrisy of hypnosis. He attempts to synthesize his theories and to synchronize them with Scripture, but it is a false alchemy.

PIT.

Dr. Cecil Osborne is a psychotherapist who practices a form of Primal Therapy (P.T.) that he calls Primal Integration therapy (P.I.T.). Primal Therapy was invented and popularized by psychotherapist Dr. Arthur Janov. Because PIT is based upon PT, we will first describe Primal Therapy. We describe Janov's approach elsewhere as follows:

> The sacred words of Primal Therapy are *Primal Pain*, which are always capitalized for emphasis. It is around these words that the central doctrines of Primal Therapy revolve. According to Janov, as the child grows he has a dilemma between being himself and conforming to the expectations of his parents. During this period of development, the child accumulates Pain from the injuries of unmet needs, such as not being fed when hungry, not being changed when wet, or being ignored when needing attention. Primal Pain occurs as a result of the conflicts between self need and parental expectation. Through the process of growth, as conflicts continue to occur, the accumulation of Primal Pain results in what Janov calls the "Primal Pool of Pain."
>
> When the Pool gets deep enough, just one more incident supposedly pushes the child into neurosis. This single

significant incident is labeled the "major Primal Scene."
Janov contends: "The major Primal Scene is the single
most shattering event in the child's life. It is that moment of
icy, cosmic loneliness, the bitterest of all epiphanies. It is
the time when he begins to discover that he is not loved for
what he is and will not be." It is at this point that the child
finally gives up the idea of being himself in order to gain
his parents' love. In the process of gaining parental
approval, the child supposedly seals off his real feelings
and becomes an unreal self. Janov calls this dissociation
from one's feelings "neurosis."[111]

Janov believes that the Primal Scene occurs between the ages of
five and seven and is buried in the unconscious. Primal Therapy
requires a return to the early years of life in order to find healing
and help. Janov's single-cause-single-cure formula is simple.
Blocked pain causes neurosis; PT cures it.

To be cured the neurotic is led back to his major Primal Scene in
order to experience the emotions associated with it and to suffer the
Primal Pain. The intense, acted out emotions associated with this
event are called a "Primal."

This is a feeling therapy in which feelings are encouraged and
emotions dominate. Screaming and crying are necessary ingredients to change, and verbal aggression is a mandated part of the
package. Screaming, screeching, sobbing, gagging, thrashing,
writhing, gurgling, choking, and wailing are all promoted and
practiced.

Janov claims a 95 percent cure rate for his customers. His claims
for cures are impressive. Mental, emotional, and even physical
cures and transformations are promised. He claims cures for everything from asthma to arthritis and from migraines to menstrual
cramps. Janov even claims that "about one-third of the moderately
flat-chested women independently reported that their breasts
grew."[112]

Osborne's PIT approach is a derivative of PT and is a blend of
Freudian theory, rebirthing,[113] and just a dash of "I'm not OK"[114]
from Transactional Analysis. As one reads the PIT approach, one
sees the principles, practices, and promises of PT (Primal Therapy). Though he does not make as rigid a claim as Janov does,
Osborne nonetheless uses the single-cause-single-cure idea.

Osborne states his central theme about "human ills" in this way: "A lack of proper love in childhood is the cause; Primal Integration therapy in a loving Christian atmosphere is the solution for emotional distress."[115]

Both Janov and Osborne offer their Primal promises in the same pattern with the same zeal. Testimonies of persons who tried other methods that failed and then "found it" in PT or PIT are presented by both Janov and Osborne. Osborne tells about a case of a man with a doctorate who had tried all kinds of psychotherapeutic approaches and even one Christian approach. However, nothing helped until he tried PIT. Osborne quotes the man as saying, "Primal Integration has become for me the equivalent of the Holy Grail, the Fountain of Youth. I've found it!"[116]

Osborne, like Janov, is long on promises, but short on independent scientific research to support his claims. Claims of cure by Osborne and Janov are based upon their own say so and not upon independent research and follow up.

Osborne, like Janov, is quick to make glib, unscientific and unsubstantiated claims. Osborne's book presents many unscientific, unsubstantiated statements offered as fact with minimal or no justification. Some examples are:

> . . . parental failure to love properly . . . is the root cause of all neuroses.[117]

> Everything that has ever happened to us, including the birth experience, is stored in some portion of the mind.[118]

> It is axiomatic that virtually all neuroses (all over-reactions) *have roots that go back to childhood*.[119] (Emphasis his.)

> Feelings do not age.[120]

> Time does not diminish childhood hurts. Those memories are inscribed indelibly. They do not erode or disappear. Adult insight in no way lessens them.[121]

> The unconscious never forgets.[122]

> Some women, deprived of a father when quite young,

become sexually frigid, or partly so, not having had an opportunity to live through the Oedipal stage—the period when the small girl falls in love with daddy, and fantasizes marrying him.[123]

Osborne rattles off these and other statements to validate his PIT approach—never mind that the statement is scientifically inaccurate or untrue or debatable.

Osborne, like Janov, claims one cure after another to entice people into treatment. His use of the Freudian opinions about the past, the unconscious determinants, and the emotions are unfortunate in an age that is more and more criticizing Freudian ideas and where even therapists are using them less and less. *Free Inquiry*, a secular humanist publication, ran an article on "The Death Knell of Psychoanalysis."[124] Psychiatrist E. Fuller Torrey wrote a book entitled *The Death of Psychiatry*.[125] And, Adolf Grunbaum, in his book *The Foundations of Psychoanalysis*, seems to have placed the last nails in the coffin of Freudian theory.[126]

Nevertheless, Osborne and other Christian psychotherapists seem bent on proclaiming PIT and other such therapies as the Holy Grail of help. PIT is at best a mammoth example of extreme hysteria and at worst an open door for demons. Doubly unfortunate is the fact that Jesus is dragged into PIT and especially into the melee that results from the cacophonous and cataclysmic combination of convulsions, cataplexies, calamaties, and claimed cures.

THE FALSE ROOT OF REJECTION.

Dr. Charles Solomon of Grace Fellowship International has written several books about his own approach to counseling. He describes his position in his book *Counseling with the Mind of Christ*. He says:

> Rare, indeed, is the individual who employs psychology exclusively for purposes of understanding the psychodynamics of the behavior in question while allowing the Spirit of God to apply the Word of God to produce a child of God and that child being "conformed to His image" (See Romans 8:29).[127]

Solomon approaches the understanding of problems of living

through psychological, not biblical, eyes. And, his psychological understanding of man is seen almost exclusively through the concept of rejection. Just as Freud viewed human problems through the early life Oedipus Complex, Solomon sees human problems through an early life rejection syndrome.

The Rosetta stone of rejection is to Solomon what the Oedipus Complex was to Freud. Rejection is the cornerstone of Solomon's theoretical amalgamation. And, just as Freudian analysts' patients report the Oedipal ideas and feelings to them, so do Solomon's patients report the rejection syndrome to him and his followers.

Solomon says:

> . . . the majority of mental and emotional symptoms have roots traceable to childhood rejection which has limited the person's options in coping with responsibility and stress.[128]

Solomon outdoes Freud in how far back he is willing to carry the possibility of rejection. In his book *The Rejection Syndrome* he says:

> Research has also substantiated a cause-and-effect relationship between a mother's rejection of the unborn child and the psychological difficulties of the child in later life.[129]

While this might be an interesting psychological idea, research has not substantiated any such cause-and-effect relationship. A single phone call to any medical school with faculty in child development or pediatric neurology will reveal this. Though Solomon proposes a spiritual solution to the rejection syndrome, his model of man is definitely psychological.

PSYCHO-CONFUSION.

Because of the multitude of theories and myriad of techniques it would be exhausting to be exhaustive in order to exemplify the confusion (and even quackery) that exists in psychotherapy. Over 7000 psychiatrists, psychologists, and social workers attended a recent meeting described by its organizer as "the Woodstock of psychotherapy." Psycho-celebrities such as Carl Rogers, Albert Ellis, R. D. Laing, Bruno Bettleheim, and Joseph Wolpe were present. Carl Rogers, who has influenced more therapists in America than anyone else, received a standing ovation. The full range from compliments to criticisms of psychotherapy were voiced throughout the convention. Criticisms by the speakers themselves included reports that most of the present distinct schools of psychotherapy are doomed to fizzle, that psychiatry is not a science, and that nothing new in human relations has surfaced from a century of psychotherapy.[130]

The various debates and differences of opinion led behavior therapist Dr. Joseph Wolpe to confess that "an outside observer would be surprised to learn that this is what the evolution of psychotherapy has come to—a Babel of conflicting voices."[131] The rifts which resulted from the range of therapies and therapists could easily lead one to title the conference "Babble from Babel."

From the unconscious determinants of Freud to the congruence, accurate empathy and positive regard of Rogers, and from the archetypes of Jung to the I'm-OK-You're-Ok of Harris, the field of psychotherapy is saturated with confusion and subjectivity. The whole array is simply subjectivity garbed in the pseudosophistication of a scientific sounding vocabulary and garmented by academic degrees and licenses. But it nonetheless stands naked before the eyes of true science and research.

Subjectivity exists wherever psychotherapy exists whether in or out of the church. Just because this subjective (supposedly scientific) practice is used by Christians and sometimes baptized by adding Scriptures does not raise it to the level of truth. Attempting to sanctify psychotherapy by adding Bible verses only secularizes Scripture.

The result of all attempts to sanctify psychotherapy has only led to as great a confusion of approaches concocted by Christian practitioners as by non-Christians. Behind all the rhetoric supporting the marriage of Scripture and psychotherapy is the reality of confusion. There is almost as wide a diversity of theories and techniques amongst Christians as amongst non-Christians. Differences between Christian professionals exist on even the most basic and important elements of psychotherapy. For example, one group emphasizes the unconscious determinants of behavior and another group avoids them all together. One group of Christians will use a system such as primal therapy and another group will call it demonic. It is perplexing and paradoxical how such a mess could have mesmerized Christians.

It is clear that the prevailing psychotherapeutic systems merely reflect the current culture. In fact, American psychotherapeutic approaches are almost nonexistent in other parts of the world. They are not universal but rather socio-culturally restricted. We know that the truths of Scripture transcend culture and time. They are eternal. Which so-called truths discovered only by psychotherapists are eternal?

If psychotherapists would spend more time reading the research on outcomes in psychotherapy and less time defending their psychotherapeutic faith, they would see that the "rock" on which they stand is sinking sand. As we have shown earlier, psychotherapy is not science and does not involve scientific theory. We will later demonstrate that it rests upon the erroneous assumption that problems of thinking and living constitute illnesses and therefore require cures by psychologically trained counselors.

Amalgamania has spread from the counseling room to nearly every aspect of the Christian life. Distinctions between the ways of the world and the ways of God have blurred so that psychological ideas are accepted as biblical truth. The psychologists are not the only ones who are busy attempting to merge messages; the clergy have joined them. William Kilpatrick has said that "most popular psychology flatly contradicts the Christian message, and yet many priests and pastors seem hellbent (if I may use that term) on blending the two."[132]

The error committed by these well-intentioned, but ill-informed psychologizers is that they take what each regards as the best and seemingly biblical of the psychological wisdom of man and amalgamate it with the Word of God. Never mind that each psychologist sees it differently. Never mind about the confusion of theories and techniques. And, never mind the lack of scientific proof or justification. There is no need for amalgamania! Problems of living in the lives of Christians require Holy Spirit led, biblical solutions; not wisdom-in-the-flesh psychological solutions. The fact is that many Christian psychologists have become popular through their speaking and writing. And, popularity has taken precedence over purity in the church.

These individuals have psychologized the church with their

unscientific and unproven ideas, have trivialized the Word of God, and have almost paralyzed the body of Christ. Christians would be better off entirely to listen to pastors trained and experienced in the Word of God than psychologists who are trained and experienced in psychology. Pastors and parishioners alike have not only capitulated to the psychologizers; they have sadly catapulted them to the place of high priests over the problems of living.

It is tragic that Christians have followed the psychological way and its false solutions to real problems. Not only have the psychologists succumbed to the deception of amalgamation, but pastors, leaders, and congregations have been deceived. As author W. Phillip Keller aptly puts it, "All of them together have put their confidence in the wrong cure, i. e. in the 'couch' instead of 'In Christ.'"[133]

The Lord Himself is sufficient. His Word is living truth. He has given His Holy Spirit and His Word to guide believers in all matters concerning how to live and relate to others. He continues to call believers who are struggling with the challenges of life to come to Him.

> Why do you spend money for what is not bread,
> And your wages for what does not satisfy?
> Listen carefully to Me, and eat what is good,
> And delight yourself in abundance.
> Incline your ear and come to Me.
> Listen, that you may live. . . .
> Seek the Lord while He may be found;
> Call upon Him while He is near.
> (Isaiah 55:2, 3, 6)

6

A Way that Seemeth Right

> And when I came to you, brethren, I did not come with
> superiority of speech or of wisdom, proclaiming to you the
> testimony of God. For I was determined to know nothing
> among you except Jesus Christ, and Him crucified. And I
> was with you in weakness and in fear and in much trem-
> bling. And my message and my preaching were not in
> persuasive words of wisdom, but in demonstration of the
> Spirit and of power, that your faith should not rest on the
> wisdom of men, but on the power of God. (1 Corinthians
> 2:1-5)

No matter how personable and well-meaning a Christian
therapist may be, he has been heavily influenced by the ungodly
psychological perspective. Psychology thus becomes the means
for both interpreting Scripture and applying it to daily living.
When one reads the Bible from the psychological perspective of
Freud, Jung, Adler, Maslow, Rogers, et al, he tends to conform the
Bible to those theories and methods. Rather than looking at life
through the lens of the Bible, he looks at the Bible through the lens
of psychology.

Amalgamators add the wisdom of men to fill in what they think is missing from the Bible. They take an age-old problem, give it a new name, such as "mid-life crisis," and give solutions from the leavened loaf.[1] They integrate psychological ideas with a Bible verse or story here and there to come up with what they believe to be effective solutions to problems they think are beyond the reach of Scripture.

One human problem after another is confronted with an integrated approach. This conveys the idea that one is getting the best of both worlds, and underneath this is the not-so-subtle idea that the Bible is insufficient and must be propped up by a strong psychology. Each psychological counselor decides which of the over 250 often-contradictory psychological approaches and which of the 10,000 not-always-compatible techniques he will integrate with the Bible. Does anyone notice the contradictions in all of these integrations?

Even Christian psychologists chase one trendy idea after another just like Don Quixote pursuing the parade of tilting windmills. Freud is not quite as popular among Christians as Jung, Rogers, Adler, and Maslow are right now. As Berne became less popular, Ellis gained in popularity among Christian therapists. It all depends on which ideas and methods are in vogue and how well they are couched in Christian terminology. And, unfortunately the church pursues both blindly and eagerly the psychological purveyors of perverse and unproven ideas and opinions with the same kind of loyalty and naivete as Don Quixote's servant Sancho.

PROFESSIONALISM.

Christians have given significant concerns of life over to the ever-bulging ranks of professionalism. C. P. Dragash complains that "The 20th century has seen the professionals take over from families and communities many of their ancient responsibilities." He refers to the high price paid as "the loss of autonomy in families and the decay of community identity and responsibility."[2] This is not simply a secular problem. Christians are included in the ranks. The most repeated advice among Christians for problems of living is "get some counseling," and by this they mean professional psychological counseling.

Professionalism is especially true in the field of counseling. The "loss of autonomy," "decay of community identity," and loss of responsibility have gone so far that professional help is now considered necessary for problems that used to be solved by common sense and caring friends. A *Newsweek* article states, "Sometimes even the obvious solution requires the blessing of a therapist."[3] In other words, people are now paying professionals to tell them what common sense would dictate. And, while training and licensing are unnecessary to dispense obvious solutions to sometimes simple problems, loss of individual responsibility and confidence have necessitated it. However, it is loss of responsibility and confidence fostered by the therapists themselves, and now therapy is necessary to encourage individuals to do what common sense would have caused them to do in the past. One sees this psychological mentality in a great variety of places and the examples one could give are pandemic.

Psychological therapy has thus encouraged the very problems it claims to cure. It has fostered dependence on the professional and it has given psychological excuses for a person not to take responsibility for his own decisions and actions. People have inadvertently been robbed of dignity and personal responsibility in the name of therapy. Perhaps we could add some new "mental illnesses" to the expanding list: such as the disease of psychotherapeutic mentality, the disease of dependence on therapists, the disease of shifting responsibility onto professionals, and the disease of psychotherapy. As someone once said, "Psychotherapy is the disease of which it pretends to be the cure."

PASTORS UNDERMINED.

The cancer of psychotherapy has not only hit the church, but has metastasized to all its members. More and more Christians are looking to psychologists as though they are the wise men of the twentieth century. Psychologists have taken the position of priests and have replaced the pastors as "experts" in all matters pertaining to life. Freud and Jung et al speak for us instead of the apostles and prophets.

Psychotherapist Dr. Loriene Chase concedes that pastors can deal with "ecclesiastical confusion and can assist in the maturation of your spiritual belief systems as well as offering a workable and compatible philosophy in your search for inner harmony." But, according to Chase, the pastor without psychotherapeutic training should be limited to those matters.[4] Dr. Chase, like many psychologists, does not see the Bible as the authoritative Word about all matters of the human heart, soul, mind, and behavior. Yet her advice is almost identical to Christians who have made psychology their standard and guide for values, attitudes, emotions, thoughts, actions, and relationships. If the Bible does not speak to the crucial issues of life and if Jesus has not come to indwell and transform believers, then we are to be pitied. The psychological answers do not give life. They merely manipulate according to the whim of the human heart and the bias of the therapist.

Mary Vander Goot, a professor of psychology at a Christian college, lists a litany of reasons why preachers should not minister to individuals with "deeply-rooted, life-crippling psychological problems."[5] Her bias is obviously psychological. She lists reasons why pastors should not counsel, such as their lack of psychological training, qualifications, and experience. They do not usually charge a fee, and they do not set prescribed time limits on appointments. Furthermore, she fears that if pastors counsel they risk church unity.[6]

By the end of the article Vander Goot has made it sufficiently clear that no self-respecting minister who is ethical and logical would counsel because of the incompatibility of the roles of pastor and therapist. Evidently the biblical answers to life's problems and complexities are only appropriate on Sunday mornings; psychological ideas are the fare for the rest of the week. Thus Vander Goot recommends: "The pastor should be taught how to assemble a list of professionals in his community who will serve his parishioners well."[7]

The early church survived without professional psychologists. And, throughout the centuries Christians found victory in Jesus without the help of twentieth-century psychologists. Pastors ministered to the problems of living through preaching, teaching, and counseling the Word of God. However, today psychological ideas about life and how to live happily and successfully have replaced and/or supplemented the age old truths by which the saints through the ages have lived. And, if pastors have not been trained in those psychological ideas and methods they are no longer considered able to minister to the most crucial challenges of life. And, the psychologists have placed themselves beyond reproach, because unless a person is trained in the theories and methods of psychology he supposedly doesn't know what he is talking about if he questions the psychological way.

Contrary to the general, acceptable, cultural view, psychotherapy is riddled with myths. Psychiatrist Garth Wood, in his book *The Myth of Neurosis*, describes the bankruptcy of psychotherapists:

> Cowed by their status as men of science, deferring to their academic titles, bewitched by the initials after their names, we, the gullible, lap up their pretentious nonsense as if it were the gospel truth. We must learn to recognize them for what they are—possessors of no special knowledge of the human psyche, who have nonetheless, chosen to earn their living from the dissemination of the myth that they do indeed know how the mind works, are thoroughly conversant with the "rules" that govern human behavior.[8]

In testifying at a murder trial (for the prosecution) psychiatrist Lee Coleman said, "I think common sense wins hands-down in a race with psychiatry."[9]

Wood is not cowed by the sacred cow of psychotherapy. He says, "Freudian theories, and their offspring, are irrelevant where they are not actually dangerous."[10] Psychiatrist Thomas Szasz says.

> Perhaps most, so-called psychotherapeutic procedures are harmful for the so-called patients . . . all such interventions and proposals should therefore be regarded as evil until they are proven otherwise.[11]

In spite of the research, psychological counselors continually spread rumors about persons being harmed by pastoral or biblical counseling. One wonders if they are acquainted with the research about people being harmed by psychological counseling. There are numerous horror stories hidden away in psychological therapy closets related to misdiagnosis, maltreatment, and other failures.

Archibald Hart, Dean of the Graduate School of Psychology at Fuller Seminary, illustrates his concern by listing a host of problems associated with pastors as counselors. And of course, most of those reasons evaporate if the pastor is psychologically trained. Hart says, "When people sit in the pew, they want to know truth.

When they sit in the counseling room, they want to be understood."[12] And yet, in Jesus there is both grace and truth. The Bible
does not separate truth from love. And who understands better than
God? And what does Hart mean when he says "understood"? Does
a psychologically trained individual understand people any better
than any one else? There is no evidence that he does. Professional
therapists have even been notoriously poor at diagnosis.[13]

Hart expresses his ideas about counseling and counseling relationships as if his statements were scientific and based upon
research, when, in fact, he is espousing only his own personal
opinion. For example, he says, "The most important way we have
for understanding the self is through the exploration of feelings."[14]
Not only does the Bible not support that statement; one can easily
find a great number of professionals, including Christian psychologists, who would deny this. Nevertheless, Hart's personal point of
view is printed as if it were a scientific gospel.

In addition, Hart promotes the work of Carl Rogers by saying,
"Carl Rogers has identified and articulated, *perhaps better than
any other theoretician*, the essential qualities of a good human
interaction."[15] (Emphasis added.) Evidently it doesn't matter that
Carl Rogers is a humanistic psychologist who has espoused secular
humanism and spiritism and even consulted the Ouija Board and
been involved in necromancy.[16]

In spite of his questionable involvements and unbiblical ideas
and practices, Rogers is emulated by many who call themselves
"Christian psychologists."[17] In fact, Rogers was rated in first
place in a ranking survey of CAPS (Christian Association for
Psychological Studies) in reference to influence in counseling
practices. One could excuse this ignorance on the part of Christian
psychologists except that Carl Rogers, while having departed
severely from his early Christian background, has erected a system
that is a pale imitation of what one could more richly find in
Scripture. For example, Carl Rogers's crowning discovery is that of
love.[18] Why would anyone need to ask Carl Rogers about love? In
his description of the man of the future, he writes:

> The man of the future . . . will be living his transient life
> mostly in temporary relationships . . . he must be able to
> establish closeness quickly. He must be able to leave these
> close relationships behind without excessive conflict or
> mourning.[19]

What does this say about commitment of relationship in love between persons? Furthermore a secular humanist knows nothing about the love of God that passes understanding. And the kind of love that is Christian has no counterpart or parallel in humanistic psychology.

Why Christians need to find out about love from Carl Rogers boggles the mind. Love is a constant theme of Scripture. God is love. Jesus loves. The Bible teaches love. How could anyone miss it? It is heartbreaking to hear Christian psychologists say that they did not know about love until they read Rogers. One wonders if they could truly know Jesus or the love of God since Rogers's brand of love is limited to the self-serving carnal flesh.

Could it be that Christian psychologists spend so much time reading psychological texts and so little time reading the Bible that they do not see love in Scripture? Have they so spiritualized the Bible that they do not see the practicality of God's love and Christ's Words about love? Do they not realize the power of the gospel of Christ to deal with all problems of living?

Hart ends his comments by saying, "As a general rule, whenever possible, get some therapy yourself—not necessarily because you have problems, but to develop a greater self-understanding."[20] This would not have been the advice of the saints throughout the centuries. They would have said, "Know God." It is Socrates rather than the Bible that declared that we should know ourselves. The Bible constantly encourages us to know God. Paul prayed for the Christians that:

> . . . the God of our Lord Jesus Christ, the Father of glory, may give to you a spirit of wisdom and of revelation in the knowledge of Him. I pray that the eyes of your heart may be enlightened, so that you may know what is the hope of His calling, what are the riches of the glory of His inheritance in the saints, and what is the surpassing greatness of His power toward us who believe. (Ephesians 1:17-19)

The only kind of self understanding Christians must come to is that which follows knowing God. And that is the kind Job came to when he encountered the Living God.

> Then Job answered the Lord, and said,

> "I know that Thou canst do all things,
> And that no purpose of Thine can be thwarted.
> 'Who is this that hides counsel without knowledge?'
> Therefore I have declared that which I did not understand,
> Things too wonderful for me, which I did not know."
> 'Hear, now, and I will speak;
> I will ask Thee, and do Thou instruct me.'
> "I have heard of Thee by the hearing of the ear;
> But now my eye sees Thee;
> Therefore I retract,
> And I repent in dust and ashes." (Job 42:1-5)

The Bible teaches that we are transformed into the image of Christ not by looking at ourselves or at our feelings, but rather by looking at Him.

> But we all, with unveiled face beholding as in a mirror the glory of the Lord, are being transformed into the same image from glory to glory, just as from the Lord, the Spirit. (2 Corinthians 3:18)

Can you imagine the apostle Paul seeking self-understanding through exploring his feelings?

> But whatever things were gain to me, those things I have counted as loss for the sake of Christ. More than that, I count all things to be loss in view of the surpassing value of knowing Christ Jesus my Lord, for whom I have suffered the loss of all things, and count them but rubbish in order that I may gain Christ. (Philippians 3:7-8)

There are some very basic differences between the psychological ideas invading the church and the doctrines of Scripture, both in direction and emphasis. The psychological way seeks to enhance the self, through self-love, self-realization, self-esteem, self-actu- alization, self-understanding, and other selfisms. The Bible teaches loving God and neighbor and the application of the cross to the self so that believers may confidently say with Paul,

> I have been crucified with Christ; and it is no longer I who live, but Christ lives in me; and the life which I now live in

the flesh I live by faith in the Son of God, who loved me, and delivered Himself up for me. (Galatians 2:20)

In contrast to the fears of Vander Goot and Hart, Bernie Zilbergeld, who does not even profess the Christian faith, suspects that even lay people (regardless of their religious persuasion) do a good job of counseling. He admits that if professional therapists were pitted against lay therapists and research done on the results, "I would worry until the results were in," as far as the survival of his own profession is concerned.[21] Besides noting the research that does not support the use of professionally trained therapists, Zilbergeld says:

> If counseling does indeed produce great changes, the results should be easy to observe in therapists, for they have received more therapy than any other group of people and they have also had extensive training in methods of personal change, methods they could personally use on themselves.[22]

If therapy is all that it is supposed to be, the lives of therapists should advertise its benefits. However, the lives of therapists do not support the claims made by them for their psychological surgery. There is no book that surpasses the Bible in giving an accurate understanding of the human condition. There is no one else who can transform a life like Jesus can. He has given believers His Word and His Holy Spirit and He has chosen to minister through His people in such a way that the glory goes to the Father. That was the basis of our previous book *How to Counsel from Scripture.*[23]

SUBVERTING THE FAITH.

The antagonism towards Christianity subtly seeps through psychological ideas about why people are the way they are, how they should live, what they need, and how they change. Such ideas, promoted by sincere Christians who believe and promote the psychological way, actually subvert the claims of Christ. Rather than denying the claims of Christ directly, they simply place Him alongside their favorite psychological theorists. Instead of denying the validity of the Word of God, they merely say that ministers of the Word are not qualified to minister to the deep levels of human need.

Psychological counselors undermine the counseling of pastors and have developed a formula for referral: (1) Anyone who is not psychologically trained is not qualified to counsel those people with the really serious problems of living. (2) Refer them to professional trained therapists. This is one predictable and pathetic pattern of the psychological seduction of Christianity.

Pastors have been intimidated by the warnings from psychologists. They have become fearful of doing the very thing God has called them to do: to minister to the spiritual needs of the people through godly counsel both in and out of the pulpit. Some of that intimidation has come from psychologically trained pastors. A spokesman for the American Association of Pastoral Counselors, a psychotherapeutically trained group of pastors, says "Our concern is that there are a lot of ministers who aren't trained to handle their parishioners' psychotherapy."[24] And of course, if the pastors are not trained they are not considered qualified. Therefore, the predictable benediction to the litany is: "refer to a professional."

And, just as referral is the offering to the parishioner, it is the so-called answer for the missionary who needs rehabilitation. An article in a conservative Christian magazine recommends the possibility of sending missionaries away from a church to a treatment center "which specializes in missionary restoration."[25] In checking the staff of this restoration-for-missionaries center, we found— you guessed it— professional psychotherapists.

Can you imagine Paul turning to the ideas of men after his first missionary journey, after he had been persecuted and nearly stoned to death? Paul refused to put any confidence in the flesh. Without ever turning again to the philosophies of men and without the benefit of twentieth-century psychology, Paul rejoiced in the knowledge of Jesus Christ and in the great privilege to serve Him and to suffer for Him.

The number of examples of the referral formula is endless. It would be repetitious and eventually boring to continue adding examples. Everyone knows that the church has become one gigantic referral system. Nationally-known evangelist Jimmy Swaggart says of the church, "God help us, we've become nothing more than a great referral bureau." This same evangelist criticizes psychology which is "papered over with a thin veneer of the Word of God"

and wonders "whether this isn't the greatest Trojan horse of all."[26]
One pastor rightly challenges other pastors by saying:

> . . . we pastors have, like the rest of society, forgotten who
> we are and what we do. We are ministers of the Word. As
> such, everything we do, including counseling, is to be
> guided by the Word.
>
> We have confused ourselves with secular counselors and
> psychologists. We have different goals! Their goal is to see
> the counselee restored to normalcy as recognized by soci-
> ety. Our goal is to see the counselee restored to a right
> relationship with God, and then, as a result of that restora-
> tion, to see him live as a child of God. Just as secular
> counseling and biblical counseling have different goals,
> they have different methods.[27]

This pastor also says, "Pastors either 'farm out' counseling situations to 'professional counselors,' or use secular counseling methods themselves." Then he asks a very important question: "How
can we expect our people to see the relevance of God's Word on
Sunday morning if we use a different standard during the week?"[28]
This type of spiritual schizophrenia elevates the psychological over
the theological and therapy over sanctification.

No conservative members of any world religion would ever seek
answers to life's problems outside of their faith. Instead, they
would look to their families and religious leaders for counsel. For
example, Moslems seek answers from their religious scholars or
"ulema."[29] However, conservative Christians now seek answers
from psychotherapists. That this is true is seen in the previous
writers quoted as well as others. In a well-known Christian newsletter on cults, a professor of psychology from the University of
California in Berkeley, who obviously has excellent academic
credentials, was interviewed. She was given center stage in the
publication and spoke as an authority in the field of cults.[30] The
trouble is that this psychologist, who is a non-Christian, advocated
psychology while explaining some helpful information about cults.
All in all, while this article had some valuable observations,
psychology came out ahead and Christianity came out behind.

THEOLOGY OR PSYCHOLOGY?

In the past fifty years there really has been a gradual but dramatic shift from a conservative to a liberal view of the Scriptures in the church—from a theology of life to a psychology of life. Pastor Ben Patterson admits, "But of late, we evangelicals have out-liberaled the liberals with our self-help books, positive thinking preaching, and success gospels."[31] The psychological way is not limited to the counselor's office; it greatly influences the way Christians think and talk. Psychological ideas are interspersed with Scripture. In most cases those Scriptures that would directly oppose the popular psychological ideas are either forgotten or reinterpreted.

It is obvious that the morals of society and the biblical standards of the church have been strongly influenced by psychology and that much of the moral decay and outright rebellion are directly attributable to the psychological way. One writer says of Freud's influence:

> Probably no single individual has had a more profound effect on twentieth-century thought than Sigmund Freud . . . for better or worse he has changed the face of society.[32]

This can even more strongly be said of psychological counseling and psychological ideas about mankind. And, as the church has become psychologized, its standards have been compromised.

Psychologist William Kirk Kilpatrick aptly describes the situation he experienced:

> The point I wish to make here is that religion and psychology had become nearly indistinguishable for me. Freud and the church fathers, faith in God and faith in human potential, revelation and self-revelation—all slid together in an easy companionship. As for God, He began to take shape in my mind along the lines of a friendly counselor of the nondirective school. I never balked at doing His will. His will always coincided with my own.[33]

Later Kilpatrick says:

> It sometimes seems that there is a direct ratio between the increasing number of helpers and the increasing number of

those who need help. The more psychologists we have, the more mental illness we get; the more social workers and probation officers, the more crime; the more teachers, the more ignorance.

One has to wonder at it all. In plain language, it is suspicious. We are forced to entertain the possibility that psychology and related professions are proposing to solve problems that they themselves have helped to create. We find psychologists raising people's expectations for happiness in this life to an inordinate level, and then we find them dispensing advice about the mid-life crisis and dying. We find psychologists making a virtue out of self-preoccupation, and then we find them surprised at the increased supply of narcissists. We find psychologists advising the courts that there is no such thing as a bad boy or even a bad adult, and then we find them formulating theories to explain the rise in crime. We find psychologists severing the bonds of family life, and then we find them conducting therapy for broken families.[34]

In another book Kilpatrick says that "what psychology gives with the one hand, it takes away with the other."[35]

Kerry Koller, director of the Center for Christian Studies, asks the following question: "Do psychological theories and therapies see life from an angle that Christians can accept?" He points out how psychology "has come to take a central position in man's understanding of himself and the world he lives in."[36] He then goes on to discuss how most psychological theories contradict biblical truth. He contends that "One could even argue that it is precisely because of the use of these therapies in Christian settings that Christian ethical norms have gotten considerably weaker."[37] He concludes by saying, "If Christians wholeheartedly accept current psychological theories they will probably take on the values of the surrounding society which psychology embodies."[38] We believe this has already happened.

Two comments from the Christian Booksellers' Association (CBA) convention speak to this point. A book publisher's representative says, "It's one of the most upbeat CBA's I've been to. It's fulfill yourself, do it all, have it all—in a Christian way, of course."

Is it possible to fulfill self, do it all, have it all in a Christian way?
A. W. Tozer stressed the inadequacy of what he called "Instant
Christianity." He wrote:

> The American genius for getting things done quickly and
> easily with little concern for quality or permanence has
> bred a virus that has infected the whole evangelical church
> in the United States and, through our literature, our evan-
> gelists and our missionaries, has spread all over the world.
>
> Instant Christianity came in with the machine age. Men
> invented machines for two purposes. They wanted to get
> important work done more quickly and easily than they
> could do it by hand, and they wanted to get the work over
> with so they could give their time to pursuits more to their
> liking, such as loafing or enjoying the pleasures of the
> world. Instant Christianity now serves the same purposes
> in religion. It disposes of the past, guarantees the future
> and sets the Christian free to follow the more refined lusts
> of the flesh in all good conscience and with a minimum of
> restraint.[39]

How does this compare with the fellowship of Christ's sufferings
into which we are called? How does this fit with Jesus' words?

> If anyone wishes to come after Me, let him deny himself,
> and take up his cross, and follow Me. For whoever wishes
> to save his life shall lose it; but whoever loses his life for
> My sake shall find it. (Matthew 16:24-25)

In reference to the CBA convention, one historian-author notes that
"evangelical Christians are trying to keep their young people by
adapting their faith to the forms of the majority culture."[40] The
majority culture is a psychological culture with (to quote a well-
known book) "new rules" and is "searching for self-fulfillment in
a world turned upside down."[41]

We live in the most ego-enlarged, self-indulged, navel-exam-
ined society since the days of Babylon, and the psychological way
of dealing with problems of living has been the major source of this
self preoccupation. Unless we seek a spiritual understanding (bib-

lical model of man) and a spiritual solution (biblical methodology) in all matters of life and of ministering to one another, we are in serious danger of "holding to a form of godliness" having "denied its power."

7

Broken Cisterns or Living Waters?

For even though they knew God, they did not honor Him as God, or give thanks; but they became futile in their speculations, and their foolish heart was darkened. Professing themselves to be wise, they became fools, and exchanged the glory of the incorruptible God for an image in the form of corruptible man and of birds and four-footed animals and crawling creatures. Therefore God gave them over in the lusts of their hearts to impurity, that their bodies might be dishonored among them. For they exchanged the truth of God for a lie, and worshiped and served the creature rather than the creator, who is blessed forever. Amen. (Romans 1:21-25)

Twentieth-century idols are more sophisticated than the false gods of the Canaanites and Babylonians. Rather than idols made of wood and stone, modern man makes idols of the mind and heart. By elevating his own conceptions of personhood, purpose, and power for change above what God has already said, man directly or indirectly raises himself to the status of godhood. In his own limited wisdom man has attempted to form a psychological model of mankind in place of the biblical model and a psychological

117

methodology of change and growth in place of sanctification. In other words, psychologists have contrived ways of explaining man other than the fall, ways of saving man other than the cross, and various ways of transforming man other than through Christ. The temptation to seek help from sources other than God comes in the same way as Satan enticed Eve to eat the forbidden fruit. The twentieth-century tree of the knowledge of good and evil contains much psychological fruit which looks like "a delight to the eyes and desirable to make one wise."

Isaiah warned the people about following the teachings of those who have perverted the faith with other ideologies, other vocabularies, other explanations, and other systems of morality:

> Woe to those who call evil good, and good evil;
> Who substitute darkness for light and light for darkness;
> Who substitute bitter for sweet, and sweet for bitter!
> Woe to those who are wise in their own eyes,
> And clever in their own sight! (Isaiah 6:20-21)

There has been a reversal in the meanings of words and phrases. The change is subtle. The word *sin* has been substituted with less convicting words such as *shortcoming*, *mistake*, or *reaction to past hurt*. Words such as *healed* and *whole* replace *sanctified* and *holy*. In fact, the word *holy* has been redefined to mean some kind of psychological wholeness. What is literal in Scripture often becomes metaphorical for the psychologizers. And what is metaphorical becomes literal.

Light is dark and dark is light, all depending on the psychological ideas that are in vogue. With the advent of Adler and Maslow the self has been elevated so high that if one does not regard himself highly he is suffering from serious mental problems. Whereas the Bible teaches men to esteem others, psychologizers of Christianity insist that all must esteem themselves. All kinds of classes both in and out of Christianity have made self-esteem almost the highest virtue of all. Whereas pride has always been a deadly sin in Scripture, the psychologizers of Christianity have redefined self-centered pride into some kind of compensation for low self-esteem. The psychologizers of the church would not want anyone to think too poorly of himself. But little is said about how highly one is to think of God and of how lowly of mind one should be.

Although some people repudiate God directly and choose a totally different path to fulfill their desires, others deny God indirectly when they conclude that He is not available or not enough. Although they claim to depend upon God, they add other ways with other philosophies and other gods. In other words, they claim to know the God of the Bible, but seek help from sources outside of God Himself in matters which are the exclusive domain of God in relationship to the values, attitudes, thoughts, and actions of His children. They have amalgamated God's ways with the ways of the world.

IDOLATRY IN THE CHURCH?

After Aaron formed the golden calf he announced, "This is your god, O Israel, who brought you up out of the land of Egypt." (Exodus 32:4) Then Aaron said, "Tomorrow shall be a feast to the LORD." (Exodus 32:5) Notice that he calls this false god by the name which is translated LORD in the Old Testament. This designation, when in capital letters, was solely used for the God of Israel, Jehovah. In mixing God with other religious ideas and idols, Aaron called a god that was no god by the very name of the God of Israel. That is the height of amalgamation. One system swallows another.

Exactly the same thing has happened in the church. The psychological systems of theories and therapies have swallowed up the true faith and replaced it with idols of men's minds. The blatant idolatry of Israel is easy to see. But isn't any substitution or addition to the Word of God idolatry? Idolatry is easy to miss when it wears the respectable garb of science. It is even easier to miss when it is practiced by Christians who honestly want to help others. Those who utilize the systems of psychotherapy do so because they have not found the Bible and the Holy Spirit sufficient. Perhaps they are looking for something easier than complete transformation into the image of Christ. Perhaps they are looking for easy answers or for a quick fix. Or, perhaps they are looking to solutions that do not require them to suffer the personal discomfort that comes with change. Perhaps they are not willing to go the true way of the cross. Thus they attempt to enhance the cross with psychology. They have thus turned to "science falsely so-called" and to philosophical structures which are in opposition to the Bible.

THE DOMAIN OF SCRIPTURE.

The Bible is the most practical, relevant, and life-changing guide to living. Those who insist on incorporating the theories of men evidently believe that the Bible and the Holy Spirit are not sufficient for life-transforming work. In fact, many of them restrict the Bible exclusively to an explanation of God and as a guide only in what they refer to as "spiritual matters," when in fact the *psyche* or soul and all of its concerns are spiritual matters.

Psychotherapy intrudes upon some of the most important themes of Scripture: how to know and understand man, why he behaves the way he does, and how to help him change. In the Bible this understanding is given from God's point of view. In fact, true understanding of the human personality only comes through the Holy Spirit and through God's Word. And since God is central in the revelation of wisdom, the focus should be on God rather than on self, on theology rather than on psychology. Self understanding through psychotherapeutic theories and techniques will only lead to error because of the severe limitations of the human heart and mind. To dress these in biblical terminology and call them Christian is to compound the evil.

The overwhelming majority of problems for which people seek professional psychological help are those of marriage, family, personal distress, depression, and addictive behaviors. The Bible addresses all these areas. In fact, the Bible indicates that God is the source of all peace and also works mightily through tribulation.

> Therefore having been justified by faith, we have peace with God through our Lord Jesus Christ, through whom also we have obtained our introduction by faith into this grace in which we stand; and we exult in hope of the glory of God.
>
> And not only this, but we also exult in our tribulations, knowing that tribulation brings about perseverance; and perseverance, proven character; and proven character, hope; and hope does not disappoint, because the love of God has been poured out within our hearts through the Holy Spirit who was given to us. (Romans 5:1-5)

What psychological system justifies a person before God and

gives him peace with God? What psychological system gives the kind of faith in which a person can live by all of God's promises? What psychological system fulfills its promises the way God fulfills His? What psychological system gives the hope of which Paul speaks? What psychological system enables a person to exult in the midst of tribulation? What psychological system increases the kind of perseverance that builds proven character, gives hope, and produces divine love? Throughout the centuries there have been individuals who have suffered from extremely difficult problems of living who have sought God, and they have found Him to be true and faithful. They looked into the Word of God for wisdom and guidance for living with and overcoming the problems of life. The lives of those saints far outshine the lives of such pitiful souls as those who have followed the siren song of psychology.

GOD'S MERCIFUL WARNINGS.

Throughout the history of Israel God warned His people about following the customs of the nations around them. He warned them because He loved them and desired His best for them. He particularly warned them about running after false gods and called such idolatry "adultery" because Israel belonged to Him. Israel had developed its own amalgamation of Jehovah, Baal, Ashtoreth, and other gods and goddesses of the surrounding nations. Israel had picked up the thinking, the philosophies, and the religions of the world. The Israelites sought to combine the best of the pagan practices with the worship of Jehovah. For awhile such amalgamation appeared to work for them. However, embracing pagan practices led them into great suffering. Israel became contaminated again and again. And, each time, the only way back was to turn away from idolatry and to return exclusively to God in their need.

Israel failed when it trusted in the idols of the surrounding nations. In reference to the apostasy of idolatry, The Lord spoke through Jeremiah:

> Has a nation changed gods,
> When they were not gods?
> But My people have changed their glory
> For that which does not profit.
> Be appalled, O heavens, at this,

> And shudder, be very desolate . . .
> For My people have committed two evils:
> They have forsaken Me,
> The fountain of living waters,
> To hew for themselves cisterns,
> Broken cisterns,
> That can hold no water.
> (Jeremiah 2:11-13.)

Psychological counselors and ministers who follow their lead offer psychological systems which have more in common with false religion than with science. They are offering other religions—religions created by fallen, unredeemed men and religions based upon such philosophies as determinism, atheism, agnosticism, secular humanism, gnosticism, and occultism. They are offering the dregs of broken cisterns.

God warned Israel not to trust in mankind, but to trust in God alone.

> Thus says the LORD,
> "Cursed is the man who trusts in mankind
> And makes flesh his strength,
> And whose heart turns away from the Lord.
> (Jeremiah 17:5.)

> Blessed is the man who trusts in the LORD
> And whose trust is the LORD.
> (Jeremiah 17:7.)

Every psychotherapeutic system puts more trust in the minds and hearts of the theorists than science permits. Nevertheless the twentieth-century church is trusting in the theories of men and adding them to their understanding of the Bible, when God alone can reveal to us who we are and who we are meant to be in Him.

The amalgamation not only lurks in the therapies of Christians, it has permeated every ministry in the church. We have to wonder if the church is involved in the same kind of amalgamation as the Israelites were. When the Israelites lost sight of God through their own disobedience and hardness of heart, they lost sight of His power and grace to save. God removed Himself from them until they were ready to repent. In the meantime they needed help. Instead of turning back to God they turned to other gods. However, they never quite realized how much they had turned away from God because they generally merged the idols of their minds and hands with their limited concept of God.

In this century God's people have been quenching the Holy Spirit by devaluing the Bible and its supreme place in evaluating and transforming a person's mind, will, emotion, and behavior. They have turned to the religions of psychology for answers to the problems of living and provided psychological help rather than the whole counsel of God. Rather than recognizing the religious nature of psychology, they have mistakenly believed it to be another form of revelation by giving it the status of objective science. In doing so they have relied more on the faulty ideas of men than on the inspired Word of God.

Throughout the entire Old Testament, God called alliances with other religions "adultery." And, in each instance He brought judgment upon His people in the form of national and personal weakness. When under the judgment of God for spiritual adultery, Israel was continually oppressed by the surrounding nations. Only as they repented of their sin and cried out to God for deliverance did God deliver them and revive their strength as a nation.

The church has become weak in the area of the personal lives of its members. More and more Christians are turning to psychological answers for spiritual problems which they have thought to be psychological problems. The psychological way is promoted as "God's truth" in even the most conservative Christian colleges and seminaries. Only God Himself in His mercy and grace can reverse the tide. And we pray for His mercy and His grace to send a revival which will cleanse the church of the abominations of psychological amalgamations. J. I. Packer in his book *Keep in Step with the Spirit* says:

> Revival is God turning his anger away from his church. For God's people to be impotent against their enemies is a sign that God is judging them for their sins. In the Old Testament the cry for revival springs from the sense of judgment (see Psalms 79:4-9; 80:12-14; 85:4-7; Habakkuk 3:2) and the coming of revival is God comforting his people after judgment. In the New Testament Christ counsels the

Laodiceans to seek revival from his hand as an alternative
to the judgment he would otherwise inflict on them (Revelation 3:14-22).[1]

These are searching words when we look at the failure of Christians
to live in such a way as to show forth the life of Christ dwelling
within. Many are relying on self and psychology rather than on
Christ. They deny their faith every time they turn to the religions of
psychology for help rather than to the One True God.

The divorce rate, the incidents of all kinds of abuse in the home,
fornication, and licentiousness all indicate that something is wrong
in the church. Worldliness has crept in so subtly and profusely that
it is difficult to distinguish between the lifestyle of unbelievers and
professing Christians. Many are failing in their personal lives and
have been turning to broken cisterns for help rather than repenting
and seeking God to forgive and renew His church.

Is it possible that the very profession that claims to hold answers
to the problems of living includes some of the false teachers that
Peter warned about?

> But false prophets also arose among the people, just as
> there will also be false teachers among you, who will
> secretly introduce destructive heresies, even denying the
> Master who bought them, bringing swift destruction upon
> themselves.
>
> And many will follow their sensuality, and because of
> them the way of the truth will be maligned; and in their
> greed they will exploit you with false words. . . .
>
> These are springs without water and mists driven by a
> storm, for whom the black darkness has been reserved.
>
> For speaking out arrogant works of vanity they entice by
> fleshly desires, by sensuality, those who barely escape
> from the ones who live in error, promising them freedom
> while they themselves are slaves of corruption; for by what
> a man is overcome, by this is he enslaved.
>
> For if after they have escaped the defilements of the world

by the knowledge of the Lord and Savior Jesus Christ, they are again entangled in them and are overcome, the last state has become worse for them than the first. (2 Peter 2:1-3, 17-20)

Many sincere Christians who have desired to serve God and help people have become entangled in psychological ideologies and religions. They have become enslaved by the psychological way and in turn enslave those that they are trying to free. They have fallen into the maze of opinions masquerading as facts and are dragging others along with them.

We are not saying that everyone in the church has gone this far with the psychotherapeutic theories and the baggage of religion that they drag along. Nevertheless, unless the church turns back to God as the source of wisdom and direction for living, as the means of help for life's problems, and as the guide for understanding mankind and how a person grows and changes, the church will lose sight of the Living God. The church needs to discard the various psychological world views and operate again from a biblical world view.

Christians and Christianity do not need the theories and therapies of psychological systems. They will not be lost without them. Instead there is a very strong possibility that Christians will become entangled by them. By not standing firm in their faith, Christians may become swallowed up in the secular systems of psychological services.

Peter Schrag sees the helping professions, therapeutic methods, and mental health as national and international means for controlling behavior and thus controlling society. He introduces his book *Mind Control* with these words:

> In the past generation, there has been a fundamental shift in the way government and other organizations control the lives and behavior of individuals. . . . In general, it is a shift from direct to indirect methods of control, from the punitive to the therapeutic, from the moralistic to the mechanistic, from the hortatory to the manipulative. More specifically, it is reflected in the replacement of overt and sometimes crude techniques—threat, punishment, or incarceration—with relatively "smooth" methods: psy-

chotropic drugs; Skinnerian behavior modification; aversive conditioning; electronic surveillance; and the collection, processing, and use of personal information to institutionalize people outside the walls of institutions.[2]

Through government social agencies it is possible to extend intervention (control) to millions of people. In many instances, personal problems are no longer dealt with in a private way. They are becoming areas of public domain and imposed help. Persons may be required or intimidated to involve themselves in some kind of therapy "for their own good" and become locked into a system of external control. Schrag says:

> Impositions before or which had been possible only within closed institutions now become possible in the community at large. The vision is a kind of sanitized social efficiency; its language is clinical; its most important symbol is mental health.[3]

All such methods lead to greater government intervention and control in personal affairs. He goes on to reveal the secular humanistic myth that man can make himself and his society good.

> At the heart of the change lies a transcendent faith that with the proper environment or the proper methods, any individual can be reshaped, reformed, or at the very least, controlled with psychological or chemical methods, and alongside that faith, the chemical, mechanistic, behavioristic view of man that sustains it.[4]

Such a social climate may appear very humane. However, freedoms are taken away without due process of law for the so-called benefit of the individual: to change his thinking, to change his belief system, to change his behavior all to what would be socially acceptable to those who are in charge. Although it may not seem at all serious right now, the implications of psycho-social interventions are mind boggling.

Dr. Philip Zimbardo, a professor of psychology at Stanford University, in writing about George Orwell's book *Nineteen Eighty-Four* says,

The most telling of Orwell's predictions are to be found not in the heavy-handed practices of the Ministry of Justice, but in the treatment programs of the Ministry of Love.

As an illustration from Orwell, Zimbardo quotes the following:

The party is not interested in the overt act: the thought is all we care about. We do not merely destroy our enemies, we change them.

Zimbardo confesses:

The current practitioners in our Ministry of Love come from the ranks of the mental health establishment (psychiatry and my own field, psychology), social welfare agencies, education and business. [5]

All of these systems attempt to do what only Jesus can do: save souls, transform the heart, make a person righteous before God. Nevertheless the church is following the Pied Pipers of secular humanism, atheism, and determinism under the colors of science.

How did the church go wrong in the matter of its own psychologizing? It all began by accepting the psychological definitions of life's problems. It proceeded to using psychological diagnostic terms and then resulted in psychological solutions. We need to restore biblical definitions to life's problems and use biblical terms so that we can provide biblical solutions. As we say in our previous book, *How to Counsel from Scripture,*

Confusion arises when mental-emotional-behavioral problems are dealt with from a psychological rather than, or in addition to, a spiritual perspective. To attempt to combine the biblical truth that mankind is born in sin with a model that says, "Man is intrinsically good" (Rogers), or "Man begins from a position of I'm Not OK—You're OK" (Harris), or "Human love and human worthwhileness are man's greatest needs" (Glasser), or any other humanly contrived model, will bring confusion and distortion.

The Bible clearly states that man's condition is fallen until he is redeemed by Jesus to live by the indwelling Holy

Spirit in relationship to God the Father. To develop a model
of man with explanations such as primal anxiety, need for
transcendence, or cosmic loneliness is to avoid the sin
question and thereby to miss the only lasting means of
restoration: the death and resurrection of Christ. Mankind's condition is not due to the birth process (Otto Rank),
nor from early "psychosexual stages of development"
(Sigmund Freud), nor from the "primal pool of pain"
(Arthur Janov). Nor is it due to any of the other hundreds of
guesses and opinions of men about man. Problems of
living are basically spiritual because in some way they
involve the fallen or redeemed condition of man. And the
way to meet those problems is spiritual. [6]

We need to dare to believe that the Word of God ministered by the
Holy Spirit through one who has been transformed by the cross of
Christ to one who will receive it is a more powerful way to minister
than any psychological therapy administered by the most highly
trained psychotherapists. We need to double dare to believe that
this is the only way to deal with problems of living.

James Turner, in his book *Without God, Without Creed*, deals
with how disbelief in God became an option for millions of Americans. He says it wasn't because of Darwinism, scientific natu-
ralism, industrialization, urbanization, and technological changes
in themselves, but rather because of the response of religious
leaders to these developments. He says:

In trying to adapt their religious beliefs to socioeconomic
change, to new moral challenges, to novel problems of
knowledge, to the tightening standards of science, the
defenders of God slowly strangled Him. If anyone is to be
arraigned for deicide, it is not Charles Darwin but his
adversary Bishop Samuel Wilberforce, not the godless
Robert Ingersoll but the godly Beecher family. [7]

Adapting the Christian message to the culture actually changes the
message. Adapting the Christian message to psychological theories has changed the message from the cross to the couch.

One therapist who has repudiated his psychological training
wrote to us. He said:

> My experience has been that the major obstacle to estab-
> lishing Scriptural, spiritual counseling is not from psycho-
> therapy professionals . . . but from churches themselves.
> Pastors and laymen enamored with the psychological way
> back away from any suggestion that the Word of God,
> ministered through an untrained person, empowered by
> the Holy Spirit, is sufficient for all nonorganic problems
> presented in counseling. As my unbelief in the psycholog-
> ical way has grown, I feel I've been running against the
> current of contemporary Christian thought.[8]

Because psychology, which gives rise to psychotherapy, is not
science and has not proven itself in either research or reality, and
because it has unnecessarily replaced religious cures, it would be
appropriate to label it "psychoquackery" and to regard it as psychoheresy. Psychoquackery becomes psychoheresy when it is
combined with Christian verbiage. Psychotherapy and its philosophical and practical implications and influence could very well
be intrinsic to the great seduction in preparation for the antichrist.

Rather than turning to the unproven, unsubstantiated, unnecessary, unscientific, often conflicting psychological systems of
understanding the meaning of life, the measure of man, or the
means of transformation, the church needs to pray for a revival.
The church needs to listen to God's instruction:

> [If] My people who are called by My name humble them-
> selves and pray, and seek My face and turn from their
> wicked ways, then I will hear from heaven, will forgive
> their sin, and will heal their land. (2 Chronicles 7:14)

The entire church must follow this instruction, for if one member is
hurting, the whole body is affected. The reaching out in love to one
another in times of crisis must be undergirded by seeking God.
And although there are some in the church who faithfully pray for
revival, too many are caught up in a psychological world view to
turn to the one true source of help.

When true revival comes, instigated and fulfilled by the Holy
Spirit, the church will be cleansed. Then Christians will not even
be interested in psychology. Their eyes will be opened to the Lord
of life and the indwelling Holy Spirit so much that the high

pronouncements of psychology will appear as dung. The real thing will easily replace the false when revival comes.

The revival of the Holy Spirit will be characterized by deep conviction and a renewed realization of Jesus Christ in every area of life. He will be recognized as the answer and the source, the Lord and Savior of every aspect of life.

> Seek the LORD while He may be found;
> Call upon Him while He is near.
> Let the wicked forsake his way,
> And the unrighteous man his thoughts;
> And let him return to the LORD,
> And He will have compassion on him;
> And to our God
> For He will abundantly pardon.
> "For My thoughts are not your thoughts,
> Neither are your ways My ways," declares the LORD.
> "For as the heavens are higher than the earth,
> So are My ways higher than your ways,
> And My thoughts than your thoughts.
> "For as the rain and the snow come down from heaven,
> And do not return there without watering the earth,
> And making it bear and sprout,
> And furnishing seed to the sower and bread to the eater;
> So shall My word be which goes forth from My mouth;
> It shall not return to Me empty,
> Without accomplishing what I desire,
> And without succeeding in the matter for which I sent it.
> "For you will go out with joy,
> And be led forth with peace. . . . (Isaiah 55: 6-12)

Part Three
PSYCHOBABBLE

It is currently estimated that approximately 34 million of this Nation's citizens (15%) suffer diagnosable mental disorders each year.

Morris Parloff[1]

What kinds of people seek counseling? Do they really have a mental illness or are they experiencing problems of living? Do they need treatment or education or possibly spiritual change? The terms *mental illness*, *mental disease*, and *mental disorder* are too casily used to describe those who are suffering in the mental-emotional-behavioral realm.

In view of the prolific use of the term *mental illness*, we will attempt to show that there is no such disease and that not even brain disease or other diseases with symtoms of distorted thinking and behaving can properly be labeled "mental illness." The reason we are concerned about these terms is because words affect thinking. Erroneous terminology—a metaphor taken literally—can lead into error. Jesus always dealt with truth because He knew that the truth sets people free to do the Father's will.

Part Three

PSYCHOANALYSIS

8

The Misnomer of Mental Illness

The terms *mental disease*, *mental illness*, and *mental disorder* are popular catch-alls for all kinds of problems of living, most of which have little or nothing to do with disease. As soon as a person's behavior is labeled "illness," treatment and therapy become the solutions. If, on the other hand, we consider a person to be responsible for his behavior, we should deal with him in the areas of education, faith, and choice. If we label him "mentally ill," we rob him of the human dignity of personal responsibility and the divine relationship by which problems may be met.

Because the term *mental illness* throws attitudes and behavior into the medical realm, it is important to examine its accuracy. In discussing the concept of mental illness or mental disease, research psychiatrist E. Fuller Torrey says:

> The term itself is nonsensical, a semantic mistake. The two words cannot go together . . . you can no more have a mental "disease" than you can have a purple idea or a wise space.[1]

To begin with, the word *mental* means "mind" and the mind is not the same as the brain. Also, the mind is really more than just a function or activity of the brain. Brain researcher and author

Barbara Brown insists that the mind goes beyond the brain. She
says:

> The scientific consensus that mind is only mechanical
> brain is dead wrong . . . the research data of the sciences
> themselves point much more strongly toward the existence
> of a mind-more-than-brain than they do toward mere
> mechanical brain action.[2]

Arthur Custance, in his book *The Mysterious Matter of Mind*
presents,

> . . .the experimental findings of recent research which
> have led some of the most renowned scientists in the field
> to conclude that mind is more than matter and more than a
> mere by-product of the brain.[3]

The Bible raises the level of human dignity far above that of a
physical organism. Not only has God created humans with minds
which can think, reason, choose, and direct action, He has created
man in His own image with a spiritual dimension.

> And God created man in His own image, in the image of
> God He created him; male and female He created them.
> (Genesis 1:27)

God created the human mind to know Him and to choose to love,
trust, and obey Him. In the very creative act, God planned for
mankind to rule His earthly creation and to serve as His represen-
tatives on earth. Because the mind goes beyond the physical realm,
it goes beyond the reaches of science and cannot be medically sick.

Since the mind is not a physical organ, it cannot have a disease.
While one can have a diseased brain, one cannot have a diseased
mind, although he may have a sinful or unredeemed mind. Torrey
aptly says:

> The mind cannot *really* become diseased any more than
> the intellect can become abscessed. Furthermore, the idea
> that mental "diseases" are actually brain diseases creates a
> strange category of "diseases" which are, by definition,
> without known cause. Body and behavior become inter-

twined in this confusion until they are no longer dis-
tinguishable. It is necessary to return to first principles: a
disease is something you *have*, behavior is something you
do.[4] (Emphasis his.)

One can understand what a diseased body is, but what is a diseased
mind? It is obvious that one cannot have a diseased emotion or a
diseased behavior. Then why a diseased mind? Nevertheless,
therapists continually refer to mental-emotional-behavioral conditions as diseases.

Thomas Szasz criticizes what he calls the "psychiatric
imposter" who "supports a common, culturally shared desire to
equate and confuse brain and mind, nerves and nervousness."[5] Not
only are brain and mind not equal; nerves and nervousness are not
equal either. One might nervously await the arrival of a friend who
is late for an appointment, but the nerves are busy performing other
functions. Szasz further argues:

> It is customary to define psychiatry as a medical specialty
> concerned with the study, diagnosis, and treatment of
> mental illness. This is a worthless and misleading defini-
> tion. Mental illness is a myth . . . the notion of a person
> "having a mental illness" is scientifically crippling. It
> provides professional assent to a popular rationalization—
> namely, that problems in living experienced and expressed
> in terms of so-called psychiatric symptoms are basically
> similar to bodily diseases.[6]

Although a medical problem or brain disease may bring on mental-
emotional-behavioral symptoms, the person does not and cannot
rationally be classified as "mentally ill." He is medically ill, not
mentally ill. The words *psychological* and *biological* are not syn-
onymous. In the same way *mental* and *medical* cannot be syn-
onymous either. One refers to the mind, the other to the body.

Psychological counseling does not even deal with the brain
itself. Instead, it deals with aspects of thinking, feeling, and
behaving. Therefore, the psychotherapist is not in the business of
healing diseases, but rather of teaching new ways of thinking,
feeling, and behaving. He actually is a teacher, not a doctor.
Harvard psychiatrist Shervert Frazier, who is chairman of the APA

Joint Commission on Public Affairs, says, "Psychotherapy is a form of education."[7] Nevertheless, many psychotherapists perpetuate the concept of "mental illness" and people follow the fallacy.

Many have dishonestly used the term *mental illness* to describe a whole host of problems of thinking and behaving which should be labeled as "problems of living." Though the term *mental illness* is a misnomer and a mismatch of words, it has become firmly ingrained in the public vocabulary and is glibly pronounced on all sorts of occasions by both lay and professional persons. Jonas Robitscher says:

> Our culture is permeated with psychiatric thought. Psychiatry, which had its beginnings in the care of the sick, has expanded its net to include everyone, and it exercises its authority over this total population by methods that range from enforced therapy and coerced control to the advancement of ideas and the promulgation of values.[8]

The mistake is reinforced continually until one sees mental illness wherever he turns and turns whatever he sees into mental illness.

Behavior that sickens is often called "sick." In such a context the word is used as a metaphor to describe something that is disgusting or pathetic rather than ill or diseased. Thus, the metaphor "sick" can be used as a label to criticize behavior that is bothersome. But, if such a label moves from a definition of "disgusting" or "pathetic" to one of "illness" or "disease" the original meaning of the word is altered or lost, and erroneous thinking follows when a metaphor becomes literal. The confusion of terms, such as *mental illness*, *sick behavior*, and *mental disease*, is illustrated in the following examples of people who exhibit irresponsible behavior but are not necessarily ill.

A man with a problem known as pedophilia wrote to Ann Landers. He complained that homosexuals can find satisfactory outlets for their desires, but not the pedophiliac. He wrote, "I am a professional man (certified public accountant), 40 years of age and the father of four young boys." Then he confessed, "I am attracted to little girls." Ann replied, "When people are sick the only advice I can give is 'See a doctor,' and you are among the sickest."[9] Ann Landers quite regularly describes certain behavior as "sick." And, since she refers the person to a doctor, she obviously is not simply using a metaphor, but uses the word in the literal, medical sense. However, she just says what the psychotherapists have proclaimed for years and what the public has come to believe: that behavior can be diseased.

Jim Jones started an experimental community in Guyana. As the result of a threatened investigation, Jones led members of his community into mass suicide. The final body count of hundreds included Jones himself. Before the awful incident in Guyana, all sorts of responsible and respectable persons praised Jim Jones. In fact, San Francisco medical doctor Carlton Goodlett had praised Jones as a person and complimented the Guyana experiment. Rosalyn Carter dined with Jones in 1976, sent him a complimentary letter about a medical aid proposal of his, and later invited him to her husband's inauguration.

Numerous other dignitaries and celebrities admired both the man and what he was doing. However, the diagnosis by psychotherapists after the death drink orgy was predictably "mental illness." And, the public predictably parroted that the man was sick. However, according to the many people closest to him, Jones was not sick before the incident. The only thing that changed about Jones before and after the Guyana incident (besides the fact that he died) was the opinion that people had about him.

Ann Landers printed a letter from a woman who described herself as a twenty-year-old woman with a problem. Her problem was that in addition to living with a twenty-three-year old man she had "an obsession to go to bed with other men." She said, "It seems I can't be satisfied with one." She signed her letter, "Never Satisfied." Ann responded, "You sound like a nymphomaniac," and promptly referred her to a health professional "to help you get over this illness."[10]

A twenty-nine-year-old businesswoman was a passenger on a San Francisco cable car when it rolled backwards and crashed. She sued the Municipal Railway for $500,000, claiming that the accident had resulted in the mental "disease" nymphomania. During her trial she told of having over one hundred lovers since the accident and confessed that at one point she had engaged in sexual intercourse fifty times in five days. The psychiatric explanation suggested that the pole she was thrown against in the accident represented her stern Lutheran father and that this somehow led to severe "psychic trauma."[11]

The mental illness game has erected a safe scapegoat for human problems and, at the same time, has financially enriched psychotherapists, lawyers, and clients. Since such court settlements are usually paid for by large insurance companies, everybody wins except those who continue to pay escalating insurance premiums.

The greatest tragedy of the misnomer of mental illness is that persons who are experiencing problems of living seek help outside of the church. And, when they do seek such help from a church leader, they are generally referred to those professionals specializing in "mental illness" and "mental health." It has become as easy to send a person with marriage or family problems to a mental health professional as to send a person with a broken leg to a doctor.

Problems of living are spiritual problems which require spiritual solutions, not psychological problems which require psychological solutions. The church has been duped into believing that problems of living are problems of the brain which require scientific solutions, rather than problems of the mind which require biblical solutions. This conclusion was reached through the use of the term *mental illness* which is a metaphor that is molded to fit everything from brain diseases to problems of living. This chameleon-like concept is the crux of the confusion that causes committed Christians to be conned into catastrophic conclusions about counseling. Problems of living are NOT mental illnesses!

Have we forgotten that the church should be equipped with the necessary spiritual abilities to lead people out of darkness into new life and to encourage persons to put off the old ways of the self and to put on the new life in Jesus, whereby a person can be transformed in attitude and behavior? As long as we call problems of living "mental illness" we substitute responsibility with therapy.

9

Mental Illness by Ballot

To further confuse the "mental illness" issue, the Supreme Court has given additional support and credence to this nonexistent illness on the basis of vote. Previous to this psychotherapeutic era, drug addiction and alcoholism were considered to be social problems. In 1962 the Supreme Court ruled that drug addiction was a disease. Therefore a criminal sentence for having such a disease would violate the Eighth Ammendment prohibition against cruel and unusual punishment. The court said.

> It is unlikely that any State at this moment in history would attempt to make it a criminal offense for a person to be mentally ill, or a leper, or to be afflicted with a venereal disease . . . in the light of contemporary human knowledge, a law which made a criminal offense of such a disease would doubtlessly be universally thought to be an infliction of cruel and unusual punishment. [1]

In Powell v. Texas, a 5 to 4 Supreme Court vote determined that alcoholism is a disease. Two former social problems have now been transformed into illnesses by vote of the Supreme Court. Harold Mulford, Director of Alcohol Studies at the University of Iowa, says:

> I think it's important to recognize that the alcohol disease

concept is a propaganda and political achievement and not
a scientific achievement. Science has not demonstrated
that alcoholism is a disease by defining it, nor has science
or technology demonstrated it to be a disease by coming up
with an effective treatment or preventative.[2]

One professor says, "Labeling alcoholism a disease is like blaming
the devil for our sins—it absolves us of responsibility for our
actions."[3] R. E. Kendall says, "The disease concept of alcoholism
[is] out of tune with the facts and a serious obstacle to rational
solutions."[4]

We are all familiar with the fact that 58 percent of the psychiatrists voted in favor of deleting homosexuality from the list of
mental illnesses. Apparently human behavior is vulnerable to votes
of judicial and professional bodies in deciding what behavior is and
what behavior is not a "disease." Bruce Ennis and Thomas Litwack say of this psychiatric vote:

> If all that is needed to remove large numbers of individuals
> from the ranks of the mentally ill and grant them the status
> enjoyed by the rest of society is a vote by the American
> Psychiatric Association, then surely other diagnostic
> labels are also highly suspect.[5]

The measles, mumps, and chicken pox have not been subject to
such a vote.

The buffoonery of the "mental illness" labeling game is further
revealed when one considers the reason for the American Psychiatric Association decision about the status of homosexuality. Those
who supported the removal of homosexuality from the list of
illnesses did so on the grounds that the label "mental illness"
should only apply to those who experience conflict about their
condition. In other words, a homosexual who is disturbed about his
condition is "mentally ill"; but, if he is comfortable with this
orientation, he is not ill.

In the light of such voting, a person's subjective evaluation about
his own condition has now become a measure of whether or not he
is sick. We want to make it clear that we are not recommending that
homosexuality again be listed as a mental illness. We are merely
showing how fraudulent the mental illness labeling game is.

Such reasoning on the part of the APA extends the diagnostic authority to the person's own subjective evaluation of his condition, but this privilege of self diagnosis is only granted to the homosexual. For, if one is consistent, every condition considered to be a disease by the APA should be seen in the light of whether or not distress is present. If this subjective criteria were to be extended equally to all, such bizarre disorders as necrophilia (being sexually aroused by dead bodies) would only be considered a "mental Illness" if the person felt disturbed about his condition. If the APA extended subjective criteria across the board there could be no involuntary confinement of anyone who did not consider himself "mentally ill."

The whole classification scheme is a blatant testimony to the myth of mental illness and the unscientific nature of psychotherapy. The latest adopted classification scheme of the American Psychiatric Association's *Diagnostic and Statistical Manual of Mental Disorders (DSMIII)* excludes those conditions which "have strong cultural or subcultural supports or sanctions."[6] This criteria was used in the new classification scheme to keep homosexuality off the list of diseases. However, this criteria was not uniformly applied to all forms of behavior.

The lopsidedness of the scheme is apparent in that caffeinism is now a mental disease along with alcoholism, but child abuse is a condition "not attributable to a mental disorder."[7] To further compound the ludicrousness of the ritual of psychic labeling, the *Comprehensive Textbook* says that its definition of mental disorder "may need to be changed in future years to correspond with a change in the attitude of society and the psychiatric profession toward certain conditions."[8]

It is a strange disease that is determined by personal distress, cultural acceptability, and changing attitudes. In the biological sphere a disease is a disease regardless of personal distress or cultural acceptability. Not only are mental illnesses strange diseases; they are in fact not diseases at all. There are organic illnesses involving the brain and its functions, but those are physical diseases, not *mental* diseases.

10

Disease, Diagnosis, and Prognosis

If a person has a disease, he needs proper diagnosis and treatment. On the other hand, if a person is experiencing problems of living, he needs to know what choices he can make to overcome the problems within the limitations of his own abilities and circumstances. If a Christian is experiencing problems of living, he can turn to the Bible and to other Christians for guidance. He has the Holy Spirit to help him choose God's way through the problems and exercise God's enablement for change.

DISEASE.

Once the disease concept takes hold, the so-called patient is treated by any number of psychological therapies. Most of these can easily lead a person away from God and into self effort or dependence on the counseling relationship. A physically sick person needs medical treatment, but a person with problems of living needs knowledge, wisdom, guidance, and loving support. Strangely enough, however, in psychological counseling the person may be labeled "mentally ill" and receive treatment. But, the treatment has the same basic ingredients as exist in biblical counseling: rhetoric (talking) and religion.[1]

The disease concept for problems of living calls for professional treatment rather than personal responsibility. Such treatment falls under the category of medical services, which fall into the category of health insurance coverage. Problems of living, therefore, must be transformed into illnesses to be eligible for health insurance payments. Jonas Robitscher points out how vague the concept of mental illness is and how unstable the definitions:

> The decision to see these people, and many others, as mentally ill or not so is entirely arbitrary, related not to the patient but to political and economic factors. [2]

In addition to the fraudulent confusion of mental "disease" with physical disease for purposes of health insurance payments, there is the use of the mental "disease" concept for disability payments. Psychiatrist Leonard Kurland describes what he calls a "colossal rip-off" scheme in which lawyers and psychiatrists "cooperate" for their own financial advantage, but to the disadvantage of the taxpayers. He says:

> Psychiatric disability in workers' compensation cases is a creation of lawyers, and is almost always a fraud—one that could not succeed without the participation of psychiatrists who sell their degrees as "medical adversaries." [3]

Kurland explains:

> The psychiatrist knows what to do: provide the attorney with a diagnosis of psychiatric disability and ascribe its origin to the patient's work situation. [4]

The term *mental illness* is confusing and deceptive and promotes cures for diseases which do not even exist. Robitscher concludes his chapter on defining mental illness by saying:

> The concept of mental disease remains vague, but the pragmatics of social functioning dictate that psychiatrists will continue to deal with people as if they are diseased whether or not the disease concept makes good sense . . . since psychiatry has never been able to define mental disease, the medical basis for psychiatric authority must

continue to be questioned, and the psychiatric decisions that rely on medical authority must always be scrutinized.[5]

The concept of sickness is a convenient psychological device to confuse people and to place great power and authority in the hands of the psychotherapists. Once people are confused, it is easy to talk them into "treatment" and offer a "cure." Therefore, the psychotherapist must sustain the delusion of sickness in order to sell his supposed cures. As one psychologist puts it,

> Once we concede that people passively "catch" bad behavior from their environment in the same way they "catch" measles or bubonic plague, then it is up to the specialists to diagnose the disease and prescribe the cure.[6]

As society has trusted psychotherapy more, its practitioners have upped the ante on the number of individuals in need of psychological help. Some years ago the national figure was ten percent and now some have estimated it to be as high as ninety-five percent.[7]

In the *Diagnostic and Statistical Manual of Mental Disorders* published in 1952 there were sixty types and subtypes of mental illness. Sixteen years later this number had mushroomed to 145, and presently it includes a whopping 230 separate conditions. George Albee, past president of the American Psychological Association, says:

> Clearly the more human problems that we label mental illnesses, the more people that we can say suffer from them. And, a cynic might add, the more conditions therapists can treat and collect health-insurance payments for.[8]

Is this cynicism or realism?

DIAGNOSIS.

If the illness concept worked in practice, we might excuse its semantic inaccuracies. One measure of the usefulness of a medical concept of behavior is whether or not such a concept enables one to diagnose illness or wellness. Walter Reich refers to diagnosis as "the central psychiatric act." He says that the psychiatrist's privilege to diagnose "gives him the power to control and to influence."[9] Since diagnosis is the illness concept put to the test, the question is: How good are psychotherapists at diagnosis?

In our book *The Psychological Way/The Spiritual Way* we quote research to show that psychological diagnosis is a disaster. It involves massive errors and nonprofessionals are as good or better at it than professionals.[10] Psychiatrist Hugh Drummond admits, "Volumes of research have been done to demonstrate the absolute unreliability of psychiatric diagnosis."[11] In addition, studies have shown that the system cannot be relied upon to distinguish the sane from the insane in either civil or criminal matters.[12]

Albee tells how different therapists from different countries will disagree when presented with the same individuals. He refers to the usual psychiatric disagreements on mental fitness of the same defendants in court cases. The psychiatrists for the defense predictably have different opinions than those for the prosecution. And, it is consistently true that those considered affluent are generally given a more favorable diagnosis than those who are poor. Albee concludes, "Appendicitus, a brain tumor and chicken pox are the same everywhere, regardless of culture or class; mental conditions, it seems, are not."[13]

The system of diagnosis for mental illness in psychotherapy operates the opposite way from the system of guilt in jurisprudence. The court system protects the innocent party to such an extent that many who are guilty go free. This generosity in jurisprudence is reversed in psychotherapy. According to researcher D. L. Rosenhan, who has done a classic study on psychological diagnosis and treatment, the therapist is more inclined to label a healthy person "sick" than a sick person "well."[14] While jurisprudence bends over backwards to protect the innocent, psychotherapy is inclined to condemn the innocent for fear of making a mistake. Szasz sadly states:

> There is no behavior or person that a modern psychiatrist cannot plausibly diagnose as abnormal or ill.[15]

Christopher Lasch points out that:

> The psychiatric perversion of the concept of incompetence

nullifies the rights of the accused. . . . He could prove his innocence, even in a rigged system of justice, more easily than he can establish his mental competence.[16]

In terms of justice, one is obviously better off being tried as a criminal than being diagnosed for mental illness. It is apparently more acceptable to have a criminal walking the streets than one with the dubious condition called "mental illness."

PROGNOSIS.

Worse than the disaster of diagnosis is the problem of prognosis or prediction. After researching the ability of professional psychotherapists to predict a client's behavior, Einhorn and Hogarth conclude:

> It is apparent that neither the extent of professional training and experience nor the amount of information available to clinicians necessarily increases predictive accuracy.[17]

Psychotherapists have shown little validity in analysis of past behavior or in their predictions concerning future behavior of their clients. There is a paradox that "in spite of the great fallibility in professional judgment people seem to have unshakable confidence in it."[18] Robitscher says:

> Judges, juries, and the general public do not realize that many of the statements made by psychiatrists are based on common sense applied to data available to everyone. Because the opinion is expressed by an expert and because it is couched in an elaborate scientific vocabulary, its fallibility and its lack of special probative value are obscured.[19]

Forensic psychiatrist Ronald Schlensky reveals what many have suspected all along: "Psychiatrists are no better than other citizens in predicting a human being's conduct."[20]

Even the American Psychiatric Association has publicly admitted that psychiatrists cannot predict future dangerous behavior of their clients. In a court case involving murder committed by a

person who had just seen a psychiatrist, the APA presented an
amicus curiae brief. The brief stated that research studies indicate
that psychiatrists cannot accurately predict the future potential
dangerousness of a client.[21]

In a well-publicized Texas murder case the American Psychiatric Association "told the Supreme Court that psychiatrists should
be excluded from a part of the criminal process because their 'false
claims to expertise' might mislead jurors."[22] Two psychotherapists urged a California Legislature Committee "to ban all
psychiatric testimony in criminal trials." One attorney told the
committee, "Psychiatrists will say, quite frankly, anything you
want them to say."[23] These statements and others led Idaho to
eliminate mental illness as a defense in criminal cases, making it
the first state to do so since the 1930's.[24]

Another paradox is evident when one compares physical diseases (medical) with metaphorical diseases (mental). In medicine
when one has a real disease there exists the possibility for a real
cure. In the area of the mind we are often dealing with nondiseases
and noncures. In medicine where real diseases exist and real cures
may be available, the patient has the freedom to refuse treatment.
However, where so-called mental diseases are diagnosed and some
type of therapy is offered, the person, once labeled and committed,
has no freedom to refuse treatment. Szasz says:

> In the one area in which there is no real illness, and no real
> treatment, both the diagnosis and the treatment are com-
> pulsory. It's ironic, to say the least.[25]

Harold Mavritte, assistant director of programs for the Los Angeles
County Department of Mental Health, says:

> When you come to rights, the mentally ill are the only ill
> people that can be detained against their will.... If a
> person is physically ill, you had better not treat him against
> his will unless it's a life or death matter and he's
> comatose.[26]

Psychiatrist Lee Coleman says:

> There's no other business where you can force someone to
> take your services—and then charge him for it. A medical

doctor cannot force a patient into a cast. But there are all sorts of legal procedures to enable a psychiatrist to force treatment on a patient.[27]

11

The Labeling Game

Besides vast errors of psychotherapeutic diagnosis and the inability to apply treatment with any certainty of cure, psychological diagnosis and treatment are fraught with other problems. Much of what is currently considered psychiatric illness is culture-bound.[1] Behavior which is considered abnormal in one culture may be seen as normal in another culture. Even today, with the current interest in altered states of consciousness, behavior which would have previously been relegated to the mental illness category is now seen as something to be desired. For instance, "out-of-the-body" or certain types of hallucinatory experiences would have served as symptoms of mental illness just a few years ago. What was considered a symptom in the past may be considered a solution today. Also, what may be considered "well" behavior today may be considered "mental illness" tomorrow.

Torrey declares that "cures" are also both culture-bound and class-bound.[2] Studies have shown that those of the lower socio-economic class are given the label "mentally ill" much more readily than those of the middle and upper classes. Drummond reports:

> The more the doctor likes the patient, which by and large means the closer they are in social class, the more likely he is to diagnose the patient as neurotic rather than psychotic.

151

> Poor people, blacks and Hispanics are quickly labeled "psychotic" or "character-disordered" for the *same behavior* that earns white, middle-class patients the label "neurotic" (i.e. relatively healthy).[3]

One book reports how "the mental health movement is unwittingly propagating a middle-class ethic under the guise of science."[4]

In the Soviet Union the psychiatric label has been an insidious tool of the government to punish and incarcerate political dissidents. *Time* quotes exiled writer Vladimir Bukovsky as saying:

> It is not easy for the ordinary person to get admitted for treatment in a psychiatric hospital. For a political case, though, it is very easy. They are taken to a hospital without making any request.[5]

In fact he says that the accused is not allowed to attend his own trial because he is "mentally ill." Thus, the label "mental illness" is used instead of a fair trial and the length of sentence can be extended as long as the person is labeled "mentally ill."

Similar abuses are evidenced in our society; this shows to what extent a contrived disease and so-called cure can be manipulated. Lasch says:

> Today the state controls not merely the individual's body but as much of his spirit as it can preempt; not merely his outer but his inner life as well; not merely the public realm but the darkest corners of private life formerly inaccessible to political domination.[6]

With the rise of psychotherapy there has been a reduction of personal freedom through the use of the label "mental illness."

Besides the problems of mental illness as a concept, of diagnosis as a practice, and of the political-social-economic implications, there are further problems which come from hanging a diagnostic label on an individual. Such labeling can promote a self-fulfilling prophecy. That is, if someone is treated in a particular manner, he may begin to act accordingly. Also, once a label is placed on a person, other people tend to react to that person according to the label. If told that someone is "mentally ill," people are apt to view what he says or does in terms of his so-called illness.

Once the label has been attached, professionals tend to use every statement and action as a kind of confirmation of that label. In one study, sane, emotionally stable individuals signed themselves into mental hospitals as "patients" in order to investigate whether or not the hospital staffs could distinguish the sane from the insane. In this study the hospital staffs consistently viewed the pseudo-patients according to the labels of the assigned diagnosis.

Each action or word was received through the distortion of the label. During the time that the pseudo-patients were taking notes on their experiences, the staff suspected nothing. Instead, they saw the behavior as part of the "sickness." Activities resulting from boredom were generally thought to be generated by nervousness.[7] Reich refers to the self-confirmation involved in the process of diagnosis and says that "anything a diagnosed patient says or does, even in his own defense, can be cited as a symptom of his illness— even if the diagnosis itself is incorrect."[8] Studies show a common tendency to view behavior according to the presence or absence of a label.[9]

Drummond gives an example to reveal how easy it is to become entangled in the whole process of viewing a person as abnormal. He refers to a study which used verbatim transcripts of individuals who "led normal lives and had average scores on psychological tests." A group of psychiatrists were told that the individuals were patients and were asked for a diagnosis. Drummond reports, "Forty percent of the psychiatrists chose 'acute paranoid schizophrenia' to describe these examples of normal verbal behavior." He goes on to say,"One result of the study was particularly upsetting: the more experienced the psychiatrist, the more likely he or she was to choose a more pathological diagnosis." Drummond states, "While schizophrenia is considered a 'medical diagnosis' like pneumococcal pneumonia or appendicitus, it actually functions as a degradation ritual imposed upon those who have broken some rules of propriety."[10]

The label "mental illness" may be used to excuse and/or condemn persons with some form of unacceptable behavior. Quite often elderly adults, who may be very strong willed and who might not be willing to act the way relatives and neighbors want them to act, come under such diagnostic labels. Rather than helping them cope with life, labeling and treating often make them confused and unable to cope as well as before such "help."

Reich describes such a case of a woman whose main problem was that she was "negative and disagreeable" in that she was more dogmatic about her opinions and made remarks that embarrassed family members. The diagnosis by the chief psychiatrist upon hospital admission was "organic brain syndrome." However, a young resident could see no reason for that label. He was over-ruled and no matter how hard the woman denied having the difficulties ascribed to her, she continued to be treated as mentally ill. Incarcerated in a ward without anyone to pay real attention to what she was saying, she was continually misunderstood. Reich says, "The more she denied illness, the more powerfully the diagnosis was maintained."[11]

Then, when the woman decided to cooperate with the hospital procedure, her change of behavior went unnoticed. Finally she became discouraged and angry and was thus further diagnosed as having a "catastrophic reaction." The "solution" was to put her on a heavy tranquilizer, which calmed her down and further "proved" the original diagnosis. No one, except the young resident, even thought to doubt the original diagnosis, and all subsequent behavior was seen and treated in the light of "organic brain syndrome."[12] Unfortunately stories like this abound, much to the chagrin of the professionals and much to the distress, despair and destruction of the victims.[13]

The very term *mental illness* has become a blight to society. The mystique surrounding it has frightened away people who could be of great help to those suffering from problems of living. Many people who want to help individuals with problems of living feel "unqualified" to help a person labeled "mentally ill." The confusion inherent within this strange juxtaposition of terms has led to errors which have often been more harmful than helpful to those thus labeled. Nevertheless, the profession continues to proliferate the false concept of mental illness, to allign it with medicine, and consign it to science—and the public follows.

12

Mental Illness or Irresponsibility

In addition to the inherent weaknesses and problems associated with the concept of mental illness, such a concept violates certain biblical principles, particularly those of free will and responsibility. The concept of illness, disease, or sickness in the mental realm conveys the idea that the person is not responsible for his behavior. If we really believe that a person with a mental-emotional-behavioral problem is sick, then we have admitted that he is no longer responsible for his behavior. And, if he is not responsible for his behavior, who is? Where does one draw the line?

The disease metaphor easily slips into other areas of life and takes on such literal meaning that personal responsibility for behavior is overshadowed. Henry Fairlie suggests that therapies have exonerated man from responsibility. He says:

> A hundred little -ologies spawn a thousand little therapies, for ourselves and our societies, and what we think we have discovered for the first time we place before all the knowledge of the past, thus further releasing ourselves to do simply what we will.[1]

The psychoanalytic, behavioristic, and humanistic psychological approaches directly or indirectly free individuals from responsibility for their behavior.

The psychoanalytic and behavioristic approaches preach that man's behavior is fixed by forces outside of his control. In the psychoanalytic approach man is controlled by inner psychic forces; in the behavioristic approach man is controlled by outer environmental forces. If man's behavior is determined by internal or external uncontrollable forces, it follows that he is not responsible for his behavior. The only freedom left under these approaches is the possible freedom of escape by means of a therapist.

The seeming freedom of the humanistic approach and its "messiah" Carl Rogers is only a delusion. This system teaches that man is basically good but corrupted by his environment. Here man has choice to be good, but he is not responsible for the evil in his life. In brief, this system contends that man is not evil by choice; he is evil by circumstances.

Such a system robs man of responsibility for his condition and reinforces the secular humanistic notion that man is basically good and that the evil in his life is due to his surroundings. This particular approach provides a wider latitude of choice to escape the past than the psychoanalytic and behavioristic approaches, but the standards of choice are subjective rather than biblical.

In terms of will, it is obvious that those who are experiencing only problems of living, not complicated by biological involvement, have a much greater degree of choice in thought and action than those who have organic brain disease. God holds each person responsible to the extent that choice exists for him. It is naive to state that all men have the same level of choice and are therefore equally responsible.

In the no-man's-land between a high degree of responsibility (sanity) and no responsibility (insanity), the California court system now permits a defense plea called "diminished capacity." This was the plea of Dan White after he murdered both San Francisco Mayor George Moscone and San Francisco Supervisor Harvey Milk. The court agreed that White could not be tried for first degree murder because of diminished capacity. Instead, he received a light sentence on manslaughter charges, was released from prison, and later committed suicide. Now the door is wide open for similar pleas, and criminals who know exactly what they are doing will escape whatever just punishment they deserve through the loophole of diminished capacity. This plea is the understandable result of the misnomer of mental illness and the influence of secular humanism. The combination of these two mistakes results in a pseudosickness which is supposedly caused by society rather than self, since man is seen as good but corrupted by circumstances.

With respect to the insanity plea, Szasz says it succinctly in the following:

> What is wrong with the insanity plea is that it creates an impression that it is not the person but the insanity that does something.[2]

One medical doctor, for example, refers to the "psychosis which apparently led John Hinckley, Jr., to his despicable attack on our president."[3] Rousas Rushdoony says:

> If my criminal behavior is not a moral fault in me but a social disease for which a disorderly society is to blame, I am then a victim, not an offender.

He concludes:

> Men find it easier to claim a sickness for which society is held responsible, than to affirm a moral model, which requires them to confess, "I acknowledge my transgressions: and my sin is ever before me. Against thee, thee only, have I sinned, and done this evil in thy sight." (Psalm 51:3-4)[4]

Elsewhere Rushdoony says, "The cult of victimization is perhaps the most popular religion of our time."[5]

Psychotherapy deals with individuals almost entirely as victims, rarely as sinners. Everyone is a victim of one sort or another, past or present. It is therefore easy to identify and to magnify the victim role, and soon it becomes the sole orientation of the individual. Rushdoony says:

> A great deal of our bigotry comes from a concentration on the wrongs we have suffered rather than on the wrongs we inflict on other people. No lying is involved, only an

emphasis on one aspect of our lives.

Rushdoony reminds us, "There is not a group in society which has not suffered some indignities and also inflicted indignities on others." He asks, "Can you convince any group of their sins?" and concludes, "They have to major in the sins of others."[6] Treating a person as a victim will only amplify the problem. Leading a real victim through a process of biblical repentance and biblical forgiveness will free him from the past.

Human will and responsibility go hand in hand. If a person makes choices, then he is accountable for his behavior. Individuals have different degrees of freedom of choice because of biological limitations, environmental background, habits established through past choices, and the other effects of the Fall. However, God holds each person responsible for the degree of choice he possesses. A person is not responsible for all that happens to him, but he is responsible for his reactions. The Bible makes it clear that persons do make choices and are held accountable for their behavior.

According to Scripture, man chooses his thoughts, attitudes, and actions. Man chooses to love and to hate, to forgive and to accept forgiveness, to act responsibly or irresponsibly, and to think biblically or unbiblically. If a person is not capable of such choices, why has his Creater commanded and exhorted him regarding love and forgiveness, thoughts and actions? The concept of personal accountability is a critical biblical doctrine which is essential for change.

When Nancy Reagan was asked how she felt about the use of psychiatry, she responded that in some cases it may be necessary but, "I feel that getting psychiatric treatment means that you are not really trying to get hold of yourself. It's sloughing off your own responsibilities."[7]

Comedian Sid Caesar became a multimillionaire through his talents. In need of help for personal problems, he spent hundreds of thousands of dollars for psychiatric help. He says, "You know what they did for me? They put me to sleep instead of curing the problem, prescribing Valium and Equinol." He continues, "Once the shrinks get you addicted to drugs, they own you lock, stock and barrel. They keep you coming back day after day, year after year, putting their kids through college on your neuroses and drug dependence on them."

While Caesar recognized his own responsibility for his problems, he declares, "The guys I really blame are the shrinks. I got a great education on how to destroy yourself with self-pity, wallowing in it." Caesar tells how he escaped this psychiatric nightmare which he describes as "being the walking dead." He says, "I willed myself to get better."[8] Man does have volition; he can choose and he can change.

There are some psychological systems which declare that people make choices and should be held responsible for their behavior. However, those psychological systems which do teach personal responsibility do not reveal the additional, but essential biblical truths. The psychological way generally misses man's ability to choose and his responsibility to do so because of the concept of mental illness.

Calling someone a pedophiliac, egomaniac, nyphomaniac, alcoholic, or drug addict with the added label "mentally ill" denies willful choice. It removes moral responsibility and thus reduces the possibility for improvement. Increasing a person's awareness that he can and does choose and that he is responsible for his thoughts and behavior increases his possibility for change. Robitscher says that people are labeled:

> . . .as mentally ill for social reasons that have nothing to do with concepts of health and disease. We label people mentally ill to give them the benefit of a psychiatric excuse: so a student can continue in college even though he has not taken his examinations, or so a woman will not be sent to prison even though she has murdered her baby. Whether these people are mentally ill or not does not seem very important; the label of mental illness is needed to justify what we feel needs to be done.[9]

Labeling a person's behavior as "sick" and giving him the accompanying psychological excuse reduces the possibilities for improvement. Treating a person's behavior as an illness only convinces him that he cannot choose to change on his own. The responsibility for behavior and change is thus transferred from the person to the therapist. Therapy then replaces responsibility. Psychiatrist Peter Breggin, founder of the Center for the Study of Psychiatry, says:

It becomes increasingly difficult to help patients take responsibility for their lives because psychiatry itself is telling them that they aren't responsible.[10]

Unless a person is held responsible for his behavior, he will tend not to be responsible. Teaching an individual that he can choose and is responsible for his behavior will set the stage for needed change. Once a person accepts the fact that he does have a choice and that he is accountable, improvement follows. Larry Thomas, a professor of journalism, says:

We have fabricated physiological, psychological, and sociological causes for the woes that beset mankind. We have created a guiltless society in which people are no longer responsible for their actions. We have ignored sin and found either a medical, emotional or social phenomenon to blame for our problems.[11]

The confusion of psychotherapy with science and the misnomer of mental illness have deceived the church beyond measure. Because of this deception, the church has not only withdrawn its ministry of counseling, but readily refers individuals to the psychotherapist's office. This is unfortunate because the church is called to minister to the mental-emotional-behavioral needs of its members. That is part of what is involved in the saving and sanctifying work of the Lord. Jesus taught His disciples how to live and imbued them with spiritual power to live the crucified life. In the Great Commission He instructed His disciples:

Go therefore and make disciples of all the nations ... teaching them to observe all that I commanded you; and lo, I am with you always, even to the end of the age. (Matthew 28:19-20)

Part Four
PSYCHOQUACKERY

The number of therapies and the variety of techniques continue to increase, the ranks of putative therapists swell, and the volume of consumers rises. The limits of this burgeoning enterprise give no signs of having been reached.

Morris Parloff[1]

Because of the great faith in what is believed to be science and the ever expanding numbers of people labeled "mentally ill," psychotherapy continues to flourish with promises for change, cure, and happiness. Assurances of help are undergirded by testimonies and confidence in psychological models and methods. On the other hand, the outcome research tells us something quite different about the effectiveness and the limitations of psychotherapy.

The research in Part Four is only the "tip of the iceberg" of what is available to show that psychotherapy is not a panacea or a palliative but may be a powerful placebo. While much research is presented we minimized the amount so as to make a point without overwhelming the reader.

13

Is Psychotherapy a Panacea?

> The psychologizing of the American public has created an expanding market. . . . As a result of the psychologizing of the American public, people who have marital problems, sex problems, problems with their children, who are having psychological "discomfort" increasingly look for psychological help. It is an infinitely expanding market.
>
> Alan Stone[1]

Psychological counseling and its underlying psychologies are a powerful force in this century. They have virtually subdued biblical counseling or the cure of souls. Because of this overwhelming takeover, an important question must be asked: Does psychological counseling and its accompanying psychologies have something better to offer Christians than the ministry which the church provided since its inception?

DOES RESEARCH SUPPORT PSYCHOTHERAPY?

The best-known early research on the success and failure rates of psychotherapy was reported in 1952 by Hans J. Eysenck, an eminent English scholar. In his research Eysenck compared groups

163

of patients treated by psychotherapy with persons given little or no treatment at all. Eysenck found that a greater percentage of patients who did not have psychotherapy improved over those who did undergo therapy. After examining over 8000 cases, Eysenck concluded that:

> . . . roughly two-thirds of a group of neurotic patients will recover or improve to a marked extent within about two years of the onset of their illness, whether they are treated by means of psychotherapy or not.[2]

What Eysenck showed was that for the subjects he examined little differences in results could be found between those treated and those not treated. Since his study failed to prove the advantage of psychotherapy over no formal treatment, he remarked:

> From the point of view of the neurotic, these figures are encouraging; from the point of view of the psychotherapist, they can hardly be called very favorable to his claims.[3]

The significance of Eysenck's statement is overwhelming! Why refer people to psychological counseling if they will do just as well (on the average) without treatment?

Since 1952 the controversy has been raging over the difference, if any, between counseled and not counseled persons. In 1979 a symposium was conducted on "The Outcome of Psychotherapy: Benefit, Harm, or No Change?" During the symposium, Eysenck reported the results of reviewing the history of the cures for mental patients in the hospital in which he works. He discovered that as far back as the late seventeenth century (1683-1703) about two-thirds of the patients were discharged as cured. Psychotherapy did not exist at that time, and yet the improvement rate was about the same as it is today. The so-called treatment consisted of the use of fetters, cold baths, solitary confinement, and even extraction of teeth for extreme punishment.

In his presentation Eysenck gave additional evidence for his earlier statement that about the same number of individuals will improve over a two-year period of time whether or not they receive therapy. He confirmed, "What I said over 25 years ago still stands."[4] Later, in 1980 Eysenck wrote a letter to the *American Psychologist* supporting his original position[5] Since then Eysenck has even more strongly supported his original position.[6]

A few years ago Smith and Glass did a review of a large number of research studies. Psychotherapists were encouraged because the review seemed to indicate that psychotherapy was indeed more effective than no treatment at all. Smith and Glass reviewed such a vast amount of research and used such sophisticated statistical methods that many who read the conclusions thought that finally, once and for all, the proof for psychotherapy had been established. However, psychiatrist Sol Garfield, in the book *Psychotherapy Research*, criticizes that conclusion which is based upon the approach used by Smith and Glass called meta-analysis. Garfield says that "instead of resolving forever the perennial controversy on the efficacy of psychotherapy, meta-analysis seemingly has led to an increased crescendo in the argument."[7]

The controversy over whether or not psychological counseling really helps people continues to rage in spite of the increase in research.[8] Garfield concludes a review of the research activities in psychotherapy by stating:

> Admittedly, we have a long way to go before we can speak more authoritatively about the efficacy, generality, and specificity of psychotherapy. . . . The present results on outcome, while modestly positive, are not strong enough for us to state categorically that psychotherapy is effective, or even that it is not effective. . . . Until we are able to secure more definitive research data, the efficacy of psychotherapy will remain a controversial issue.[9]

S. J. Rachman, Professor of Abnormal Psychology, and G. T. Wilson, Professor of Psychology, in their book *The Effects of Psychological Therapy*, also critique the Smith and Glass report. Rachman and Wilson point out its many serious errors and violations of sound statistical procedure. They say:

> Smith and Glass are naive in prematurely applying a novel statistical method to dubious evidence that is too complex and certainly too uneven and underdeveloped for anything useful to emerge. The result is statistical mayhem.[10]

After evaluating the Smith and Glass review as well as other disagreements with and criticisms of Eysenck, Rachman and Wilson support Eysenck's original position that there is no advantage of treatment over no treatment. Eysenck also mentions a study done by McLean and Hakstian which used a variety of treatment methods for depressed patients. One conclusion of the study was that, of the treatment methods used, psychotherapy was the least effective.[11]

For any form of psychotherapy to meet the criteria for efficacy, that therapy must show that its results are equal to or better than results from other forms of therapy and also better than no treatment at all. It must meet this criteria through standards set by independent observers who have no bias towards or against the therapy being examined. Also, the study must be able to be repeated and confirmed to indicate whether a therapy can be said to be helpful.[12]

Professor of psychiatry Donald Klein, in his testimony before the Subcommittee on Health of the U. S. Senate Subcommittee on Finance, said, "I believe that, at present, the scientific evidence for psychotherapy efficacy cannot justify public support."[13] As a result of the hearings, a letter from Jay Constantine, Chief, Health Professional Staff, reports:

> Based upon evaluations of the literature and testimony, it appears clear to us that there are virtually no controlled clinical studies, conducted and evaluated in accordance with generally accepted scientific principles, which confirm the efficacy, safety and appropriateness of psychotherapy as it is conducted today.
>
> Against that background, there is strong pressure from the psychological and psychiatric professions and related organizations to extend and expand Medicare and Medicaid payment for their services. Our concern is that, without validation of psychotherapy and its manifest forms and methods, and in view of the almost infinite demand (self-induced and practitioner-induced) which might result, we could be confronted with tremendous costs, confusion and inappropriate care.[14]

After summarizing a variety of research studies, Nathan Epstein and Louis Vlok state:

> We are thus left to conclude with the sad and paradoxical fact that for the diagnositc category in which most psychotherapy is applied—that of ncurosis—the volume of satisfactory outcome research reported is among the lowest and the proven effectiveness of psychotherapy is minimal.[15]

Michael Shepherd from the Institute of Psychiatry in London summarizes the outcome studies in psychotherapy:

> A host of studies have now been conducted which, with all their imperfections, have made it clear that (1) any advantage accruing from psychotherapy is small at best; (2) the difference between the effects of different forms of therapy are negligible; and (3) psychotherapeutic intervention is capable of doing harm.[16]

The following statement from Rachman and Wilson, after extensive review of the research on the effects of psychotherapy is both revealing and shocking:

> It has to be admitted that the scarcity of convincing findings remains a continuing embarrassment, and the profession can regard itself as fortunate that the more strident advocates of accountability have not yet scrutinized the evidence. If challenged by external critics, which pieces of evidence can we bring forward? ... The few clear successes to which we can point, are out-numbered by the failures, and both are drowned by the unsatisfactory reports and studies from which no safe conclusions can be salvaged.[17]

These authors conclude their book by saying:

> ...it is our view that modest evidence now supports the claim that psychotherapy is capable of producing some beneficial changes—but the negative results still outnumber the positive findings, and both of these are exceeded by reports that are beyond interpretation.[18]

The *Handbook of Psychotherapy and Behavior Change* reports:

> . . . it is disheartening to find that there is still considerable controversy over the rate of improvement in neurotic disorders in the absence of formal treatment.[19]

Psychotherapy has not shown positive results in cases of substance abuse. *Newsweek* magazine reveals, "Individual psychotherapy, the rehab experts agree, is notoriously ineffective in treating addiction."[20] Stanton Peele, a top addiction researcher says:

> Among people in therapy to lose weight, stop smoking, kick a drug or drink addiction, as few as 5% actually make it.[21]

Peele believes that "therapy itself may inadvertently impede cure."[22] He summarizes his remarks by saying, "But here's the irony and the hope: Self-cure can work, and depending on someone else to cure you usually does not."[23]

We believe that there is some justification to conclude that for all problems of living the best way out is by individual effort. The next best help is the informal support group, then the formal support group, and finally least effective is individual psychotherapy.

In the treatment of agoraphobia, the authors of one book make the following statements:

> Patients often attribute progress to the help that they receive from the therapist, and thus they feel dependent on continuing contact with him/her.

> Possibly as a result, progress does not usually continue after treatment has ended even though most patients still have some residual symptoms and disability.

> Patients who later experience a recurrence of acute anxiety may be unable to cope successfully without the help of the therapist, and so they relapse.

For these and other reasons, the authors conclude:

Treatment should emphasize the practice that patients carry out by themselves; it should either involve non-professional helpers *or better still encourage complete self-reliance.*[24] (Emphasis added.)

The psychotherapeutic environment fosters reliance on the therapist. It may do so unintentionally, but it prolongs the treatment and creates a continuing source of income for the therapist. And, when relapse occurs, return visits. No matter how one may try to avoid it, therapist dependency is a factor to be considered when seeking therapeutic help.

SELF HELP AND SOCIAL SUPPORT.

One solution to the need for help is a self-help group. Self-help groups are made up of individuals with the same or similar problems or needs who meet together to help each other. There are a number of local and national self-help groups that are available to aid individuals with a great variety of problems of living. Best known of the self-help groups is Alcoholics Anonymous. The success rate is very much related to the support that is provided by such an environment. An even better rate of improvement occurs in Teen Challenge, where the principles— unlike A.A.—are very specifically biblical.

In addition to self-help groups there is the social support provided by one or more friends. Leonard Syme, professor of epidemiology at the University of California at Berkeley, investigated disease and mortality rates throughout the world. He found that Japan had the best record for health and longevity. After he had eliminated many of the possible reasons for this high rating, such as food and physical environment, he came to the conclusion that the social, cultural, and traditional family and group ties contributed to the health and longevity. He believes that the more social ties one has the healthier he is bound to be, and the more isolated a person is the greater possibility for poor health and earlier death.[25]

One important element in social support involves speaking and listening to one another. It is a matter of hearing others and being heard by them. Dr. James Lynch says:

Our research has revealed that virtually all forms of

dialogue—even a pleasant chat about the weather—can alter the cardiovascular system, particularly blood pressure. Although a great many factors contribute to chronic high blood pressure, or hypertension, I believe the condition is most deeply connected to problems in human communication.[26]

If our bodily functions can be affected by human communication, it follows that our mental outlook can also be affected. Social support as described by Syme and human conversation as described by Lynch provide two powerful antidotes for problems of living. It may be that these two ingredients alone account for the majority of help provided in therapeutic settings. A number of organizations have sprung up nationally that recognize the importance of such ingredients and provide friends for those suffering from mental anguish.[27]

Annette Leavy says, "Patient-therapist compatibility is the best indicator of outcome."[28] Notice that the important factor is compatibility not therapy, not technique, not training, not degrees, not licenses. At four days of hearings in Washington, D.C., John Docherty, former Chief of the Psychosocial Treatment Research branch of the National Institute of Mental Health, said that the rapport between patient and therapist is the only variable that has been shown to be reliably significant in psychiatry.[29] Lester Luborsky and his colleagues report in the *Archives of General Psychiatry* that success in psychotherapy is due to a "helping alliance" between therapist and patient, not the type of therapy.[30]

There is so much fixation on professionalism that simple human interaction is ignored. And yet, it is this human interchange that is of utmost importance. This is precisely the area about which the Bible says so much. The Bible teaches how one person should regard another, encourage another, and even correct another. No license, no degrees, and no professional training are necessary to learn and apply the most powerful factors in human change available to man. They are found in the most readily available Textbook in the world and the Teacher has been given as a gift from God. The Teacher never sleeps and is thus always available. His fee is the most reasonable in the industry.

It seems to us that the first and best way of help is deciding to do it and doing it. If one needs help from others, then the next should be family and friends who hold the same spiritual world view, and then a support group. The last resort (which we do not recommend) would be professional psychological help. It is obvious in the case of alcoholism that individual choice works, whereas individual psychotherapy does not. Since alcoholism is the number one mental health problem for men,[31] it seems that this priority of individual effort, family and friends, and a support group would apply to other problems of living identified as "mental health problems."

We believe that there is some justification to conclude that for all problems of living the best way out for a Christian is by individual choice in cooperation with God; the next best help is the informal support group made up of Christian friends and family; then the formal support group of a local Christian fellowship; and individual biblical counseling within the context of the church body.

DOES PSYCHOTHERAPY WORK?

Many think that the answer to the question of "Does psychotherapy work?" is obvious, but it is not. Hans Strupp, Suzanne Hadley, and Beverly Gomes-Schwartz, three eminent researchers in the field of outcomes in psychotherapy, conclude that "the urgent question being pressed by the public—Does psychotherapy work?—goes unanswered."[32] Suzanne Hadley, in response to a letter sent to her, said that "the question itself, 'Does psychotherapy work?' is at best a simplistic approach which defies an answer."[33]

A book entitled *Psychotherapy Research: Methodological and Efficacy Issues*, published by the American Psychiatric Association, indicates that a definite answer to the question, "Is psychotherapy effective?" may be unattainable. The book concludes by stating: "Unequivocal conclusions about causal connections between treatment and outcome may never be possible in psychotherapy research."[34] In reviewing this book, The *Brain/Mind Bulletin* says, "Research often fails to demonstrate an unequivocal advantage from psychotherapy." The following is an interesting example from the book:

> ... an experiment at the All-India Institute of Mental Health in Bangalore found that Western-trained psychia-

trists and native healers had a comparable recovery rate. The most notable difference was that the so-called "witch doctors" released their patients sooner.[35]

Researcher Allen Bergin admits that it is very hard to prove things in psychotherapy.[36] Because of the difficulties involved, Judd Marmor says that there is a "paucity of sound research in this area."[37] Two writers indicate that "the paucity of 'outcome' data leaves the profession vulnerable to the familiar charge that it is not a science at all, but rather a 'belief system' that depends on an act of faith between the troubled patient and a supportive therapist."[38]

If top researchers feel uneasy about the question, why do Christians believe that psychological counseling is necessary for people suffering from problems of living? If it is so difficult to perform studies and prove things in psychological counseling, why do Christians place such confidence in it? If both the American Psychiatric Association and the American Psychopathological Association give mixed reports about efficacy, why do Christian leaders promote the promises of the psychological way? And if there is little sound research, why are Christians so eager to substitute theories and therapists for the Word of God and the work of the Holy Spirit? If no one can say how much better psychotherapy is than other forms of help or even if it works at all, is it worth the over 17 billion dollars spent annually for mental health care? Why has the church permitted the cure of souls ministry to be replaced by the cure of minds?

CAVEAT EMPTOR.

We often hear about the possible help given by psychotherapy, but we rarely hear about its potential harm. A book by Richard B. Stuart entitled *Trick or Treatment, How and When Psychotherapy Fails* is filled with studies and reviews that show "how current psychotherapeutic practices often harm the patients they are supposed to help."[39] One group of researchers after surveying the "best minds in the field of psychotherapy" conclude:

> It is clear that negative effects of psychotherapy are overwhelmingly regarded by experts in the field as a significant problem requiring the attention and concern of practi-

tioners and researchers alike.[40]

Stuart is not alone in his concern about potential negative effects in therapy. Many other researchers are noting this danger zone in therapy. Bergin and Lambert say that "ample evidence exists that psychotherapy can and does cause harm to a portion of those it is intended to help."[41] Morris Parloff, chief of the Psychosocial Treatments Research Branch of the National Institute of Mental Health, declares:

> In my view, it seems fair to conclude that although the empirical evidence is not firm, there is now a clinical consensus that psychotherapy, if improperly or inappropriately conducted, can produce psychonoxious effects. Most studies do not contemplate the possibility of negative effects.[42]

Carol Tavris warns:

> Psychotherapy can be helpful, especially if the therapist is warm and empathic, but sometimes it slows down a person's natural rate of improvement. In a small but significant number of cases, psychotherapy can be harmful and downright dangerous to a client. Most of the time it doesn't accomplish much of anything.[43]

The average figure of harmful effects is about ten percent.[44] This provides some support for a *caveat emptor* (buyer beware) warning to prospective patients. Michael Scriven, when he was a member of the American Psychological Association Board of Social and Ethical Responsibility, questioned "the moral justification for dispensing psychotherapy, given the state of outcome studies which would lead the FDA to ban its sale if it were a drug."[45]

Even after considering the most recent research on the subject, Scriven still refers to psychotherapy as a "weak possibility."[46] If psychotherapy can be harmful to one's mental health, some written warning (equivalent to the one on cigarette packages) ought to be given to potential buyers. When one considers the research which reveals detrimental effects of psychological counseling, one wonders if the overall potential for improvement is worth the risk.[47]

Many therapists are reluctant to publicize and advertise anything but the positive results of psychological counseling. We
agree with Dorothy Tennov, who says in her book *Psychotherapy:
The Hazardous Cure*:

> . . . if the purpose of the research is to prop up a profession
> sagging under the weight of its own ineffectiveness in a
> desperate last-ditch effort to find a rationale for its sur-
> vival, we might prefer to put our research dollars else-
> where.[48]

Bergin once accused two well-known writers in the field of being
too concerned about harming the image of psychotherapy in the
eyes of government, insurance companies, and consumers. He
said:

> The implication is that "harmful effects" will impinge
> upon our pocketbooks if we are not more careful about
> publishing evidence on therapy-induced deterioration.[49]

We wonder to what extent money, academic rank, and vested
interests in training programs influence the outlook and reaction of
therapists to research detrimental to the psychological way.

OTHER FACTORS.

How many of the positive results of psychotherapy are due to the
"experimenter effect"? The experimenter effect is the tendency of
a researcher (mostly unintended) to bias results in the direction of
his expectation or beliefs. Derek Freeman, in his book *Margaret
Mead and Samoa*, and Martin Gardner, in the *Skeptical Inquirer*,
document how much the distinguished anthropologist Margaret
Mead biased data in the direction of her own beliefs. This experimenter effect occurred in her investigation of the Samoan culture,
UFO's, dowsing, psychic powers, and trance behavior.[50]

One text on the subject presents "evidence that an experimenter's expectancy may serve as self-fulfilling prophecy of his
subject's responses."[51] It has been found in various research settings that expecting a result or a certain kind of behavior increases

the probability of it occurring (self-fulfilling prophecy). Teachers have learned that if they expect certain students to do well they probably will. And, on the other hand, if they expect a certain student will do poorly he probably will. It would be natural for a therapist to expect positive results from psychotherapy and therefore either encourage it or interpret the results positively.

Another factor which would cause questionability is that studies determining the efficacy of psychotherapy are usually based upon the use of the best therapists. When one is doing a study, he ends up with a select group of therapists. The therapists are asked because they are known to be good therapists or the therapists agree to participate because they are confident in their counseling abilities. Bergin and Lambert, in reference to the positive results that they have found of treatment over no treatment, say:

> ... we believe that a major contributor to these newer findings is that more experienced and competent therapists have been used in recent studies.[52]

The use of above-average therapists would tend to inflate outcome results greatly.

Allen Bergin reports how outcome studies depend on the use of good therapists and not those who are average or below.[53] This raises several questions which research does not answer. First: "Does the use of average psychotherapists yield better results on treated patients than no treatment at all?" Second: "How much more deterioration occurs with average psychotherapists on treated groups compared with no treatment at all?" And, finally: "How many good therapists are there?" No one really knows how many good therapists there are. Nor does anyone know whether no treatment would yield better results than the use of average or below-average therapists. Furthermore, no one knows how high the harm rate is with average or below-average therapists.

However, there is some doubt as to whether there are many good therapists. Researchers Truax and Mitchell say, "From existing data it would appear that only one out of three people entering professional training has the requisite interpersonal skills to prove helpful to patients."[54] Two other researchers estimate that only one-fifth of the therapists are competent.[55] On top of this, some studies have indicated that while "warmth and empathy are highly important variables in determining client benefit ... graduate programs do not help students to greatly increase their interpersonal skills.[56] The authors of *Psychotherapy for Better or Worse* note that "the therapist himself was one of the most often cited sources of negative effects in psychotherapy."[57]

The research studies are not only based upon the use of above-average psychotherapists. They use almost exclusively other-than-private-practice therapists. One review of psychotherapy research revealed only fifteen private-practice studies were done during a twenty-five-year period of time. There are few such studies because private-practice psychotherapists are reluctant to participate.[58]

One additional factor which would inflate improvement results in favor of treatment over no treatment is that of research procedure. Generally the therapist, the patient, and the one evaluating the results all know that research is being conducted. It has been shown through other studies that such knowledge tends to inflate results. Arthur Shapiro says:

> The design of almost all studies does not fulfill the essential prerequisite for an adequate or double-blind study, which requires that there is no possibility that patients, clinicians, researchers, and statisticians can break the code before the statistical results are completely tabulated and analyzed.[59]

Often research results are biased by the researcher himself. Greenwell and King, after analyzing a questionnaire, report:

> We are now reasonably sure that scientists' notions of reality are influenced not only by objective conditions but also by subjective considerations.[60]

Morris Parloff declares:

> You have to ask "Who does research?" By and large those motivated to do research have a point they want to prove, and generally they do the kind of research that will prove it.[61]

George Miller says:

> People do not usually try to disprove their own ideas. . . .
> People seldom find anything they're not looking for. All
> research is done where the light is best.[62]

David Myers notes:

> Even when observing purely random events, people easily
> become convinced that significant relationships are occur-
> ring— when they expect to see them.[63]

It may be that this illusory correlation is the influencing factor in
many of the research results which are favorable towards psychotherapy.

Myers, in his book *The Inflated Self*, indicates that there is an
illusion of efficacy which often occurs when people go for psychotherapy. The illusion of efficacy is an illusory belief about causation.[64] Testimonies are given about self-improvement after intense
journal workshops, Gestalt therapy, transactional analysis, body
work, est, Senoi dream education, etc., etc., etc. There seems to be
a cause and effect here: a workshop or other experience is followed
by an improvement. Therefore the person concludes that the workshop must have caused it, whether there was any connection or not.
Psychotherapist Allan Fromme claims that any change will usually
result in improvement, no matter what it is.[65] Myers explains:

> The principle of "regression toward the average" also
> contributes to the illusion of efficacy. Since people tend to
> seek help when things have hit bottom, any activity that is
> then undertaken may seem to be effective—to both the
> client and the therapist.[66]

In summary, it cannot be said categorically that psychotherapy
itself is or is not effective, or that there is a possibility of greater
improvement with or without treatment, or how much harm may
occur during the treatment. However, these are serious considera-
tions for anyone recommending or seeking treatment, especially
when the research indicating that treatment may be helpful could
have inflated results due to the use of the best therapists or due to
biased results.

14

Is Psychotherapy a Palliative?

In spite of the research, many people believe that psychotherapy does help individuals. And, indeed, people do improve with therapy as well as without. If, indeed, psychotherapy does help, what might be the factors which could lead to client improvement?

PROFESSIONALS VERSUS NONPROFESSIONALS.

Many people assume that psychological training is the most important pre-requisite for improvement. However, the conclusions of researchers suggest that if psychotherapy does help it has little to do with techniques or training. Researcher Ruth Matarazzo says:

> It has never been established that high levels of education and/or training are necessary to the development of an effective psychotherapist.[1]

According to Ernest Havemann, William Glasser (the originator of Reality Therapy) "says he could teach any bright young trainee all he needs to know about the theory in a day."[2] Truax and Mitchell contend:

> There is no evidence that the usual traditional graduate

training program has any positive value in producing therapists who are more helpful than nonprofessionals.[3]

After reviewing a vast amount of psychotherapy outcome research, Parloff admits that there is no

> ... convincing evidence that these procedures can be uniquely applied only by members of professions who have completed specified training programs and have honed their skills by lengthy experience.[4]

Dr. Joseph Durlak evaluated research projects in which the psychotherapeutic effectiveness of paraprofessionals was compared with that of mental health professionals, such as experienced psychiatrists, psychologists, and social workers. The training of the paraprofessionals ranged from none to fifteen hours. Therefore, it would be more appropriate to think of those individuals as nonprofessionals. Durlak says,

> Overall, outcome results in comparative studies have favored paraprofessionals. . . . There were no significant differences among helpers in 28 investigations, but paraprofessionals were significantly more effective than professionals in 12 studies. . . . In only one study were professionals significantly more effective than all paraprofessionals with whom they were compared. . . . The provocative conclusion from these comparative investigations is that professionals do not possess demonstrably superior therapeutic skills, compared with paraprofessionals. Moreover, professional mental health education, training, and experience are not necessary prerequisites for an effective helping person.[5]

According to Jerome Frank, over six-and-a-half million persons see mental health specialists during a single year. Frank reveals the shocking fact of:

> ... the inability of scientific research to demonstrate conclusively that professional psychotherapists produce results sufficiently better than those of nonprofessionals.[6]

A study of trained and untrained therapists by Hans Strupp at Vanderbilt University compared the mental-emotional improvement of two groups of male college students. Two groups of "therapists" were set up to provide two groups of students with "therapy." The two student groups were equated on the basis of mental-emotional distress as much as possible. The first group of therapists consisted of five psychiatrists and psychologists. "The five professional therapists participating in the study were selected on the basis of their reputation in the professional and academic community for clinical expertise. Their average length of experience was 23 years."

The second group of "therapists" consisted of seven college professors from a variety of fields, but without therapeutic training. Each untrained "therapist" used his own personal manner of care, and each trained therapist used his own brand of therapy. The students seen by the professors showed as much improvement as those seen by the highly experienced and specially trained therapists.[7]

Bergin and Lambert report on a "nationwide interview survey conducted for the Joint Commission on Mental Illness and Health." The survey shows:

> ... that of those persons who actively sought help for personal problems, the vast majority contacted persons other than mental-health professionals, and that generally they were more satisfied with the help received than were those who chose psychiatrists and psychologists.

Bergin and Lambert remark that the no-treatment success rate "may therefore result from seeking and obtaining therapeutic help from nontherapists!"[8]

Other researchers have noticed possible improvement from non-professional sources. Frank found that "over a period of years approximately 50 percent of a group who had sought psychotherapy had also sought help from a variety of non-mental-health sources." Frank suggests that the improvement which occurred "over a long period of time when they were not in therapy was the result of the effects of this nonprofessional 'treatment.'"[9] Gurin et al commenting on such nonprofessional "treatment" state:

> These findings underscore the crucial role that non-

psychiatric resources—particularly clergymen and physicians—play in the treatment process. They are the major therapeutic agents. . . .[10]

Bergin and Lambert say:

> Perhaps psychotherapists are not unique. Perhaps selected helping persons in the "natural" social environment provide adequate or better coping conditions for neurosis than do trained mental health experts.[11]

When one considers the great variety of psychotherapies and the research comparing the different approaches, it appears that the personal qualities of the therapist are far more important than training, techniques or approach.

ALL THERAPIES WORK, BUT SO DOES CONVERSATION.

There are over 250 different approaches in the field of psychotherapy. Generally when psychotherapies have been tested and compared, it has been found that they are about equally effective. Parloff refers to the "disconcerting finding that all forms of psychotherapy are effective and that all forms of psychotherapy appear to be equally effective."[12] He says:

> No consistent differences are found among different forms of therapy in terms of type or degree of benefit with comparable patients.[13]

A six-year, ten-million-dollar study coordinated by the National Institute of Mental Health (NIMH) compares two forms of talk therapy with drug treatment. The two approaches used were a cognitive behavioral therapy and an interpersonal therapy. Both forms of talk therapy worked equally well. *Time* reports:

> The general finding that the two different talk therapies are about equally effective strengthens the hand of those who believe that since most therapies get about the same results, the hotly debated differences among talk treatments are basically irrelevant.[14]

In *American Health* Morris Parloff, former Chief of the Psycho-social Treatment Research branch of NIMH says:

> Nearly 500 rigorously controlled studies have shown with almost monotonous regularity that all forms of psychological treatment . . . are comparably effective.[15]

Some researchers admit that this is like the Dodo in *Alice in Wonderland* who declares, "Everybody has won, and all must have prizes." Bergin says, "Comparative studies reveal few differences across techniques, thus suggesting that nontechnical or personal variables account for much of the change."[16] Smith, Glass and Miller, in analyzing 475 outcome studies found little influence of results due to technique factors.[17] Psychotherapist Eugene Gendlin admits:

> The omniscient and totally self-assured psychotherapist exists only in the movies. Of course each school of therapists has its own ideas and techniques, but they all know that they stumble around confusedly when their techniques don't work, which is more often than not.[18]

Donald Klein, New York State Psychiatric Institute, and Judith Rabkin of Columbia University have examined the area of specificity versus generality. They say that "specificity usually implies that the specific technique is necessary so that the particular outcome simply cannot be accomplished without it."[19] They say:

> A core, covert issue in the specificity debate is the uncomfortable realization that if all psychotherapies work about the same then all of our elaborate psychogenic etiological hypotheses are called into question.[20]

And, if all hypotheses are called into question, then all third party payments should be too. Of course that is the life blood of most psychotherapists. Their worst nightmare would be the termination of such a lucrative and easy source of payments.

Dr. Joseph Wortis, State University of New York, reduces the problem of generality down to its lowest common denominator. He says, "The proposition of whether psychotherapy can be beneficial can be reduced to its simplest terms of whether talk is very helpful." He goes on to say, "And that doesn't need to be researched. It is self evident that talk can be helpful."[21] What a simple yet profound statement. It is transparently true with devastating implications not only for third party payments, but for all payments to psychotherapists.

Researcher James Pennebaker, an associate professor at Southern Methodist University, showed a relationship between confiding in others and health. He showed that lack of confiding is related to health problems. One could conclude from his research that, to paraphrase an old adage, the conversation of confession is good for the soul—and apparently for the body too.[22]

Dr. Robert Spitzer, Columbia University and New York State Psychiatric Institute, takes this concept a bit further by giving a hypothetical example of someone proving efficacy for a specific psychotherapeutic technique. He then goes on to speak of those who might provide this service "for the lowest dollar." He continues his hypothetical example by supposing that a "mental health aide" can perform the service for $6 per hour rather than $30 or $50 or $120. He concludes by challenging his colleagues on how they would feel about a mental health aide providing the service for $6 per hour rather than the higher paid psychotherapist.[23] It is certain that such a conclusion, which is a highly likely one, if established under research conditions, would be rejected by the psychotherapeutic community.

INTERPERSONAL QUALITIES.

Researchers are becoming more and more aware that the interpersonal qualities of the counselor far outweigh his training and techniques. E. Fuller Torrey reports:

> The research shows that certain personal qualities of the therapist—accurate empathy, non-possessive warmth, and genuineness—are of crucial importance in producing effective psychotherapy.

He notes that:

> . . . therapists who possess these qualities consistently and convincingly get better therapeutic results than those who

do not possess them.[24]

When Sloane et al compared psychotherapy and behavior therapy, they found that:

> Successful patients in both therapies rated the personal interaction with the therapist as the single most important part of their treatment.[25]

Jerome Frank contends:

> Anyone with a modicum of human warmth, common sense, some sensitivity to human problems, and a desire to help can benefit many candidates for psychotherapy.[26]

Bergin says that "change appears to be a function of common human interactions, including personal and belief factors."[27] Lewis Thomas says:

> Most psychiatrists of my acquaintance are skilled in therapy, but the therapy, when it works, is really plain friendship.[28]

Daniel Hogan, a social psychologist at Harvard, published a four-volume series called *The Regulation of Psychotherapists*. Hogan analyzed the traits and qualities that characterize effective psychotherapists. Hogan says,

> Contrary to much professional opinion . . . the effectiveness of therapists is more determined by the presence or absence of certain personality characteristics and interpersonal skills than technical abilities and theoretical knowledge.

Hogan goes on to say, "The necessary qualities that make a superb psychotherapist are very similar to those one looks for in a good friend." In half of the studies examined by Hogan, paraprofessional (nonprofessional) therapists did better than professionals.[29]

Frank says that "the effectiveness of a psychotherapeutic method depends more on the therapist than the technique."[30] Bergin suggests that it is not psychotherapies that help people get better, but rather psychotherapists.[31] In other words, it is not the system which is important, but rather the person. Bryce Nelson says:

> Many patients now use their psychotherapist as a substitute for someone who might, in an earlier day, have filled the need for intimate conversation—a good friend, a wise relative, a priest.[32]

Jay Haley says:

> . . . the exploration of the human psyche may be irrelevant to therapeutic change . . . it is argued here that change occurs as a product of the interpersonal context of that exploration rather than the self-awareness which is brought about in the patient.[33]

Frank agrees that the "personal qualities of the therapist and the way he behaves soon outweigh symbols of his therapeutic role."[34] The *Handbook* states:

> So far we can probably safely say that psychological good health, flexibility, open-mindedness, positive attitudes toward people, and interpersonal skill are associated with success as a psychotherapist.[35]

However, these characteristics are not restricted to psychotherapists. They are characteristics of all helping individuals.

WHAT WORKS?

When evaluating formal treatment, one needs to remember that the patient's environment and activities outside of the treatment sessions may have more to do with improvement than the treatment itself. Any factors which influence the no treatment improvement rate may be at work to influence the success rate in therapy. Eysenck, in reporting on the well-known Sloan study of outcomes in psychotherapy, mentions how this study showed a 77 percent spontaneous remission rate. He declares, "Whatever you do [whatever treatment] spontaneous remission will do the work for you or most of it."[36] Spontaneous remission is due to such factors as change in circumstances (e.g. new job), a personal change (e.g. thinking different thoughts or deciding to change), or the help of nonprofessionals (e.g. friends or relatives).

Psychiatrist E. Fuller Torrey claims that "psychotherapy *does* work and that its effectiveness is primarily due to four basic components—a shared worldview, personal qualities of the therapist, client expectations, and an emerging sense of mastery."[37] All of these factors are at play in all effective human relationships. None of these factors requires psychological training, psychological techniques, psychological degrees, or psychological licensing. All of these factors may be at work whether a person is in therapy or not. The same factors which lead to improvement outside of formal treatment also work inside of formal treatment, or along side it, which adds more questionability to the whole psychotherapeutic mind game.

15

Is Psychotherapy a Placebo?

Arthur Shapiro, clinical professor of psychiatry at Mount Sinai School of Medicine, suggests that the power of psychological counseling may be the effect of a placebo. The placebo effect takes place when one has faith in a pill, a person, a process or procedure, and it is this faith that brings about the healing. The pill, person, process, or procedure may all be fake, but the result is real. Shapiro says:

> Just as bloodletting was perhaps the massive placebo technique of the past, so psychoanalysis—and its dozens of psychotherapy offshoots—is the most used placebo of our time.[1]

Eysenck dramatically states:

> It is unfortunate for the well-being of psychology as a science that . . . the great majority of psychologists, who after all are practising clinicians, will pay no attention whatsoever to the negative outcome of all the studies carried on over the past thirty years but will continue to use methods which have by now not only failed to find evidence in support of their effectiveness, but for which there

is now ample evidence that they are no better than placebo
treatments.

He goes on to ask:

> Do we really have the right to impose a lengthy training on
> medical doctors and psychologists in order to enable them
> to practise a skill which has no practical relevance to the
> curing of neurotic disorders? Do we have the right to
> charge patients fees, or get the State to pay us for a
> treatment which is no better than a placebo?[2]

All of this and more add an exclamation mark to the question mark
hanging over psychotherapy.

If psychotherapy indeed operates as a placebo, the psychological approach one uses does not matter. The patient will interpret
what he is receiving as helping him whether it does or not. His
thinking will then influence the result. Lewis Thomas says:

> Protests against bleeding had been raised as early as the
> 1830's, and a few eminent physicians wrote papers assert-
> ing that it generally did more harm than good, but it took a
> long time to pass from favor.[3]

Could it be that psychotherapy will go the way of bloodletting?
William Kroger says:

> The fact that there are contradictory theories being
> employed with identical results in a wide variety of psy-
> chotherapies indicates that here, too, a placebo effect is in
> operation![4]

Kroger notes that faith and the placebo effect have been constant
over a period of time while there have been a variety of new and
different therapeutic approaches. He concludes that "it is certain
that our present cure rate for many of the psychogenic entities
would not differ appreciably from that of any other period."[5]
Thomas Kiernan, author of *Shrinks, Etc.*, says:

> In the end, psychotherapy is a state of mind. If you are
> convinced it can help you, the likelihood is that it will; if
> you are convinced of the opposite, the likelihood is that it
> won't.[6]

A number of studies support the idea that mental, emotional, and even physical change may occur simply because of expectations. Simply expecting to improve will often set the stage for improvement. In fact, the authors of a book on the placebo effect say, "It may be that interventions differ in effectiveness because they differentially elicit expectancy of benefit."[7] D. A. Shapiro calls this the "expectancy arousal hypothesis," which is that "treatments differ in effectiveness only to the extent that they arouse in clients differing degrees of expectation of benefit."[8]

A study of the use of acupuncture at one university indicates that expectation of relief on the part of the patient can influence the results. The researchers concluded that acupuncture "requires a specific psychological attitude on the part of the recipient to potentiate its effect." The remarks that the experimenters made to the patients encouraged higher expectations. The researchers found that:

> Acupuncture significantly reduced pain only when administered in conjunction with procedures designed to enhance subjects' expectation for successful treatment.[9]

Other studies have shown that a variety of anxiety and stress symptoms can even be reduced by giving false information to subjects. Through the use of false feedback with biofeedback devices, a patient receives a sense of self control. As the false feedback communicates increasing levels of success the patient believes that he has greater self control. Over a period of weeks the subjects report a decrease in stress symptoms.[10] One reason for such improvements is suggested by two studies which indicate that "paying attention to your body at specific times, not the physiological changes biofeedback produces, may be responsible for its success."[11] Another study reported that false information about room temperature can influence bodily comfort. The study showed that "misinforming people about room temperature can lead them to feel warmer or cooler than they might if they knew the actual temperature."[12]

One form of psychotherapy, called Social Influence Therapy, purposely uses false feedback in order to achieve success. One practitioner of this brand of therapy says:

> Humanitarian fervor aside, it's the therapist's job to take

> power over the patient, push ahead with solving the prob-
> lem, then convince the patient he or she is better, even if it
> means being devious.[13]

This therapist claims, "Successful therapy can almost be reduced
to a formula." The main part of the formula is to convince the
"client that the therapy is definitely working apart from any objective evidence of change."[14] In this form of therapy flattery, distortion, lies, and all forms of what is euphemistically called "false
feedback" are used, and with success. Ethics aside, this form of
therapy is a testimony to the power of the placebo.

If one out of three individuals finds relief through the use of a
medical placebo, what percent of the individuals who see a psychotherapist receive similar relief through a type of mental placebo? A
group of researchers at Wesleyan University compared the benefits
of psychotherapy with those of placebo treatments. The placebo
treatments were activities (such as discussion of current events,
group play reading, and listening to records) that attempted to help
individuals without the use of psychotherapeutic techniques. The
researchers concluded:

> . . . after about 500 outcome studies have been reviewed—
> we are still not aware of a single convincing demonstration
> that the benefits of psychotherapy exceed those of placebos
> for real patients.[15]

Arthur Shapiro criticized his professional colleagues at the
annual meeting of the American Psychopathological Association
for ignoring placebo effects and therefore skewing the results of
their research.[16] He believes that if placebo effects were considered
in the Smith and Glass survey mentioned earlier "that there would
be no difference between psychotherapy and placebo."[17]

The placebo not only affects the individual, but it affects those
who come in contact with the individual. Everyone tends to feel
and believe that progress will be made because something is being
done. The placebo effect, along with other factors just mentioned,
greatly diminishes the authority of any positive results reported for
psychotherapy.

If one combines the interpersonal qualities of the therapists, the
external factors involved in spontaneous remission, and the

placebo effect, one may account for much of what may be working to bring about any success in psychotherapy. In other words, the particular psychological approach is not what leads to change, nor the theories, training, or techniques. It is the interpersonal environment provided by the counselor, plus spontaneous remission factors, plus the placebo effect. And all of these, of course, pale in comparison to the individual's desire to change and his willingness to take the responsibility to do so.

16

The Emperor's New Clothes

> Psychology is burdened with a scrap heap of empirical
> results that have contributed nothing to our field except to
> increase the number of publications and to justify aca-
> demic promotions.
>
> Howard Kendler in *Autobiographies*
> *in Experimental Psychology*[1]

The psychological way provides numerous theories about dealing with problems of living. The fact that the theories are not
scientific seems to bother few people. The added fact that none of
these often conflicting, nonscientific theories has been shown to be
clearly superior to any of the others seems of little concern. No
matter what psychological approach one develops, it will seem as
valid as any other.[2] Anyone can do just about anything he wishes in
the midst of the confusion of psychological theories and techniques. One look at the multitudenous contradictory psychological
approaches with the competing claims of success should cause
even the most ardent supporter of the psychological way to throw
up his hands in despair.

For the Christian, the point is not simply whether or not psychotherapy works, but whether it works better than biblical counseling. The question for the church is this: Does psychological

counseling have something better to offer on the average than the cure of souls? To begin with, no one really knows if psychotherapy conducted by highly trained and long experienced therapists does any better than that done by untrained and inexperienced non-professionals. Additionally, no one even knows if professional psychotherapy does any better than hundreds of other promises for help, such as meditation, dog-fish-or-parakeet "therapy," laughter "therapy," or just plain blowing bubbles every day to overcome depression.[3]

The research has not advanced much beyond *attempting* to prove that psychotherapy works better than no treatment, probably because it has not even proven this very well. It is still not certain from a research standpoint whether or not psychotherapy works, and if it does, how well it works. It seems logical to conclude that, if researched, the use of biblical counseling would be shown to be as effective as the over 250 present systems of promises for help. One professor of psychology reports:

> During the first half of the nineteenth century, when moral treatment was at its peak, at least 70 percent of the patients who had been ill for a year or less were released as recovered or improved. . . . Moral treatment did all this without tranquilizers, antidepressants, shock treatment, psychosurgery, psychoanalysis, or any other kind of psychotherapy.

He adds:

> The use of moral treatment declined during the second half of the nineteenth century. The results were disasterous. Recovery and discharge rates went down as moral treatment gave way to the medical approach.[4]

It may be that in the future there will be definite research proof for the efficacy of psychotherapy. However, in its present state of confusion over its questionable successes and unquestionable failures, it seems appropriate to recommend that the church minister to people with needs rather than turning them away to a costly, often prolonged process of dubious value.

People are suffering from anxiety, shyness, marital discord, drug abuse, alcoholism, sexual disorders, depression, and a host of other problems and fears. Regardless of what claims psychotherapists may make, no one has ever shown that psychological counseling is superior to biblical counseling.

No one really knows whether psychological counseling is superior to biblical counseling. There is only a massive, but mistaken assumption that it is. And, it is this false assumption which has caused the church to abandon its ministry to the suffering soul. Mental illness is a myth and psychological counseling is not science.

Christians need not be submerged in this sea of confusion. Unfortunately psychotherapy has become entrenched in our society. It is a stronghold of the enemy to turn believers to another gospel—the gospel of "mental illness" and "mental health," the gospel of self and a myriad of other religious philosophies. Christians who suffer from problems of living need to be helped by the church, not sent away to those who believe that problems of living are mental illnesses or that the psychological counselor has scientific cures.

Our primary objection to the use of psychotherapy, however, is not based merely upon its confused state of self-contradiction, nor upon its phony scientific facade, nor on its use of the misnomer of mental illness. Our primary objection is not even based upon the attempts to explain human behavior through personal opinion presented as scientific theory. Our greatest objection to psychotherapy is that it has displaced biblical ministry among Christians without proof or justification of superiority.

The frustrating part of all this is that there is absolutely no scientific justification for the replacement of the cure of souls ministry by psychotherapy. And yet, the path from the church to the couch has become so well-worn that few self-respecting clergymen will resist the temptation to send an ailing parishioner down that broad way, in spite of the questionable results and expense of the effort. Just because the world utilizes psychological counseling, it does not follow that the church has been wise in following the trend. The Bible warns us about using the world's systems and about trying to combine the world's ways with God's ways. (2 Corinthians 6:14-18)

It is unnecessary to add psychology to the Word of God or to use psychology in place of the Word of God. Even those psychologies which seem to have elements of truth in them are unnecessary because the essential elements are already found in Scripture. The way the theory is described may entice believers into thinking that psychology has something more than the Bible. However, if stripped down to the core, each theory has some element of truth and just enough error to lead people away from God and into the ways of self and Satan.

One of the best-known behavior therapists is psychiatrist Dr. Aaron Beck. He has developed a short-term method for treating depression. The treatment is aimed at correcting three major thought distortions of depressives: "seeing themselves as deficient and unworthy; seeing the world as frustrating and unfulfilling; and seeing the future as hopeless."[5] These three aspects of one's life—the individual's view of himself, the world, and his future—are all spiritual matters. These can all be and should all be confronted biblically rather than psychologically.

Even if psychology can deal as effectively as the Bible with individual deficiencies, frustrations and hopelessness, why turn to it? The Bible will more efficiently—and more accurately—deal with such conditions. Surely the Bible has more to offer than worldly systems. Moral treatment when administered in love and truth has had positive results. And, biblical ministry has more to offer the Christian than psychological treatment.

In a *Spiritual Counterfeits Project Journal* article on the human potential movement, Frances Adeney notes:

> Sketching the development of the human potential move-
> ment in this way seems to leave the Christian little choice
> but to discard Western psychology and its myriad
> therapies altogether.[6]

Although she backs away from such a conclusion, her article certainly leads one to it. When one examines the research and ignores the myths, one could easily conclude that psychotherapy is an expensive hoax perpetrated unnecessarily upon Christians who are at a vulnerable place in life. At such a critical time they should be ministered to by the body of Christ.

It is extraordinary that so many people have spent so much money for so many years on a system which has so little to give. About all that may be proven eventually through the herculean effort of all the psychotherapies offered, purchased, and evaluated (and all the billions of dollars that have changed hands) is this: "On the average, given any problem (psychological or otherwise) doing something about it is better than doing nothing at all." (Baboyan's Law.)

In an article titled "What is Vulgar?" in *The American Scholar*, the writer says:

> Psychology seems to me vulgar because it is too often overbearing in its confidence. Instead of saying, "I don't know," it readily says, "unresolved Oedipus complex" or "manic-depressive syndrome" or "identity crisis." As with other intellectual discoveries . . . psychology acts as if it is holding all the theoretical keys, but then in practice reveals that it doesn't even know where the doors are. As an old *Punch* cartoon once put it, "It's worse than wicked, my dear, it's vulgar."[7]

Because the efficacy of psychotherapy has not been demonstrated, Alexander Astin contends that "psychotherapy should have died out. But it did not. It did not even waver. Psychotherapy had, it appeared, achieved *functional autonomy*."[8] (Emphasis his.) Functional autonomy occurs when a practice continues after the circumstances which supported it are gone. Astin is suggesting that psychotherapy has become self perpetuating because there is no support for its efficacy. Astin concludes his comments with the following dismal note:

> If nothing else, we can be sure that the principle of functional autonomy will permit psychotherapy to survive long after it has outlived its usefulness as a personality laboratory.[9]

Psychotherapy has not been affirmed by scientific scrutiny and only remains because of the usual inertia that results when a movement becomes established and then entrenched.

With the questionability of the results of psychotherapy and the certainty that damage sometimes occurs, it is difficult for many critics of psychotherapy to understand either the glib pronouncements of its practitioners or the confidence of those who refer individuals to this treatment. The suspicions of psychotherapy ARE justifiable and the sensitivities of psychotherapists to criticisms are unfortunate.

After having listened to a taped message by a well-known Bible teacher, we listened to a tape by a well-known psychologist who is a Christian. There was a gigantic difference between the two presentations. The Bible teacher elevated God, the Word of God, and the Son of God. The psychologist emphasized man, the desires of man, and how to satisfy these desires (all in a Christian way, of course, or so he said). The Bible teacher touched on the deep, significant, biblical truth of God in relationship to man. The psychologist stressed the superficial, insignificant (by comparison) opinions of men and included some Scriptures to justify his ideas.

Because of our familiarity with the research, we have come to assume certain things when we listen to what the professional psychologizers of Christianity say and when we read what they write. What we assume is based upon the research cited in the earlier chapters. The following assumptions do not all apply to all of the psychologizers. However, we find that the following should be considered when reading what they have written or listening to what they say.

1. Assume that what the psychologizer says about human relationships and problems of living is personal opinion rather than scientific fact.

2. Remember that the degrees, licenses, experience, and education in the field of counseling do not make the psychologizers experts on human behavior.

3. Assume that the psychologizer knows less about the Word and its application to problems of living than a Bible school or seminary graduate.

4. Remember that when the psychologizer mentions God or His Word he may be doing it more to give credibility to his opinions than to promote biblical understanding.

5. Remember that the psychologizer may be interpreting Scripture from a psychological perspective rather than evaluating psychology from a biblical perspective.

6. Assume that what the psychologizer is saying is contrary to what numerous other psychologizers would say.

7. Assume that case histories or examples used are not generally

representative of what normally happens.

8. Assume that the successes claimed may have had less to do with the counselor's psychological training, licenses, and experience than with factors in the counselee's own life.

9. Assume that successes claimed in counseling could be matched by persons not receiving psychological counseling.

10. Assume that for every success mentioned there are many failures and check to see if any are mentioned.

11. Remember that successes in psychological counseling are often short-termed.

12. Consider that, if someone is improved or delivered from his problems, competent biblical counseling could have done even better.

13. Consider that for every psychological solution suggested there is a better biblical solution available.

14. Remember that there is definitely a potential harm rate for every seemingly wonderful idea from the psychological systems of men.

15. Remember that there is almost no psychological idea that cannot be made to sound biblical.

16. Assume that what the psychologizer believes to be psychologically true may dictate what is theologically true for him, rather than the other way around

After reviewing all of the research, one could conclude that psychotherapy is one of the biggest and most vicious ripoffs that has ever been perpetrated on the American public and that it is one of the greatest deceptions in the church today.

In an article in *Science 86* magazine titled "Psychabuse," the author compares the results of research and the actual practice of psychotherapists. He gives examples of discrepancies between what therapists do and what scientific research reveals. He refers to these differences as abuses, thus the name of the article. He concludes by saying, "One distressing conclusion that can be drawn from all of these abuses is that psychotherapists don't care much for results or science."[10]

The largest of the four branches of psychotherapy is the humanistic one. The Association for Humanistic Psychology is the professional association of humanistic psychologists. Its president, Dr. Lawrence LeShan says, "Psychotherapy may be known in the future as the greatest hoax of the twentieth century."[11] It may also be known as the greatest heresy of twentieth-century Christianity.

In *The Emperor's New Clothes* after the little boy cried out, "He has no clothes!" the people knew that what the boy said was true. But, the greatest tragedy was not the discovery (no clothes), but the continuation of the deception by the Emperor. The story goes one:

> The Emperor squirmed. All at once he knew that what the people said was right. "All the same," he said to himself, "I must go on as long as the procession lasts." So the Emperor kept on walking, his head held higher than ever. And the faithful minister kept on carrying the train that wasn't there.[12]

And so, like the naked Emperor, psychotherapy and all its psychologies will "go on as long as the procession lasts." For many of us the procession is over. The cure of minds (psychotherapy) never was and never will be a satisfactory replacement for the cure of souls (biblical counseling).

Psychiatrist Thomas Szasz has recommended taking mental health care away from the professionals, such as M.D.'s and Ph.D.'s and giving "this whole business back to the ministers and priests and rabbis."[13] This means taking it away from the Christians who are professionals, too. We predict that if this is done both the mental and spiritual health of the nation will dramatically improve. It is time for Christians to reclaim and restore the cure of souls ministry and to do it now!

In the book of Nehemiah, Tobiah was an opposer and ridiculer of the building of the wall. When the Temple was restored, Tobiah was given a room in the house of the Lord. When Nehemiah heard of it he came and threw him out. (Nehemiah 4:3; 6:1; 13:4-9; 1 Kings 11:2, 3) This is what needs to be done with the Tobiah of psychotherapy in the church. Psychotherapy, with its facade of science needs to be purged from the church so that Christians will once more "bear one another's burdens and thus fulfill the law of Christ." (Galatians 6:2)

Part Five

THE PSYCHOLOGICAL WAY OR THE SPIRITUAL WAY?

The unbelieving counselor, seated in his plush, expensive furniture, surrounded by hundreds of books on psychology and psychiatry, with every word may seem to exude an outward confidence and certainty that one might have thought originated on Mount Olympus. Yet, unless he is incredibly naive, unless the volumes on his shelves are there for impression alone, he knows that every statement, that every judgment, that every decision that he makes in counseling is challenged and countered by scores of authors from an equal number of viewpoints. . . . The truth of the matter is that the Christian counselor who determines by the grace of God to know and use the Scriptures in his counseling is the only one who can ever have a solid basis for what he says and does.

Jay E. Adams[1]

In spite of the religious nature of psychotherapy, in spite of the evidence that problems of living are not diseases needing therapy,

203

and in spite of the research data which cannot prove that psycho-therapy is better than even the most seemingly innocuous non-professional help, the main thrust of pastoral counseling continues to be psychological and/or referral to an outside, professional therapist. The faith in the psychological way has become wedded to faith in God so completely that those persons who truly desire to help others turn to psychological studies rather than to biblical studies.

The new faith is a mixture and each Christian therapist believes that he has culled the very best from both worlds. Is it possible to combine psychological counseling theories and techniques with biblical counseling and lead a person into a deeper spiritual walk whereby problems of living may be overcome? Or must a Christian choose between the psychological way and the spiritual way?

17

"Choose You This Day"

For I am not ashamed of the gospel, for it is the power of God for salvation to every one who believes, to the Jew first and also to the Greek. For in it the righteousness of God is revealed from faith to faith; as it is written, "But the righteous man shall live by faith." (Romans 1:16-17)

Both psychological counseling and biblical counseling claim to lead a person out of problems of living and into changes in thinking, feeling, and behaving. However, they are quite different. The differences between psychological counseling and biblical counseling also include differences between psychological approaches; therefore, not all of the differences cited in this chapter can be used as an indictment against all psychological counseling. But, all psychological counseling fails in one or more of the ways described on the following pages. Many points of difference apply to psychological counseling used by Christians as well as non-Christian therapists no matter how sincere their desire to help. Psychotherapy in the hands of even the most conscientious Christian is still founded upon psychological opinions which are subject to one or more violations of biblical doctrine.

CRUCIAL DIFFERENCES.

The psychological ways of counseling are based upon man-made philosophies which teach that man is intrinsically good, that there is no personal God, that man can rise above his circumstances and become his own standard of right and wrong. Most Christians who practice psychology would not agree with one of the most basic premises of psychological theories: that man can become a better human being without God. Nevertheless, when Christians supplement Scripture with psychology they clearly give the impression that it is psychology that helps people. Since such therapies are conducted with or without God, the inference is that people can become better human beings without God. Just because God and His Word are added to the theories does not undo the unbiblical inference that man can become a better human being with psychological help, with or without God.

On the other hand, the biblical way of counseling and changing depends fully on God and is based upon the principles of Scripture. Furthermore, biblical counseling is love in relationship and truth, because the Lord is the counselor, because it follows the precepts and doctrines of the Word of God, and because it relies on the Word of God and the Holy Spirit to convict of sin and enable obedience.

Paul warned the Colossians about following the ways of men:

> As you therefore have received Christ Jesus the Lord, so walk in Him, having been firmly rooted and now being built up in Him and established in your faith, just as you were instructed, and overflowing with gratitude. See to it that no one takes you captive through philosophy and empty deception, according to the tradition of men, according to the elementary principles of the world, rather than according to Christ. For in Him all the fulness of Deity dwells in bodily form, and in Him you have been made complete, and He is head over all rule and authority. (Colossians 2:6-10)

When the Bible speaks of "philosophy and empty deception, according to the tradition of men," it is speaking to a larger bulk of psychological studies than one might suppose. Although some disciplines in the broad field of psychological study have contributed some information about people, much of the information that has filtered down into popular literature and into the psychologist's office is spurious. The most seductively dangerous area of psychology is that part which seeks to explain why people are the way they are and how they change. The theories and techniques of psychological counseling fall into this category. And although testimonials abound, the research does not support the promises or the claims of success. The many psychologies that claim to understand the nature of man and tell people how to live are full of misinformation and confusion.

The psychological way originates with man, utilizes man-made techniques, and ends with man. The biblical way originates with God, employs gifts and fruits of the Spirit and leads a Christian into a greater awareness of God and of himself as created by God. The goal of the psychological way is enhancement of the self. The motivation for change is personal benefit. The goal of the biblical way is to glorify God. The motivation for change is love for God and the desire to please Him.

The psychological way is limited to man-assisted self effort. The biblical way is accomplished through God's provision of new life and through His indwelling Holy Spirit who enables the believer to cooperate with the changes God is making within him In addition, He has provided fellowship with other believers also in the process of being transformed into the image of Jesus.

The psychological way includes many theories about why people are the way they are and how they can change. The biblical way says that problems of living are due to separation from God because of the sinful condition of mankind and the presence of sin in the world after the Fall. The biblical answer is Jesus, who has provided the only means to reestablish relationship between God and man and to enable people to live by faith in God.

A great number of the theories say that the past determines the present. That is, what a person does today is not by present choice but is rather predetermined by his past. Endless hours of searching faulty memory to find the key in the past which drives him to do what he does in the present is lengthy and costly. However, the past belongs on the cross and under the blood of Jesus. The new life begins at salvation. The old is done away with and buried. The past cannot be reconstructed. A Christian may be sorry about his past, including what he did and what was done to him, but he believes God's Word that says that he has been born again. Jesus said:

> Truly, truly, I say to you, unless one is born again, he
> cannot see the kingdom of God. . . . Truly, Truly, I say to
> you, unless one is born of water and the Spirit, he cannot
> enter into the kingdom of God. That which is born of the
> flesh is flesh, and that which is born of the Spirit is spirit.
> (John 3:3, 5-6)

The principle is also stated clearly at the beginning of the Gospel of
John:

> But as many as received Him, to them He gave the right to
> become children of God, even to those who believe in His
> name, who were born not of blood, nor of the will of the
> flesh, nor of the will of man, but of God. (John 1:12-13)

Although the Christian may have developed wrong attitudes and
habits in the past, he can deal with them in the present through the
presence of Christ within him. He can repudiate the past through
present choices, but he cannot blame the past. Any backward
glance should be one of gratitude for salvation and new life, not for
excuse of present sin. Paul repudiated his past, both the good and
the bad, and said, "But one thing I do: forgetting what lies behind
and reaching forward to what lies ahead, I press on toward the goal
for the prize of the upward call of God in Christ Jesus." (Philippians 3:13-14)

Many psychological theories include the idea that each person is
compelled by unconscious drives to do what he does not con-
sciously choose to do. The unconscious is blamed for all kinds of
behavior and problems, but God speaks to the conscious mind. The
Bible addresses human behavior from a conscious point of view.
God's Word commands a person to love, to believe, and to do.
There is no indication in Scripture that what one says or does is
determined by unconscious drives. When Paul cried out his despair
over wanting to do one thing and doing another, he did not blame
the unconscious or past determinants of behavior. He identified the
problem as sin—not only in deed, but in condition.

After many years of counseling, secular psychologist Carl
Rogers claimed that his crowning discovery was the importance of
love in relationship. Nevertheless, the love promoted by psychological theorists is from the point of needing and receiving love. Much

more is said about needing to be loved than needing to love. In other words, it ends up to be self-centered love or, at best, human love. The biblical way, on the other hand stresses God's love. Next to that, it stresses loving God and others. All biblical ministry is based upon the love of God. God has provided for the redemption of man and for all the changes that are necessary for him.

> But God, being rich in mercy, because of His great love with which He loved us, even when we were dead in our transgressions, made us alive together with Christ (by grace you have been saved). (Ephesians 2:4-5)

The entire message of the Bible is one of love. However, God's love is not sentimental, but just and righteous. Therefore, sin had to be dealt with, and by His love God has provided for all that each believer needs in order to be conformed to the image of Jesus.

The psychological way is wed to evolution, which sees humanity not in a class by itself but simply further along than the apes. But, evolution does not end here, because there is the idea that man himself is continuing to evolve. According to many theories in the humanistic and transpersonal psychologies, mankind is moving towards greater and greater potential to become divine. The biblical way teaches that man is a spiritual being created in the image of God and that man cannot find his true identity apart from God. The biblical way begins and ends with the Creator and Sustainer of the universe.

The biblical way not only teaches that man was created in the image of God. The Bible also teaches that Christians are to approach life from a different basis from nonbelievers because of the indwelling Holy Spirit. The Bible teaches that Christians have the mind of Christ. He is their life. The presence of God indwelling them through His Holy Spirit makes all of the difference.

The process of change is also different as God works from the inside and calls us to cooperate so that there are external changes as well. God is the one who has given new life and He is the one who continues to transform each of His children. The process is through relationship with God and by faith in His love and His Word, as demonstrated in obedience.

How can psychological systems of counseling which have originated in minds "excluded from the life of God" (Ephesians 4:18) be applied to those who have been given a "new self, which in the likeness of God has been created in righteousness and holiness of the truth" (Ephesians 4:24)? There is a tremendous difference between the resources of the Christian and those the world attempts to provide. Psychological diagnosis and methods do not apply to the new self created in Christ Jesus. The difference is clearly stated in Ephesians:

> This I say therefore, and affirm together with the Lord, that you walk no longer just as the Gentiles also walk, in the futility of their mind, being darkened in their understanding, excluded from the life of God, because of the ignorance that is in them, because of the hardness of their heart. . . . But you did not learn Christ in this way, if indeed you have heard Him and have been taught in Him, just as truth is in Jesus, that, in reference to your former manner of life, you lay aside the old self, which is being corrupted in accordance with the lusts of deceit, and that you be renewed in the spirit of your mind, and put on the new self, which in the likeness of God has been created in righteousness and holiness of the truth. (Ephesians 4:17-18, 20-24)

God has provided the Manual of operation and thus of change for Christians. It is the Bible. Any counseling which uses philosophies and methods other than Scripture will not nourish and build a believer's relationship with God. Such counseling may, in fact, strengthen the independent autonomous self which the Bible says to "lay aside."

Psychological counseling, which has been devised by unredeemed men with unredeemed minds for unredeemed people, can only affect and change that which has already been called "dead" in Scripture. Psychological counseling can and will work with the old nature and may even "improve" the old nature. But Christians have been told to put off the old nature (old self) and put on the new nature which has been created by God.

Biblical counseling differs drastically from psychological counseling in spite of the seeming similarities. Both systems may use information gained from accurately observed and recorded behavior. But, the biblical way submits the observations to the light of

Scripture. In the psychological way the theories and techniques are limited to human understanding, opinion, and bias. The biblical way encourages faith in God—in His faithfulness, love, power, and Word. The psychological way encourages faith in the therapist, in his professional training and status, and in the psychotherapeutic theories and methodologies. The biblical way exalts Christ. The psychological way emphasizes self. The biblical way is God-centered. The psychological way is man-centered.

THE BIBLICAL WAY OF CHANGE.

From the point of initial new life, the most fundamental choice of change is choosing to walk after the Spirit (according to the new nature) rather than after the flesh (according to the ways of the old nature). Although the believer is a new creation in Christ, he nevertheless undergoes transformation as he daily yields himself to God.

> I urge you therefore, brethren, by the mercies of God, to present your bodies a living and holy sacrifice, acceptable to God, which is your spiritual service of worship. And do not be conformed to this world, but be transformed by the renewing of your mind, that you may prove what the will of God is, that which is good and acceptable and perfect. (Romans 12:1-2)

Such yielding is choosing to walk after the Spirit as Paul spoke of believers, "who do not walk according to the flesh, but according to the Spirit." (Romans 8:4) The choice between following the flesh and following the Spirit is crucial and continual.

When one walks in the flesh (self-effort, self-rule, self-anything), he will fulfill the lust of the flesh and all of those expressions of the flesh, of pride, and of the unyielded self, as listed in Galatians 5:19-21 and elsewhere. When one walks in the Spirit, he is dependent upon the Lord.

> However, you are not in the flesh but in the Spirit, if indeed the Spirit of God dwells in you. . . . And if Christ is in you, though the body is dead because of sin, yet the spirit is alive because of righteousness. But if the Spirit of Him

who raised Jesus from the dead dwells in you, He who
raised Christ Jesus from the dead will also give life to your
mortal bodies through His Spirit who indwells you.
(Romans 8:9-11)

Those who belong to Christ have the choice to walk by the Spirit.
However, there is indeed a struggle between the flesh and the spirit.
The psychological way strengthens the flesh and the biblical way
encourages the life of the spirit. The psychological way emphasizes self with its selfisms, which include self-effort, self-evalua-
tion, an over-emphasis on feelings, and self as personal ruler. The
biblical way emphasizes God and His work within the human heart
in combination with the person's cooperation in active, obedient
dependence upon God. The psychological way emphasizes human
potential. The biblical way emphasizes faith in the God of the
universe.

The psychological way attempts to treat guilt feelings, but generally avoids or dismisses the problem of sin. It looks for other
reasons for problems rather than the sinful condition of self. The
biblical way reveals the problems of sin and leads to confession for
personal sin and forgiveness for the sins of others. Rather than
being left with remorse or a structure of rationalization, a Christian
can be transformed through repentance, a process which is more
than just being sorry for sin. The psychological way, especially
through the many self theories, has fed pride, rebellion, and self-
will. The biblical way teaches humility and submission to the
perfect will of God.

The biblical way gives real hope, not just empty promises. God
has given the believer both the instructions and the ability to follow
them. Every command is coupled with God's enablement to obey.
Every promise will be fulfilled according to all righteousness.

Grace and peace be multiplied to you in the knowledge of
God and of Jesus our Lord; seeing that His divine power
has granted to us everything pertaining to life and godliness through the true knowledge of Him who called us by
His own glory and excellence. For by these He has granted
to us His precious and magnificent promises, in order that
by them you might become partakers of the divine nature,
having escaped the corruption that is in the world by lust.

(2 Peter 1:2-4)

THE STRUGGLE BETWEEN THE FLESH AND THE SPIRIT.

God has provided a better way than the flesh. In fact, He is constantly working on our behalf to draw us into a walk by faith in the Spirit rather than onto a treadmill of rules, self effort, and defeat.

> It was for freedom that Christ set us free; therefore keep standing firm and do not be subject again to a yoke of slavery. . . .
>
> For you were called to freedom, brethren; only do not turn your freedom into an opportunity for the flesh, but through love serve one another. . . .
>
> But I say, walk by the Spirit, and you will not carry out the desire of the flesh. For the flesh sets its desire against the Spirit, and the Spirit against the flesh; for these are in opposition to one another, so that you may not do the things that you please. (Galatians 5:1, 13, 16, 17)

There is a battle going on between the flesh and the Spirit. The flesh may be defined here as everything within ourselves—our attitudes, thoughts, motivations—that places self at the center, independent from the life of the Holy Spirit. The fallen flesh, which came from the fruit of the tree of the knowledge of good and evil, is thus a mixture. It was developed as self attempted to rule and meet its own needs and desires apart from a dependent relationship with God. However, the self is not adequate to live independently from God, for it then reverts to the ways of the world and of Satan. Satan can only influence a person through the flesh and the mind. The extent of his influence is thus determined by the person's choice to walk in the flesh rather than in the spirit.

When the believer learns who he is in Christ, he discovers that the rulership of the flesh can be denied its former power. Its authority has been severed so that the believer does not have to follow its affections and lusts, motivations and drives, feelings and distorted perceptions. Nevertheless, if a believer chooses to follow the flesh he may develop its strength once again. On the other hand, if he chooses to follow the Spirit, the flesh will lose its power to influence.

Galatians presents the key: "Now those who belong to Christ Jesus have crucified the flesh with its passions and desires." (Galatians 5:24) Habits of thinking, feeling, speaking, and acting may be firmly established in the flesh, but by identifying with Christ's death we have crucified the flesh. The outworking of crucifying the flesh is following the rulership of the indwelling life of Jesus, rather than following the former inclinations of the flesh and its desires and feelings. Jesus said:

> If any one wishes to come after Me, let him deny himself, and take up his cross, and follow Me. For whoever wishes to save his life shall lose it; but whoever loses his life for My sake shall find it. (Matthew 16:24-25)

Denying self is following Jesus rather than self, obeying and following King Jesus rather than the pretender to the throne, and walking after the Spirit rather than after the flesh.

The continual activity of taking up the cross daily, putting everything that is flesh-motivated on that cross, and giving moment-by-moment rulership to Jesus affirms the fact of the believer's new identity and life. He strengthens the new life within him as he thinks according to the ways of God and obeys Christ and the Word of God instead of feelings and desires. Some of the results of walking after the Spirit are listed in Galatians:

> But the fruit of the Spirit is love, joy, peace, patience, kindness, goodness, faithfulness, gentleness, self-control; against such things there is no law. (Galatians 5:22-23)

On the other hand, a person strengthens the flesh when he listens to old thought patterns and follows the feelings and desires of the flesh. Some of the ugly results of walking after the flesh are listed in Galatians also:

> Now the deeds of the flesh are evident, which are: immorality, impurity, sensuality, idolatry, sorcery, enmities,

strife, jealousy, outbursts of anger, disputes, dissensions, factions, envyings, drunkenness, carousings, and things like these.... (Galatians 5:19-21)

The external outworkings of a person's life will reveal whether he is walking after the flesh or the Spirit. However, we must keep in mind that the flesh appears much more attractive in some people than in others.

SELF EFFORT OR FAITH IN GOD?

As important as choice is, choice alone is not enough. As important as personal involvement in change is, such personal involvement is not enough. Both choice and personal involvement must be undergirded by faith in God. Choice to do what seems right apart from faith in God may lead one away from God and into self. He may be left with self effort to accomplish what he himself believes is right and good. Jesus said that apart from Him one can do nothing of eternal value. Apart from walking by faith according to the Spirit one cannot please God. (Romans 8:5-8) Therefore a theology of counseling is crucial to a Christian rather than an imperfect psychology of counseling.

Personal involvement apart from God will ultimately fail in attempting to do God's will because there is no real power to do what is right apart from God. This is the quandry which Paul so aptly describes in Chapter 7 of Romans:

> For I know that nothing good dwells in me, that is, in my flesh; for the wishing is present in me, but the doing of the good is not. For the good that I wish, I do not do; but I practice the very evil that I do not wish. But if I am doing the very thing I do not wish, I am no longer the one doing it, but sin which dwells in me. (Romans 7:18-20)

Self effort cannot perform the will of God, but God dwelling within a person can. A Christian is able to obey God by faith rather than by self effort.

Obedience to God comes through relationship by faith and love. The law of the Old Testament was good, but it was weak in that it did not provide the ability to obey. Christians must not throw away the moral law of God, but recognize that the rules and regulations themselves do not enable one to please God. They are right and good, but powerless in themselves. The commandments of Jesus in the New Testament are actually stricter and more difficult to obey through self effort than those of the Old Testament. But, Jesus has made it possible for believers to obey.

> For what the law could not do, weak as it was through the flesh, God did; sending His own Son in the likeness of sinful flesh, and as an offering for sin, He condemned sin in the flesh, in order that the requirement of the Law might be fulfilled in us, who do not walk according to the flesh, but according to the Spirit. (Romans 8:3-4)

The coupling of obedience with faith can also be seen in Paul's admonition.

> So, then, my beloved, just as you have always obeyed, not as in my presence only, but now much more in my absence, work out your salvation with fear and trembling; for it is God who is at work in you, both to will and to work for His good pleasure. (Philippians 2:12-13)

Love for God is the motivation for obedience, and faith in God is the basis for obedience. Both faith and love are essential. And all change which should come through biblical counseling is towards greater love and obedience through faith. The counseling must be in accordance with God's will for the person and it can only be accomplished through faith in relationship to God.

> Now the God of peace, who brought up from the dead the great Shepherd of the sheep through the blood of the eternal covenant, even Jesus our Lord, equip you in every good thing to do His will, working in us that which is pleasing in His sight, through Jesus Christ, to whom be the glory forever and ever. Amen. (Hebrews 13:20-21)

Therefore, the self effort which comes from self trying to improve or change itself cannot be the biblical way of counsel or change.

Because psychological counseling majors in the ways of the self, biblical counseling must in essence be theological rather than psychological. The emphasis must be in God, not as a greater force that will change a person through some mystical magic apart from the person's cooperation, but rather as the Person who indwells, enables and guides the believer into performing His will in His way.

Faith in God is not a passive attitude of "just let God do it." Faith is active and diligent. Faith involves doing as well as believing. But rather than the self being the force behind the doing, God is the Source in whom the believer lives and moves. The writer to the Hebrews emphasizes the necessity of faith in God:

> And without faith it is impossible to please Him, for he who comes to God must believe that He is and that He is a rewarder of those who seek Him. (Hebrews 11:6)

Faith in God is not just some mental assent; nor is faith in God believing for something which the self wants. Faith in God is based upon knowledge of God, His character and His Word. The two parts of faith are trust and obey—the inner attitude and the external expression. Therefore, true faith in God leads to transformed behavior. Faith in God enables a person to become more and more like Jesus. Self effort, on the other hand, just changes the manifestations of the self.

VICTIM OR SINNER?

Most psychological systems of counseling put the counselee in the role of victim. He is a victim of circumstances, past and present. Or, he is a victim of past determinants which now control his behavior through so-called unconscious motivations. Or, he is a victim of so-called uncontrollable unconscious drives. Or, he has been victimized by people who have not treated him in the way he deserves to be treated. Or, he has reached that "primal pool of pain" from the hurts he has received. Or, he who was originally "OK" made the decision that he is "NOT OK" because of those around him. And one can go on and on.

The Bible declares that each person is born in original sin and that the only way out is through the cross of Christ. Man has not been born perfect and good, but in the condition of sin with the proclivity to sinning. He was born into the kingdom of darkness and within that kingdom he both sins and is sinned against.

Although he is a victim of the sins of others, he finds his way out of the kingdom of darkness through recognizing that he is a sinner separated from God. Therefore, the Bible does not over-emphasize the victim aspects of mankind, but rather reveals the condition of sin. It is only through admitting one's own sinful condition and confessing one's own sinful acts that a person comes into relationship with God through His provision for salvation and sanctification

After Adam and Eve had sinned in the Garden and therefore broken their relationship with God, they immediately assumed the victim role through the act of blaming. Adam blamed Eve and God. Eve blamed the serpent. And ever since the fall, people have found it easier to blame someone else than to admit their own sin and turn away from that sin.

Living as a victim may temporarily relieve a person from guilt feelings because the blame is placed elsewhere. But, when a person seeks truth he will find that he has sinned as well. Then through confession and forgiveness he not only receives freedom from guilt, but he is cleansed and enabled to do what is right.

The flesh does not like to admit wrong doing. The flesh squirms under conviction. In fact, the flesh will do much to disguise true guilt even to the point of self-condemnation (which is the ultimate victim role because now the self is a victim of its own condemnation). Generalized self-condemnation covers up true guilt and prevents a person from facing his real sin, confessing, and repenting.

Psychological counseling attempts to deal with guilt through redefining standards of right and wrong and by shifting responsibility from personal choice to such things as the "unconscious," the past, other people, circumstances, and so on, all of which encourage the victim role rather than reveal personal responsibility. Even when psychological counseling theories include "right and wrong," the basic condition of sin and God's provisions of forgiveness and restoration are ignored.

Even the biblical counselor has to be careful about encouraging the victim role through empathy or through talking more about the wrongs of others than about what the counselee can do through God's means of restoration. Whenever the conversation focuses on what the other person is doing rather than upon the counselee's actions and reactions, the counselee may remain in the stance of victim rather than move into the place of doing God's will God's way within whatever circumstances he may find himself.

REMORSE OR REPENTANCE?

Fear prevents many Christian counselors from calling sin *sin*. Their reasons are that they are afraid to be judgmental. They don't want to hurt anyone more than he may already be hurting. Besides that, the world has criticized the church for its emphasis on sin. However, Christians have a totally different frame of reference from those who have no hope. Therefore, talking about sin and leading a person to confession is not to leave him in his sin which is then worsened by guilt and remorse. No, a Christian counselor speaks of sin and encourages confession because he believes in and teaches God's total forgiveness and restoration from sin.

A Christian who counsels biblically knows that sin must be dealt with, just as a doctor knows that cancer should not be simply redefined or ignored. Confession and repentance bring about restoration and that is what Christian counseling should be about. Jesus did not come to condemn sinners but to reconcile them to the Father. However, in this restoration sin had to be taken care of. Jesus fully dealt with sin by dying in the place of every sinner so that each one might be forgiven and cleansed of sinful habits. (1 John 1:9)

Without the assurance of God's forgiveness and faith to repent, a person may indeed remain in sin and continue to experience guilt. After recognizing his own sinfulness a person may move into remorse rather than repentance, but remorse is the way of the flesh because it does not submit to the love of Christ or the truth of God concerning His provision for sin. Remorse includes such feelings as self pity, being disappointed with oneself, and self condemnation. Underneath all of those self-centered activities lies pride.

The way pride works in remorse is through a distorted self-righteousness which must pay for its own sin or which must exonerate the self through putting the blame elsewhere. The person may attempt to pay for his own sin through feeling miserable and depressed, through flagellating himself with various kinds of so-called penance, and through setting up impossible standards for himself. Remorse may lead to despair or else back into the victim response of blame, but repentance leads to life. Judas died in remorse, but Peter was restored through repentance. The difference between repentance and remorse is the difference between faith and unbelief, between God-centeredness and self-centeredness, and between life and death.

If a counselor is too reluctant to deal with sin in counseling, he may indeed help a counselee "gain the whole world" in terms of psychological means of improving the old self. But, Jesus asked, "For what does it profit a man to gain the whole world, and forfeit his soul?" (Mark 8:36) Psychological counseling may indeed avoid the whole issue of sin for fear of leaving a person in remorse and self condemnation. And, as a matter of fact, the majority of psychotherapists do not believe the biblical concept of sin anyway. Even those who attempt to combine the Bible with psychology tend to soft-pedal sin and try to help a person find other reasons for problems, or at least external reasons to explain why the person sinned.

True repentance leads a person into a place of humility where he can receive from God. He receives forgiveness, fellowship, and love from the Father. He is restored to the righteousness of Christ and given the necessary inner help from the Holy Spirit to walk in that righteousness. Repentance is an agreement with God that what He has said about a matter is true. Repentance is also an admission that one cannot walk the Christian life independently by his own goodness.

When Jesus offered to help the "weary and heavy-laden," He was speaking to all who have become weary of trying to live a good life by their own righteousness. It is impossible to live righteously without also living in relationship to God. Jesus was speaking to each person who will repent from his own ways and choose God's will.

> Come to Me, all who are weary and heavy-laden, and I will give you rest. Take My yoke upon you, and learn from Me, for I am gentle and humble in heart; and you shall find rest for your souls. For My yoke is easy, and my load is light. (Matthew 11:28-30)

There is no pride in true repentance, but rather gratitude and love. As soon as we begin to feel proud of our own good behavior or positive attitude, we become vulnerable to sin. When we begin to feel good about ourselves, we need to turn to God and "feel good" about Him. Even when we are doing our very best to do God's will, we must remember that He is the One working in us "both to will and to work for His good pleasure." (Philippians 2:13)

REFERRAL OR RESTORATION?

After Jesus rose from the dead, was seen by many, and ascended to the Father, He sent the Holy Spirit to indwell and empower believers to be His body, the church. God created the church to continue to restore people to God through preaching, through teaching, through encouraging and building up one another in the faith, and through loving one another as Jesus loved. The church is to be an expression of the wisdom of God and the love of God. Jesus did more than save men's souls from hell. Jesus died to bring them into a living relationship with the Father here on earth whereby they might live according to His design.

To subject Christians to the psychological ways of counseling conveys that the ideas of men must supplement the Bible. The underlying implication is that God has provided some help for living through His Word and through the Holy Spirit, but not enough for people who really have serious problems. To send Christians out to the psychological way says that the revelation of God concerning why man is the way he is, how he should live, and how to help him change is insufficient. Paul's answer to such nonsense is direct:

> You foolish Galatians, who has bewitched you, before whose eyes Jesus Christ was publicly portrayed as crucified? This one thing I want to find out from you: did you receive the Spirit by the works of the Law, or by hearing with faith? Are you so foolish? Having begun by the Spirit, are you now being perfected by the flesh? (Galatians 3:1-3)

If the church is not meeting human needs at the deepest and most serious levels, perhaps it has to examine itself and find out if indeed it is truly acting as the body of Christ. Perhaps a church does not have answers for human need because it has been too much in the world. A church that takes the things of the world and translates them into something identified as "Christian" would naturally send Christians with problems of living out into the world for professional psychological counseling.

On the other hand, if a church has leadership fully committed to following God and making disciples through preaching and teaching the Word, that church can minister to the personal needs of its members.

> You therefore, my son, be strong in the grace that is in Christ Jesus. And the things which you have heard from me in the presence of many witnesses, these also entrust to faithful men, who will be able to teach others also. (2 Timothy 2:1-2)

And if a church has a congregation actively involved in ministering to one another and in witnessing to those who have not yet come into the fellowship, that church has what it takes to minister to people with problems of living. A church which is empowered by the Holy Spirit for righteous living and which follows the teachings of the Word, especially the Great Commandment, will have much to give a suffering soul.

Rather than referring Christians with problems of living out into the world system of psychological counseling, the church is responsible to do all it can to restore believers to productive, god-honoring living, whereby they walk in the Spirit rather than in the flesh.

> For those who are according to the flesh set their minds on the things of the flesh, but those who are according to the Spirit, the things of the Spirit. For the mind set on the flesh is death, but the mind set on the Spirit is life and peace, because the mind set on the flesh is hostile toward God; for it does not subject itself to the law of God, for it is not even able to do so and those who are in the flesh cannot please God. (Romans 8:5-8)

How can people who are of the flesh, who are hostile toward God, who do not subject themselves to the law of God, and who cannot please God propose to explain the nature of man, tell how one should live, and help Christians change for the better?

Restoration of a fellow Christian does not necessarily involve telling him what he must or must not do in specific detail. Rather, restoration involves all of the teaching, exhortation, and encouragement he needs to find God's answers for himself and to desire to do God's will by trusting Him and obeying Him.

> Be diligent to present yourself approved to God as a workman who does not need to be ashamed, handling accurately the word of truth. (2 Timothy 2:15)

God may use a sermon or a word of personal testimony from a fellow believer to put the finger on an area of needed change. He may then use another believer to encourage and bear with him as he submits to God for transformation.

Spiritual restoration occurs when an individual sees problems of living as spiritual problems with spiritual solutions and responds to spiritual enablement. The spiritual conflict between the flesh and the spirit, between the lies of Satan and the truth of God, and between man's ways and God's ways is at the base of all problems. Therefore, God is the source of help and He gives His wisdom in the midst of conflict.

Restoration occurs when an individual takes responsibility before God and seeks and finds God's will in a situation through prayerful application of the Word of God. The counselor needs to know answers or at least where to look for them through prayer and Bible study, but his counseling will be more effective and long lasting if he helps a counselee find God's will for himself. The counselor may teach biblical principles and assign Scripture to study. He may use questions in conversation to help the one counseled to perceive the nature of the problem and to recognize what might need to be changed or confessed. But, because of the personal relationship God has with each of His children, every Christian needs to learn to solve problems of living according to the Lord's will and the Lord's way.

Restoration occurs when a person draws close to God through faith and love in trust and obedience. When a person actively obeys God in one area of life—even though it may be just a small thing in relationship to the entire problem—he brings God into the situation. For instance, if there is a great deal of hostility in marriage and one partner chooses to obey God by speaking with a soft voice instead of screaming, this one act may be the beginning of restoration of the relationship. Whenever a person chooses to change how he acts—from old ways to godly ways revealed in Scripture—there is restoration. Though others may teach, encourage, and pray, the person himself must be the one to draw close to God through faith and love.

The Bible calls believers who are walking with God to come alongside a brother or sister who is encountering difficulties through sinful behavior.

> Brethren, even if a man is caught in any trespass, you who are spiritual, restore such a one in a spirit of gentleness; each one looking to yourself, lest you too be tempted. (Galatians 6:1)

The person who seeks to help another must not think he has anything in himself to offer or that he is any better than the one who has sinned. And, if a Christian is restored, the one whom God has used is not to take any credit.

> Bear one another's burdens, and thus fulfill the law of Christ. If anyone thinks he is something when he is nothing, he deceives himself. (Galatians 6:2-3)

The major work of restoration is actually performed by God and by the repentance of the believer. Therefore what the one receiving the counsel does is more significant in bringing about change than what a counselor may say or do.

> But let each one examine his own work, and then he will have reason for boasting in regard to himself alone, and not in regard to another. For each one shall bear his own load. (Galatians 6:4-5)

Sometimes Christians who desire to minister to other Christians have no specific wisdom whereby they can give advice or counsel. Nevertheless, they can still participate in restoration. They can listen and they can love. They can encourage a person to draw close to God in prayer and to seek His will in the Bible. And, they can lift up Jesus. They can encourage faith by their own confidence in Jesus and the knowledge that "God causes all things to work together for good to those who love God, to those who are called according to His purpose." (Romans 8:28) Their greatest help may be to focus their own hearts on the greatness of God and on His great love for the one who is in the midst of problems.

GOD'S WAY OF CHANGE.

God has a plan for changing every person. His plan for change is the way of the cross. Psychological systems of counseling may lead a person along the broad way which leads to destruction, but Jesus said, "For the gate is small, and the way is narrow that leads to life, and few are those who find it." (Matthew 7:14) The entrance into new life through faith in Jesus is the small gate. The narrow way is the walk of sanctification (becoming more like Jesus). Evangelism is concerned with leading unbelievers through the small gate. Biblical counseling is one small aspect of the total ministry of leading believers along the narrow way of sanctification.

18

Beyond Counseling

Jesus understood human need and He came to meet that need. Paradoxically, however, He taught that the human response to personal need should be to seek the kingdom of God and His righteousness above all else. True personal needs are met within the context of His kingdom. There has been a great confusion over what people need beyond the bodily necessities of life. Some say security, others elevate significance, and others reach for self-fulfillment and self-actualization. The Bible, on the other hand, says that the greatest human need is relationship to God and one another as stated by Jesus when asked about the greatest commandment. "You shall love the Lord your God with all your heart, and with all your soul, and with all your mind" and "you shall love your neighbor as yourself." (Matthew 22:37, 39)

LOVE FOR GOD AND OTHERS OR LOVE FOR SELF.

Because the greatest human need is relationship with God, Jesus came to express God's love and to pay the penalty for sin, which separates man from God. Jesus came to restore relationship. Therefore, after He ascended to the Father He sent the Holy Spirit to indwell believers so that they might experience the presence of God in their lives. (John 14) Besides restored relationship with God,

Jesus formed His church, which is His body. (Ephesians 1:22, 23) And, one stellar commandment to the disciples was to love one another just as Jesus had loved them. In fact, Jesus connected the relationship of the disciples to Himself with their relationship to one another.

> Just as the Father has loved Me, I have also loved you; abide in My love. . . . This is My commandment, that you love one another, just as I have loved you. (John 15:9, 12)

When Jesus taught about love and demonstrated the supreme love of God, He was not referring to warm fuzzy feelings. He was speaking of a deep commitment of believers to each other that would surpass even natural family relationships. Just as He put the welfare of others before Himself when He went to the cross, Jesus challenged His disciples to love one another.

Putting the welfare of another person before oneself is not a popular message today, and it was not popular in Jesus' day either. Rather than just taking care of themselves, the disciples were instructed to take care of each other, to love one another with longsuffering, and to regard the needs of each other as important as personal needs. When people who have been saved by faith choose to live in love and commitment to God and to each other, there will be spiritual growth and the means to face challenges of life.

The church lives in the midst of a society that preaches a different message, a message of self-gratification. And, although someone may object to the idea that psychology has fostered this trend, the entire history of psychology has supported selfishness. Michael and Lise Wallach, authors of the book *Psychology's Sanction for Selfishness*, preface their historical analysis by saying:

> A surprisingly broad and influential range of psychological theory turns out to legitimize selfishness. Although this is usually far from what is intended, support is lent by academic thinkers as well as clinicians, by Freudians as well as anti-Freudians, by behaviorists as well as contenders against behaviorism, and by psychologists who investigate altruism as well as by those who deny its existence. Support is lent even by psychologists who themselves deplore the adverse moral impact of psychology's teachings.[1]

We are now living in the midst of a people that exalts and celebrates the self. And, because self is central, getting in touch with one's feelings is of utmost importance. Personal well-being has become the goal of life. And, even the church has moved from community to individuality and from sanctification to self-realization. The Wallachs aptly state the rule of the day:

> The proper mode of living is to be oneself—to find out who one is and let no one and nothing interfere with one's self-realization.[2]

In contrast with the Christian gospel of love in relationship and community comes the ever-increasing promotion of the "self contained person" who is described as "one who does not require or desire others for his or her completion or life; self-contained persons either are or hope to be entire unto themselves."[3] The seemingly righteous reason for this is not to burden others, but underneath there is a selfishness that takes care of number one and excuses one from the need to care for others.

Current advice encourages expressing personal desires and seeking to gratify them without undo restraint for the sake of others. In fact, the move from community to selfishness is such that:

> One has the right to assert oneself and seek gratification, but one should avoid entangling commitments and preserve one's freedom to move on without regrets or a sense of loss.[4]

The Wallachs note this trend of selfishness:

> The role of another person is, insofar as one can manage it, to serve as a means for fulfilling one's own emotional requirements. One should not be losing oneself in that other person, subordinating oneself as a part that seeks completion and meaning through another person—or through a cause or tradition outside oneself. Such superordinate loyalties tend to be viewed as an unacceptable limitation on one's own personal freedom. Rather, one should cultivate a posture of detachment and make "nonbinding commitments."[5]

But how has psychology, and particularly psychotherapeutic theory and practice, contributed to the trend of self-centeredness? Nearly all theorists view man as one whose primary motivation is to serve himself. It began with Freud's "legacy of selfishness that he bequeathed to psychology's understanding of human motivation."[6] It continued with Harry Stack Sullivan's need for being esteemed and valued playing a primary role in motivation. Karen Horney added the establishment of the victim role in "basic anxiety" of a child in a hostile world with "a feeling of being small, insignificant, helpless, deserted, endangered, in a world that is out to abuse, cheat, attack, humiliate, betray, envy."[7] Then Abraham Maslow added the so-called hierarchy of needs apexing in the need to actualize oneself. And, Carl Rogers added his faith in a person's ability to discover his own best interests and his right to follow them. Most psychological theorists believe that any altruism or community is to serve individual need and desire. Furthermore, since psychological theorists generally believe that a person is born good and it is society that harms him, they naturally conclude that the person must seek his own good if he is to continue to be good.

Carl Rogers describes a psychologically healthy and growing person this way:

> Less and less does he look to others for approval or disapproval; for standards to live by; for decisions and choices. He recognizes that it rests within himself to choose; that the only question which matters is, "Am I living in a way which is deeply satisfying to me, and which truly expresses me?"[8]

Rogers advocates selfishness, but contends that what he teaches is actually for the good of all persons and is therefore not selfish:

> ... the criterion of the valuing process is the degree to which the object of the experience actualizes the individual himself. Does it make him a richer, more complete, more fully developed person? This may sound as though it were a selfish or unsocial criterion, but it does not prove to be so, since deep and helpful relationships with others are experienced as actualizing.[9]

The faith of Rogers and others rests in the actualized self, that as the self meets its needs and fulfills its desires society benefits. Thus, although they promote ideas contrary to biblical teachings, they do so for what they believe will be the good of society.

All in the name of mental health, theorists and therapists have led us to a place where self is supreme. The Wallachs observe:

> Asserting oneself seems quite broadly accepted as a sign of mental health; guilt seems readily viewed as a form of oppression from which we are entitled to deliver ourselves in the interests of psychological soundness. To view personal gratification as the primary basis of our functioning is taken as necessary if we are not to be crippled psychologically.[10]

In fact, in view of the theories of psychology, one who does not seek personal gratification is either crazy or he's kidding himself.

Even if a church does not promote psychological counseling, it has been influenced by the culture—so much so that many of the doctrines of secular psychological theories creep in, especially those which promote self-love, self-esteem, and self-realization. And, just as the secular theorists claim that society benefits from a person who loves himself, strives to meet his own needs, and pursues his own desires; so the church is tempted to preach a gospel which stresses self-gratification—all in religious terms of course—rather than love and sacrifice.

LOVE IN THE BODY OF CHRIST.

Jesus preached another gospel, the gospel of love. And because of the greatness of God's love for humanity, He sent His Son to bear the punishment for sin so that those who believe might be set free, not free to do as they please, but free to love God and others. The Lord formed the church to be an expression of love, not an organization to promote the autonomous, self-seeking self.

The church, if it is functioning biblically, has something better to offer than the doctrines and conversations of psychological counseling. In fact, it has more to offer than just biblical counseling. The church is a place where people can actively love. Besides receiving the great love of God and receiving love from Christians, believers learn to love. They learn to love by being loved by God, they learn to love through teachings from the Bible, and they learn to love with longsuffering as they actually put up with each other and forgive each other in love. Loving God and others is the opposite from the psychological doctrines to love yourself and fulfill your own needs and desires.

God formed the church with believers with all sorts of personalities, abilities, and weaknesses to learn to love God and others. There are opportunities to practice loving God through worship, prayer, and obedience. And, there are opportunities to love each other. The amount of space given in the Epistles for instructing believers to love each other certainly indicates that one of the primary objectives of sanctification is to love as Jesus did—to love the brethren even when they are not being very lovable and also to love enemies and to do good to them.

The early Christians gathered together because of their common faith to encourage and be encouraged, to learn, to love and be loved, and to maintain and strengthen their faith. They were also thrown together by persecution so that they had to get along even when there were cultural differences and personality conflicts.

The essence of the early church was community rather than individuality. Spiritual ministry gifts were given for the sake of the entire group, not for personal fulfillment. Individuals' needs were not the focus, but they were met through giving and receiving love in the community. Each person functioned within the group, devoted to God in singleness of purpose, submitting to one another, concerned for the common good, and thereby actively loving each other.

The first church in Jerusalem was a vital, active body devoted to the Word, fellowship, worship, and prayer.

> So then, those who had received the word were baptized; and there were added that day about three thousand. And they were continually devoting themselves to the apostles' teaching and to fellowship, to the breaking of bread and to prayer. And everyone kept feeling a sense of awe; and many wonders and signs were taking place through the apostles. And all those who had believed were together, and had all things in common; and they began selling their property and possessions, and were sharing them with all, as anyone might have need. And day by day continuing

with one mind in the temple, and breaking bread from house to house, they were taking their meals together with gladness and sincerity of heart, praising God, and having favor with all the people. And the Lord was adding to their number day by day those who were being saved. (Acts 2:41-47)

What an ideal church! And yet, the description is accurate. One wonders how such a tremendously large number of people could be formed into such a cohesive group so quickly. Just as the Holy Spirit was active in both the message and the inception of new life through faith, He was active in forming the body of Christ.

The church should differ radically from simply a human organization created by human design, because the church is a spiritual entity created by God through His Holy Spirit. Furthermore, as each person received new life at conversion he also received the Holy Spirit. Thus, the cohesiveness of the early church was attained both through the inner work of the Holy Spirit and the external teaching of the apostles and the fellowship of the saints. Even so, the twentieth-century church can only be the cohesive body of Christ by the inner work of the Spirit, the faithful teaching of the Word of God, and love among the brethren.

The early Christians were *devoted* to this new life in community as "they were continually devoting themselves to the apostles' teaching and to the fellowship, to the breaking of bread and to prayer." Many churches lack this kind of devotion today. Even if a church is blessed with excellent teaching from the pulpit, it will not be the living organism it was created to be if the members do not devote themselves to the teaching. Devotion to the teaching does not mean: "Wasn't that wonderful teaching? I just love to hear our preacher speak!" Devotion implies such involvement in the teaching that it is practiced. When a person is devoted to the Word, he obeys that Word.

The early church knew that the apostles were speaking the words from God. Those who devoted themselves to the apostles' teachings understood the need for application of truth. Devotion implied living according to the very teachings which came from God's Holy Spirit through the apostles.

Besides being devoted to the Word, the early Christians were devoted to one another in fellowship. They understood that each member is a vital part of the body of Christ, and they wanted to spend time together. They wanted to break bread together. They wanted to pray together. The gospel message they heard drew them together and their love for God drew them together. Spending time with other Christians was not immediately caused by persecution, for as a group they were still in a position of "having favor with all the people." Very soon, however, persecution forced them together in such ways that they had to learn to forebear and put up with each other with longsuffering, forgiving each other as Christ had forgiven them. Love was commitment of relationship within the body of Christ rather than simply positive regard or warm feelings.

Besides relating to one another through fellowship and eating meals together, the early Christians related to God as they celebrated the Lord's Supper and prayed together. Jesus was central in their devotion. Their relationship to Him motivated them to learn more about Him, to fellowship with one another, and to worship and pray together. Within these activities and within this love relationship with Jesus "everyone kept feeling a sense of awe." Furthermore, they were experiencing miracles as God confirmed His Word among them through signs and wonders.

Lives were being transformed, not by techniques from worldly wisdom or from the great reservoir of philosophy from the Greeks or from the political maneuvers of the Romans. Lives were being changed by God without the help of twentieth-century psychology. God continues to perform His most amazing miracles within the lives of men and women as they are translated from the kingdom of darkness into the kingdom of light and as the Holy Spirit works in them to conform them into the image of Christ.

Not only were people changed through receiving the gift of the Holy Spirit; their relationship to possessions changed. Without any legislation or political system, people began to realize that all they had was truly God's, just as they themselves belonged to God. Their hold on possessions loosened so that sharing was a natural response to need within the community of Christians.

The early Christians continued learning and following the Word, fellowshipping, and worshipping God together "day by day" rather than just once a week for about an hour. They continued "with one mind in the temple" and broke bread "from house to house." They experienced a singleness of purpose. Rather than being double-minded in attempting to balance their Christianity with the philosophies of the world, they were of one mind. Although they may not have agreed on every point in every matter, the focus of the mind was on devotion to God. Their purpose was centered in doing what would be pleasing in God's sight. They were involved in what Paul later described as having the mind set on the Spirit rather than on the things of the flesh as they were learning to walk according to the Spirit rather than according to the flesh.

Although we are living in the twentieth century and although we have increased in knowledge and technology, the spiritual life still must have the same root and bear the same fruit, for "Jesus Christ is the same yesterday and today, yes and forever." (Hebrews 13:8) Although we have the privilege of reading the Bible as well as of listening to teachers and although we may have different cultural manners by which we engage in fellowship, those activities must be primary as we devote ourselves to loving God and neighbor. Although different groups of Christians may celebrate the Lord's supper in a variety of ways, it must still be a celebration and recognition that Jesus died in our place for the remission of sin, was resurrected, is our advocate with the Father, sent the Holy Spirit to indwell believers, and is coming again to set up His kingdom. Those truths are not just theological doctrines; they are essential to living the Christian life. They are essential to overcoming the problems of living. Furthermore, the acts of praying and praising God are not just religious exercises. They are God's means for enabling believers to walk in His ways, in His perspective, and by His grace.

Psychological theories and techniques pale in comparison to the greatness of God's plan for each of His children. The early Christians did not need psychological counseling. Why do we? Have we fallen so far from our first love? Perhaps we only have an inkling of the intensity of the devotion by which the early Christians were motivated in learning to live by the Word, in fellowshipping with one another, in freely giving themselves and their possessions, in worshipping God and partaking of His nature, and in communicating with Him through prayer.

If indeed Peter is right in saying that God's "divine power has granted to us everything pertaining to life and godliness, through the true knowledge of Him who called us by His own glory and excellence," the church should be able to minister to those suffering from problems of living. Have we lost the vision of what Peter meant when he continued, "For by these He has granted to us His precious and magnificent promises, in order that by them you might become partakers of the divine nature, having escaped the corruption that is in the world by lust"? (2 Peter 1:3-4) If Peter is right and if we have lost the vision, then we need to turn to God in desperation and seek His ways rather than rely on the empty promises of psychological solutions to problems of living. And, just as Moses cried out to God on behalf of the people, leaders in the church need to cry out to God for His direction and His cleansing so that the church might partake of the manna sent from Heaven, Jesus Christ, who is the Christian's source for all matters of life and godliness. (John 6:32-35)

Personal ministry in a church does not need to turn to psychological theories or techniques. In fact, a church should avoid adding the psychological way to the biblical way of counseling. We have shown earlier in the book that psychotherapy involves non-biblical religion, that mental illness is a misnomer, and that psychological counseling has not been proven to have any more to offer than biblical counseling. All that the research has consistently indicated is that conversation can help and that psychotherapy is no better than a placebo or, as some eminent researchers believe, no better than no treatment at all. Furthermore it has not been demonstrated by research that one brand of psychotherapy is better than another. Our own position is that conversation can help. Therefore, whenever conversation can help assist a Christian who is experiencing problems of living, the conversation should be biblical.

We are not recommending biblical counseling where medical science is needed. Nor are we recommending it in lieu of medicine, x-rays, etc. We may recommend biblical counseling in addition to medical attention, but never instead of or as a substitute for medical service for problems with a physical cause and cure.

FROM COUNSELING TO COMMUNITY.

When a church takes the dramatic step of faith away from psychological counseling, it actually moves beyond counseling. When problems of living are treated as spiritual problems with spiritual goals of restoration and spiritual maturity, each member of the body of Christ will be able to grow through adversity and naturally minister to one another on an informal basis as well as through teaching and counseling biblical truths in love.

The more that exists of a caring community within the church, the less the need for a formal counseling ministry. In fact, there is an inverse relationship between the church as a caring community and the need for formal counseling. As a pastor is able to develop the elements of a biblical community, the demands for formal counseling will diminish. As there are opportunities for personal care, as well as for tangible provision for those in need, formal counseling will fade into the background.

Although we speak much about community, the church in America has promoted individualism for so long that the idea of putting the group ahead of personal need and desire seems impersonal and impractical. Even the custom of sharing meals in homes has diminished because of personal inconvenience. The influence of the psychological way reveals itself through so-called personal needs being elevated above God's will and above the common good. Individualism permeates society so that "looking out for number one" is not only acceptable, but honorable. Kenneth Vaux warns against this trend of narcissism as being destructive to the individual as well as to the group:

> And true personhood means being for others, not for our solitary self. The cults of humanistic psychology, transactional analysis, winning friends and influencing people, composing impressive dossiers and interview demeaner—indeed, all fascinations with my own being—are depersonalizing because they intensify self-concentration.[11]

The church must take dramatic steps away from individualism into the kind of devotion that pulsed through the living stones of the early church. Paul emphasized the fact that believers were being built together into a holy temple of God through the Spirit. We need to regain that vision of commitment and mutual support if we are to live as Jesus has called us to live.

19

The True Vine

I am the true vine, and My Father is the vinedresser. Every branch in Me that does not bear fruit, He takes away; and every branch that bears fruit, He prunes it, that it may bear more fruit. (John 15:1-2)

The vine is the living organism of the church which finds its source in Jesus. The Father removes branches that do not bear fruit and prunes those that do. While many churches seem to be dying on the vine, we need to take heart and look to God for some drastic pruning. We believe that the leaves and branches of the psychological way need to be removed from the church if it is to operate as the body of Christ.

However, simply removing the psychological way, on which many have become dependent, is not enough. The church must operate according to the guidelines specified by Jesus, as recorded in John 15. Here Jesus developed three themes which are essential to the kind of church which fulfills His plan. The first theme concentrates on the relationship of the believer to Jesus. The second theme discusses the relationship of believers to one another in the context of being first of all related to Jesus. The third theme is the believer's relationship to the world because of his relationship to Jesus.

As Jesus developed the theme of relationship with Himself, He used the symbolism of the vine and its branches to stress the absolute dependence of the believer on Jesus if he is to do anything of lasting value in God's eyes.

> Abide in Me, and I in you. As the branch cannot bear fruit of itself, unless it abides in the vine, so neither can you, unless you abide in Me. I am the vine, you are the branches; he who abides in Me, and I in him, he bears much fruit; for apart from Me you can do nothing. (John 15:4-5)

Jesus Himself is the source of life for a believer. Therefore, relationship with Him must be nurtured above all other activities or relationships. Because of the vital significance of abiding in Jesus in attitudes, thoughts, words, and actions, the spiritual life of the believer must extend into all areas of life, so that no part is outside of relationship with Him. Everything in the world attempts to counteract this essential connection of the believer to Jesus. Every temptation will attempt to undermine faith, hope, and love, because once a believer begins to act independently from Jesus he weakens his will to do God's will.

Jesus knows that Christians need to be bonded together as one body to withstand temptation because of the influence of the world and because of the evil forces of the kingdom of darkness under the rulership of Satan. Christians need each other, not just for what the other can provide, but also because of each person's need to exercise the love of Christ. Jesus did not command us to love one another so that our own needs for love may be met, but rather so that we would have opportunities to love in relationship, in both giving and receiving.

Jesus did not set forth forms of organization. He simply commanded the disciples to love each other just as He had loved them. He commanded them to love in such an active, fully committed way that there would be eternal results.

> This is My commandment, that you love one another, just as I have loved you. . . . You did not choose Me, but I chose you, and appointed you, that you should go and bear fruit, and that your fruit should remain, that whatever you

ask of the Father in My name, He may give to you. This I
command you, that you love one another. (John 15:12, 16,
17)

Jesus could command love, because He had first loved them. And,
He continues to command believers to love one another as He
abides in them. The body of believers provides both the encouragement to live in relationship with Jesus and the opportunity to obey
His commandment to love one another. Jesus did not design a
spectator sport or even spiritual performances. He designed a
living vital body in which every member is a minister, in which
every member receives teaching, exhortation, encouragement, and
love, and in which every member also ministers God's love in grace
and truth in whatever capacity and circumstance God has provided.

The church exists in a hostile world. However, if the church is
not composed of members who trust and obey Jesus' commands,
that church may not stand in enmity with the world, but merely
reflect it. In the same subtle ways in which the philosophies,
theories, and practices of psychology have entered the church and
become "Christianized," a host of other influences of the world
and of the devil have taken on a Christian coating. If we are friends
with the world (its philosophies, psychological systems, religions,
and practices) then we have to ask ourselves about Jesus' words:

If the world hates you, you know that it has hated Me
before it hated you. If you were of the world, the world
would love its own; but because you are not of the world,
but I chose you out of the world, therefore the world hates
you. (John 15:18-19)

The church has been called to reflect Jesus, not the world. Believers
have been separated to God, and even though they are in the world,
they are not to be of the world. Thus, every ministry of the body of
Christ must be biblical and must not attempt to incorporate worldly
philosophies, theories, or techniques.

Only the church which operates according to Jesus' description
of the vine will become a place of birth and growth to maturity, a
place for restoration and discipleship, and a place of shelter and
guidance for the troubled soul. Only a church which is vitally

connected to Jesus can be a place of security and encouragement for the fearful and weak, a place of fellowship and commitment, and a place to express the love of God in relationship with one another and devotion to Him. In such a church people would not be isolated in their problems, but would be both accountable to other believers and assisted by them.

A church that does not seek God as its source but relies on the philosophical and psychological ideas and techniques of men will gradually become as secular as the world. It may exist for years and yet have no real life in it. Such a church may indeed have a form of godliness but deny the power of God.

As the body of Christ we need to pray for cleansing. We need to pray for pruning. We need to seek His face with diligence. We need to put off the old (all that is of the world, the flesh, and the devil). We need to put on the new (all that is in Christ Jesus). Jesus is the vine. We are the branches. He has given us the true manna from heaven which is Himself. Let us feed upon the true manna rather than eat the fruit from the tree of the knowledge of good and evil. Let us drink from the springs of living water instead of from the broken cisterns of psychological systems.

NOTES

Part One: PSYCHOSEDUCTION.
1. Dave Hunt and T. A. McMahon. *The Seduction of Christianity*. (Eugene: Harvest House, 1985), p.189.

Chapter One: LEAVEN IN THE LOAF.
1. Sutherland, P. and Poelstra, P. "Aspects of Integration." Paper presented at the meeting of the Western Association of Christians for Psychological Studies, Santa Barbara, CA, June 1976.
2. A. W. Tozer. *That Incredible Christian*. (Harrisburg, PA: Christian Publications, Inc., 1964), p. 11.
3. Martin Gross. *The Psychological Society*. (New York: Random House, 1978).
4. William Law. *The Power of the Spirit*. Dave Hunt, ed. (Fort Washington: Christian Literature Crusade, 1971), p. 74.

Chapter Two: PSYCHOLOGY AS RELIGION.
1. Jerome Frank, "Mental Health in a Fragmented Society," *American Journal of Orthopsychiatry*, July 1979, p. 404.
2. Viktor Von Weizsaecker, "Reminiscences of Freud and Jung," *Freud and the Twentieth Century*, B. Nelson, ed. (New York: Meridian, 1957), p. 72.
3. Carl G. Jung, "Psychotherapists or the Clergy," *Modern Man in Search of a Soul*. (New York: Harcourt, Brace, 1933), pp. 240, 241.
4. Sigmund Freud. *The Future of an Illusion*. Translated and edited by James Strachey. (New York: W. W. Norton and Company, Inc., 1961), p. 43.
5. Jay E. Adams. *What About Nouthetic Counseling?* (Grand Rapids: Baker Book House, 1976), pp. 16-17.
6. Thomas Szasz. *The Myth of Psychotherapy*. (Garden City: Doubleday/Anchor Press, 1978), p. 139.
7. *Ibid.*, p. 146.
8. Carl Jung. *Memories, Dreams, Reflections*. Edited by Aniela Jaffe, translated by Richard and Clara Winston. (New York: Pantheon, 1963), p. 55.
9. *Ibid.*, pp. 170-199.
10. Mary Stewart Van Leeuwen. *The Sorcerer's Apprentice*. (Downers Grove, IL: InterVarsity Press, 1982), p. 49.
11. Carl Rogers. *On Becoming a Person*. (Boston: Houghton Mifflin, 1961) p. 8.
12. Calvin S. Hall and Gardner Lindzey. *Theories of Personality*. (New York: John Wiley & Sons, 1957), p. 476.

243

13. Rogers, *op. cit.*, p. 8.
14. *Ibid.*, p. 8.
15. William Kirk Kilpatrick. *The Emperor's New Clothes.* (Westchester, IL: Crossway Books, 1985), p. 177.
16. Szasz, *op. cit.*, p. 188.
17. Robert C. Fuller. *Mesmerism and the American Cure of Souls.* (Philadelphia: University of Pennsylvania Press, 1982), p. 1.
18. *Ibid.*, p. 10.
19. *Ibid.*, p. 12.
20. *Ibid.*, p. 20.
21. *Ibid.*, pp. 46-47.
22. *Ibid.*, p. 104.
23. Thomas Szasz, *op. cit.*, p. 43.
24. Richard Feynman et al. *The Feynman Lectures on Physics*, Vol. 1. (Reading: Addison-Wesley, 1963), pp. 3-8.
25. Lance Lee, "American Psychoanalysis: Looking Beyond the 'Ethical Disease,'" *Los Angeles Times*, 23 March 1980, Part VI, p. 3.
26. Perry London. *The Modes and Morals of Psychotherapy.* (New York: Holt, Rinehart & Winston, Inc., 1964), pp. 11, 160.
27. Jerome D. Frank. *Psychotherapy and the Human Predicament.* (New York: Schocken Books, 1978), p. 251.
28. Julian Meltzoff and Melvin Kornreich. *Research in Psychotherapy.* (New York: Atherton Press, Inc., 1970), p. 465.
29. Thomas Szasz. *The Myth of Psychotherapy.* (Garden City: Anchor/Doubleday, 1978), p. 25.
30. Martin and Deidre Bobgan. *The Psychological Way/The Spiritual Way.* (Minneapolis: Bethany House Publishers, 1979), cover.
31. Szasz, *op. cit.*, p. 28.
32. *Ibid.*, p. 188.
33. Christopher Lasch. *The Culture of Narcissism.* (New York: W. W. Norton & Company, Inc., 1979), p. 13.
34. Kenneth Cinnamon and Dave Farson. *Cults and Cons.* (Chicago: Nelson Hall, 1979), cover.
35. Martin Gross. *The Psychological Society.* (New York: Random House, 1978), p. 9.
36. Carl Rogers, quoted by Allen Bergin, "Psychotherapy and Religious Values," *Journal of Consulting and Clinical Psychology*, Vol 48, p. 101.
37. Bernie Zilbergeld. *The Shrinking of America.* (Boston: Little, Brown and Company, 1983), p. 5.
38. Lasch, *op. cit.*, p. 7.
39. Christopher Lasch. *Haven in a Heartless World.* (New York: Basic Books, Inc., 1977), p. 98.
40. Szasz, *op. cit.*, pp. 104-105.
41. Bobgan, *op. cit.*, p. 190.
42. Szasz, *op. cit.*, p. 26.
43. *Ibid.*, p. xxiv.
44. Daniel Goleman, "An Eastern Toe in the Stream of Consciousness," *Psychology Today*, January 1981, p. 84.
45. Jacob Needleman, "Psychiatry and the Sacred." *Consciousness: Brain, States of Awareness, and Mysticism.* Daniel Goleman and Richard Davidson, eds. (New York: Harper & Row, Publishers, 1979), pp. 209-210.
46. Thomas Szasz, "Psychoanalysis as 'Pastoral Work,'" an essay to be published in forthcoming book.

47. A. W. Tozer. *The Root of the Righteous*. (Harrisburg, PA: Christian Publications, Inc., 1955), pp. 49-50.

Chapter Three: SCIENCE OR PSEUDOSCIENCE?

1. Sigmund Koch, ed. *Psychology: A Study of a Science*. (New York: McGraw-Hill, 1959-63).
2. Sigmund Koch, "The Image of Man in Encounter Groups," *The American Scholar*, Autumn 1973, p. 636.
3. Sigmund Koch, "Psychology Cannot Be a Coherent Science," *Psychology Today*, September 1969, p. 66.
4. Robert Hillman, "Psychopathology of Being Held Hostage," *American Journal of Psychiatry*, September 1981, pp. 1193-1197.
5. United States Department of Justice, "The Stockholm Syndrome: Law Enforcement Policy and Ego Defenses of the Hostage," FBI Terrorist Research Center, 15 June 1979, pp. 2-3.
6. *Webster's New Collegiate Dictionary*. (Springfield: G. & C. Merriam Company, 1974).
7. Mary Stewart Van Leeuwen. *The Sorcerer's Apprentice*. (Downers Grove, IL: InterVarsity Press, 1982), p. 91.
8. Lee Coleman. *The Reign of Error*. (Boston: Beacon Press, 1984), p. xii.
9. *Ibid.*, p. xv.
10. Jerome Frank, "Mental Health in a Fragmented Society," *American Journal of Orthopsychiatry*, July 1979, p. 404.
11. Roger Mills, "Psychology Goes Insane, Botches Role as Science," *The National Educator*, July 1980, p. 14.
12. David G. Benner, ed. *Baker Encyclopedia of Psychology*. (Grand Rapids: Baker Book House, 1985).
13. Ed Payne, "Books." *Presbyterian Journal*, December 24, 1986.
14. Gary Collins *Psychology and Theology: Prospects for Integration*. (Nashville: Abingdon, 1981), p. 15.
15. John Carter and Bruce Narramore. *The Integration of Psychology and Theology*. (Grand Rapids: Zondervan Publishing House, 1979).
16. William Law. *The Power of the Spirit*. Dave Hunt, ed. (Fort Washington, PA: Christian Literature Crusade, 1971), p. 52.
17. Charles Tart. *Transpersonal Psychologies*. (New York: Harper & Row, Publishers, 1975), p. 4.
18. Martin and Deidre Bobgan, *The Psychological Way/The Spiritual Way*. (Bethany House Publishers, 1979), p. 63.
19. Jonas Robitscher. *The Powers of Psychiatry*. (Boston: Houghton Mifflin Company, 1980), p. 8.
20. *Ibid.*, p. 183.
21. E. Fuller Torrey. *The Mind Game*. (New York: Emerson Hall Publishers, Inc., 1972), p. 8.
22. E. Fuller Torrey, "The Protection of Ezra Pound," *Psychology Today*, November 1981, p. 66.
23. Walter Reich, "Psychiatry's Second Coming," *Encounter*, August 1981, p. 68.
24. *Ibid.*, p. 70.
25. Linda Riebel, "Theory as Self-Portrait and the Ideal of Objectivity," *Journal of Humanistic Psychology*, Spring 1982, p. 91.
26. *Ibid.*, p. 92.
27. Karl Popper, "Scientific Theory and Falsifiability," *Perspectives in Philosophy*. Robert N. Beck, ed. (New York: Holt, Rinehart, Winston, 1975), pp. 343, 346.

28. Carol Tavris, "The Freedom to Change," *Prime Time*, October 1980, p. 28.
29. Jerome Frank, "Therapeutic Factors in Psychotherapy," *American Journal of Psychotherapy*, Vol. 25, 1971, p. 356.
30. Lewis Thomas, "Medicine Without Science," *The Atlantic Monthly*, April 1981, p. 40.
31. Dave Hunt. *Beyond Seduction*. (Eugene: Harvest House, 1987), p. 96.
32. Bernard Berelson and Gary A. Steiner. *Human Behavior: An Inventory of Scientific Findings*. (New York: Harcourt, Brace and World, 1964), p. 666.
33. Michael deCourcy Hinds, "Therapy that Aids Parents," *New York Times*, 13 July 1981, p. A-13.
34. David Gelman, "Finding the Hidden Freud," *Newsweek*, 30 November 1981, p. 64.
35. Jay E. Adams. *More Than Redemption*. (Grand Rapids: Baker Book House, 1979), pp. xi,xii.
36. Dave Hunt. *The Cult Explosion*. (Eugene: Harvest House, 1980), p. 70.
37. C. I. Scofield. *The New Scofield Reference Bible*. (New York: Oxford University Press, 1967), p. 1301.
38. Bobgan, *op. cit.*, pp. 43-50.

Part Two: PSYCHOTHEOLOGY.
1. George Albee quoted in "Psychology Is Alive and Well," *Santa Barbara News Press*, 23 August 1981, p. B-7.

Chapter Four: PROMISES, PROMISES, PROMISES.
1. Art Levine, "The Great Subliminal Self-Help Hoax." *New Age Journal*, February 1986, p. 48.
2. Eileen Keerdoja, "The 'Screaming Cure.'" *Newsweek*, 10 July 1978, p. 12.
3. Judy Foreman, "NLP: Is It a Breakthrough or a Pop Hustle?" *Los Angeles Times*, 9 September 1981, Part V, p. 12.
4. Byram Karasu, "Maze Bewilders Those Seeking Psychotherapy." *The Dallas Morning News*, 18 January 1981. p. F-8.
5. Bernie Zilbergeld. *The Shrinking of America*. (Boston: Little, Brown and Company, 1983), p. 159.
6. "Anger," *Santa Barbara News Press* ad, 25 January 1986, p. D-9.
7. Joan A. McCord, "A Thirty-Year Follow-up of Treatment Effects." *American Psychologist*, Vol. 33, 1978, pp. 290-291.
8. William Backus and Marie Chapian. *Telling Yourself the Truth*. (Minneapolis: Bethany House Publishers, 1980), front cover.
9. *Ibid.*, p. 25.
10. *Ibid.*, p. 10.
11. Martha Rogers, "A Family in Crisis." *Eternity*, November 1980, p. 18.
12. *Ibid.*, p. 18.
13. Paul Meier radio interview, "Issues of the Eighties," 11 October 1985, KCBI, Dallas, TX.
14. Hans Strupp in Zilbergeld, *op. cit.*, p. 159.
15. Zilbergeld, *op. cit.*, pp. 159-160.
16. *Ibid.*, p. 160.
17. Anthony Storr. *The Art of Psychotherapy*. (New York: Methuen, Inc., 1980), p. 151.
18. Jerome Frank. *Persuasion and Healing*. (New York: Schocken Books, 1974), p. 102.
19. Zilbergeld, *op. cit.*, p. 221.

Chapter Five: AMALGAMANIA.

1. John Sanderson, review of *Biblical Concepts for Christian Counseling* in *Presbyterian Journal*, 11 September 1985, p. 10.
2. Paul Bartz, "Chemical Man." *Bible-Science Newsletter*, Vol. 24, No. 2, February 1986, p. 1.
3. David G. Benner, ed. *Baker Encyclopedia of Psychology*. (Grand Rapids: Baker Books, 1985).
4. Ed Payne, "Books." *Presbyterian Journal*, 24 December 1986, p. 24.
5. J. Vernon McGee, "Psycho-Religion—The New Pied Piper." *Thru the Bible Radio Newsletter*, November 1986.
6. Letter on file, September 18, 1986.
7. Daniel Yankelovich. *New Rules: Searching for Self-Fulfillment in a World Turned Upside Down*. (New York: Random House, 1981), p. xx.
8. *Ibid.*, p. xviii.
9. *Ibid.*, jacket cover.
10. James Dobson. *Hide and Seek*. (Old Tappan, N. J.: Revell, 1974), p. 142.
11. James Dobson. *What Wives Wish their Husbands Knew About Women*. (Wheaton: Tyndale House Publishers, Inc., 1975), pp. 22-23.
12. Carol Tavris, "Coping with Anxiety." *Science Digest*, February 1986, p. 46.
13. Dobson, *Hide and Seek*, *op. cit.*, pp. 12-13.
14. Dave Hunt and T. A. McMahon. *The Seduction of Christianity*, (Eugene: Harvest House, 1985), p. 193.
15. Edward Stainbrook, quoted by Lloyd Shearer, "Intelligence Report," *Parade Magazine*, 25 November 1979, p. 6.
16. John D. Mc Carthy and Dean R. Hoge, "The Dynamics of Self-Esteem and Delinquency." *American Journal of Sociology*, Vol. 90, No. 2, p. 407.
17. *Ibid*, p. 407.
18. David Myers. *The Inflated Self*. (New York, Seabury, 1980), p 24.
19. Patricia McCormack, "Good News for the Underdog," *Santa Barbara News Press*, 8 November 1981, p. D-10.
20. Larry Scherwitz, Lewis E. Graham, II, and Dean Ornish, "Self-Involvement and the Risk Factors for Coronary Heart Disease," *Advances, Institute for the Advancement of Health*, Vol. 2, No. 2, Spring 1985, p. 16.
21. *Ibid.*, p. 17.
22. Paul Vitz. *Psychology as Religion: The Cult of Self Worship*. (Grand Rapids: Eerdmans, 1977), p. 91.
23. John Piper, "Is Self-Love Biblical?" *Christianity Today*, 12 August 1977, p. 6.
24. Jay E. Adams. *The Biblical View of Self-Esteem, Self-Love, Self-Image*. (Eugene: Harvest House, 1986), p. 65.
25. *Ibid.*, pp. 65-66.
26. J. I. Packer. *Keep in Step with the Spirit*. (Old Tappan, NJ: Fleming H. Revell, 1984), p. 97.
27. Dave Hunt. *Beyond Seduction*. (Eugene: Harvest House, 1987), p. 169.
28. John Wesley, "Who Will You Deny?" *The Last Days Newsletter*, Vol. 7, No. 4, 1984.
29. William Law. *The Power of the Spirit*. Dave Hunt, ed. (Fort Washington: Christian Literature Crusade, 1971), p. 76.
30. Ruth Graham, "By the Way." *Christianity Today*, 19 February 1982, p. 14.
31. Elwood McQuaid, "Before the Altar of 'I.'" *Moody*, November 1986, p. 15.
32. E. Fuller Torrey. *Witchdoctors and Psychiatrists*. (New York: Harper & Row, 1986), p. 27.

33. William Kirk Kilpatrick. *Psychological Seduction*. (Nashville: Thomas Nelson Publishers, 1983), p. 41.
34. Paul Brownback. *The Dangers of Self-Love*. (Chicago: Moody Press, 1982).
35. Jay Adams, *op. cit.*
36. Robert N. Bellah, Richard Madeson, William Sullivan, Ann Swidler and Steven M. Tipton. *Habits of the Heart*. (Berkeley: Univ. of California Press, 1985).
37. Michael A. Wallach and Lise Wallach. *Psychology's Sanction for Selfishness*. (San Francisco: W. H. Freeman and Company, 1983), p. 1.
38. *Ibid.*, pp. ix, xx.
39. T. A. McMahon, letter on file.
40. John Vasconcellos and Mitch Saunders, "Humanistic Politics." *AHP Perspective*, July 1985, pp. 12-13.
41. Richard Dobbins. *The Believer and His Self Concept*, film brochure, p. 6.
42. A. W. Tozer. *Man: The Dwelling Place of God*. (Harrisburg: Christian Publications, Inc., 1966), p. 72.
43. Richard Dobbins, "Anger: Master or Servant," *Pentecostal Evangel*, 6 July 1986.
44. Richard Dobbins. *Your Spiritual and Emotional Power*. (Old Tappan, NJ: Fleming H. Revell Company, 1982).
45. Dobbins, "Control Your Anger." *Pentecostal Evangel*, 20 July 1986, p. 19.
46. Dobbins, *Your Spiritual and Emotional Power*, *op. cit.*, p. 82.
47. Dobbins, "Control Your Anger," *op. cit.*, p. 19.
48. Carol Tavris. *Anger: The Misunderstood Emotion*. (New York: Simon and Schuster, 1982), p. 38.
49. Carol Tavris, "Anger Defused," *Psychology Today*, November 1982, p. 25.
50. Leonard Berkowitz, "The Case for Bottling Up Rage," *Psychology Today*, July 1973, p. 31.
51. Tavris, *Anger*, *op. cit.*, p. 128.
52. Tavris, "Anger Defused," *op. cit.*, p. 29.
53. *Ibid.*, p. 31.
54. *Ibid.*, p. 33.
55. Richard Dobbins, "Recognizing Anger." *Pentecostal Evangel*, 13 July 1986, p. 13.
56. *Ibid.*, p. 13.
57. Judy Eidelson, *EveryWoman's Emotional Well-Being*, Carol Tavris, ed. (Garden City: Doubleday and Company, Inc., 1986) p. 397.
58. Dobbins, "Anger: Master or Servant," *op. cit.*, p. 9.
59. *Ibid.*, p. 10.
60. H. Norman Wright, Christian Marriage Enrichment, Summer 1985 conference announcement.
61. *Ibid.*
62. Letter on file.
63. Myers, *op. cit.*, p. 101.
64. Lawrence Crabb. *Effective Biblical Counseling*. (Grand Rapids: Zondervan Publishing House, 1977), p. 37.
65. *Ibid.*, p. 43.
66. *Ibid.*, p. 51.
67. Erich Fromm. *Man for Himself.* (New York: Rinehart, 1947), p. 23.
68. Crabb, *op. cit.*, p. 44.
69. William Kirk Kilpatrick. *The Emperor's New Clothes*. (Westchester, IL: Crossway Books, 1985).
70. Crabb, *op. cit.*, p. 96.
71. *Ibid.*, pp 52-56.

72. *Ibid.*, p. 62.
73. *Ibid.*, p. 66.
74. A. W. Tozer. *The Pursuit of God.* (Harrisburg: Christian Publications, 1948), pp. 91-92.
75. Crabb, *op. cit.*, p. 69.
76. Paul Tournier. *The Meaning of Persons.* (New York: Harper & Row Publishers, 1957), p. 23.
77. *Ibid.*, p. 25.
78. *Ibid.*, p. 13.
79. *Ibid.*, p. 59.
80. *Ibid.*, p. 60.
81. M. Scott Peck. *People of the Lie.* (New York: Simon and Schuster, 1983).
82. M. Scott Peck. *The Road Less Traveled.* (New York: Simon and Schuster, 1978).
83. Anne Roiphe, "Gun Fight at the I'm OK Corral," *New York Times* Book Review, 19 January 1986, p. 22.
84. Ben Patterson, "Is God a Psychotherapist?" *Christianity Today*, 1 March 1985, p. 22.
85. *Ibid.*, p. 23.
86. *Ibid.*, p. 22.
87. M. Scott Peck. *The Road Less Traveled*, *op. cit.*, pp. 269-270.
88. *Ibid.*, p. 270.
89. *Ibid.*, pp. 270-271.
90. *Ibid.*, p. 273.
91. *Ibid.*, p. 281.
92. *Ibid.*, p. 282.
93. *Ibid.*, p. 283.
94. *Ibid.*, p. 283.
95. Philip Busuttil, "Hard Love," *New Age Journal*, December 1985, p. 28.
96. *Ibid.*, p. 30.
97. Thomas Harris. *I'm OK, You're OK.* (New York: Harper & Row, Publishers, 1969).
98. *Ibid.*, p. 184.
99. *Ibid.*, p. 230.
100. *Ibid.*, p. 227.
101. Gary Collins. *Psychology and Theology.* H. Newton Maloney, ed. (Nashville: Abingdon, 1981), p. 112.
102. *Ibid.*, p. 112.
103. Joseph Palotta. *The Robot Psychiatrist.* (Metairie, LA: Revelation House Publishers, Inc., 1981), p. 11.
104. *Ibid.*, p. 177.
105. *Ibid.*, p. 400.
106. Thomas Szasz. *The Myth of Psychotherapy.* (Garden City: Doubleday/Anchor Press, 1978), p. 133.
107. Martin and Deidre Bobgan. *Hypnosis and the Christian.* (Minneapolis: Bethany House Publishers, 1984), p. 42.
108. E. Fuller Torrey. *The Mind Game.* (New York: Emerson Hall Publishers, Inc., 1972), p. 70.
109. Bobgan, *Hypnosis and the Christian*, *op. cit.*, p. 53.
110. *Ibid.*, p. 54.
111. Martin and Deidre Bobgan. *The Psychological Way/The Spiritual Way.* (Minneapolis: Bethany House Publishers, 1979), pp. 86, 87.
112. Arthur Janov. *The Primal Scream.* (New York: Dell Publishing Co., Inc., 1970), p. 154.

113. Cecil Osborne. *Understanding Your Past*. (Waco, TX: Word Books, 1980), p. 200.
114. *Ibid.*, p. 142.
115. *Ibid.*, p. 10.
116. *Ibid.*, p. 15.
117. *Ibid.*, p. 10.
118. *Ibid.*, p. 16.
119. *Ibid.*, p. 21.
120. *Ibid.*, p. 21.
121. *Ibid.*, p. 24.
122. *Ibid.*, p. 24.
123. *Ibid.*, p. 64.
124. H. J. Eysenck, "The Death Knell of Psychoanalysis," *Free Inquiry*, Vol. 5, No. 4, Fall 1985, pp. 31-32.
125. E. Fuller Torrey. *The Death of Psychiatry*. (Radnor: Chilton Book Company, 1974).
126. Adolf Grunbaum. *The Foundations of Psychoanalysis*. (Berkeley: University of California Press, 1984).
127. Charles Solomon. *Counseling with the Mind of Christ*. (Old Tappan, NJ: Fleming H. Revell Company, 1977), p. 18.
128. *Ibid.*, p. 42.
129. Charles Solomon. *The Rejection Syndrome*. (Wheaton: Tyndale House Publishers, Inc., 1982), p. 21.
130. Ann Japenga, "Great Minds on the Mind Assemble for Conference," *Los Angeles Times*, 18 December 1985, Part V, p. 1.
131. *Ibid.*, p. 16.
132. William Kirk Kilpatrick interviewed by Ivan Thorn, "The Future of Modern Psychology," *Bible-Science Newsletter*, Vol 24, No. 2, February 1986, p. 2.
133. Phillip Keller, letter on file.

Chapter Six: "A WAY THAT SEEMETH RIGHT."

1. Darrell Smith, "Booked for Passages," *Eternity*, May 1980, p. 29.
2. C. P. Dragash, "Criminal Commonplaces," *Chronicles of Culture*, May 1985, p. 15.
3. David Gelman, "'Unmarried' Counseling," *Newsweek*, 17 June 1985, p. 78.
4. Loriene Chase, "Casebook of Dr. Chase," *Westways*, July 1985, p. 63.
5. Mary Vander Goot, "The Shingle and the Manse," *The Reformed Journal*, September 1983, p. 15.
6. *Ibid.*, pp. 16-17.
7. *Ibid.*, p. 17.
8. Garth Wood. *The Myth of Neurosis*. (New York: Harper & Row Publishers, 1986), p. 3.
9. Richard Aguirre, "Psychiatrist: Colleagues Too 'Naive, Trusting,'" *Santa Barbara News Press*, 18 March 1986, p. B-1.
10. Wood, *op. cit.*, p. 3.
11. Thomas Szasz. *Myth of Psychotherapy*. (New York: Anchor Press/Doubleday, 1978), p. xxiii.
12. Marilyn Thomsen and Archibald D. Hart, "Pastoral Counseling: Who, Whom, How?" *Ministry*, January 1985, p. 7.
13. Hugh Drummond, "Dr. D. Is Mad As Hell," *Mother Jones*, December 1979, p. 52.
14. Thomsen and Hart, *op. cit.*, p. 8.
15. *Ibid.*, p. 8.
16. William Kirk Kilpatrick. *The Emperor's New Clothes*. (Westchester, IL: Crossway Books, 1985), pp. 129-184.

17. Martin and Deidre Bobgan, "Psychotherapeutic Methods of CAPS Members," *Christian Association for Psychological Studies Bulletin 6*, No. 1, 1980, p. 13.

18. Martin and Deidre Bobgan. *The Psychological Way/The Spiritual Way*. (Minneapolis: Bethany House Publishers, 1979), pp. 118-124.

19. Carl Rogers, graduation address, Sonoma State College, quoted by Kilpatrick, *op. cit.*, p. 162.

20. Thomsen and Hart, *op. cit.*, p. 10.

21. Bernie Zilbergeld, "Psychabuse," *Science 86*, June 1986, p. 50.

22. Bernie Zilbergeld. *The Shrinking of America*. (Boston: Little, Brown and Company, 1983), p. 163.

23. Martin and Deidre Bobgan. *How to Counsel from Scripture*. (Chicago: Moody Press, 1985).

24. Kenneth Woodward and Janet Huck, "Next, Clerical Malpractice," *Newsweek*, 20 May 1985, p. 90.

25. David Swift, "Are We Preparing to Fail?" *Moody Monthly*, September 1984, p. 109.

26. Jimmy Swaggart, "Serious Weaknesses in the Pentecostal Message," *The Evangelist*, May 1985, p. 8.

27. Robert Illman, "Confidentiality and the Law," *Presbyterian Journal*, 26 December 1984, p. 9.

28. *Ibid.*, p. 9.

29. Elaine Sciolino, "Dear Abby, Bishop Sheen, a Psychotherapist," *Santa Barbara News Press*, 5 May 1985, p. A-14.

30. "An Interview with Dr. Margaret Thaler Singer," *Spiritual Counterfeits Project Newsletter*, Vol. 10, No. 2, March-April 1984, pp. 1, 6-8, 11-12.

31. Ben Patterson, "Is God a Psychotherapist?" *Christianity Today*, 1 March 1985, p. 23.

32. E. M. Thornton. *The Freudian Fallacy*. (Garden City: The Dial Press/Doubleday & Company, Inc. 1983), p. ix.

33. William Kirk Kilpatrick. *Psychological Seduction*. (Nashville: Thomas Nelson Publishers, 1983), p. 23.

34. *Ibid.*, p. 31.

35. Kilpatrick, *The Emperor's New Clothes*, *op. cit.*, p. 12.

36. Kerry Koller, "Psychology as a Point of View," *Pastoral Renewal*, Vol. 4, No. 2, August 1979, p. 1.

37. *Ibid.*, p. 10.

38. *Ibid.*, p. 12.

39. A. W. Tozer. *That Incredible Christian*. (Harrisburg, PA: Christian Publications, Inc., 1964) p. 23.

40. Gene Lyons, "Let There Be Books," *Newsweek*, 5 August 1985, p. 65A.

41. Daniel Yankelovich. *New Rules: Searching for Self-Fulfillment in a World Turned Upside Down*. (New York: Random House, 1981).

Chapter Seven: BROKEN CISTERNS OR LIVING WATERS?

1. J. I. Packer. *Keep in Step with the Spirit*. (Old Tappan, NJ: Fleming H. Revell Company, 1984), p. 256.

2. Peter Schrag. *Mind Control*. (New York: Pantheon Books, 1978), p. xi.

3. *Ibid.*, p. xiii.

4. *Ibid.*, p. xiv.

5. Philip Zimbardo, "Mind Control: Political Fiction and Psychological Reality," *On Nineteen Eighty-Four*. Peter Stansky, ed. (Palo Alto: Stanford Alumni Association, 1983), pp. 209-210.

6. Martin and Deidre Bobgan. *How To Counsel from Scripture*. (Chicago: Moody Press, 1985), pp. 28-29.
7. James Turner. *Without God, Without Creed*. (Baltimore: The Johns Hopkins University Press, 1985), p. xiii.
8. Letter on file.

Part Three: PSYCHOBABBLE.
1. Morris Parloff, "Psychotherapy and Research: An Anaclitic Depression," *Psychiatry*, November 1980, p. 283.

Chapter Eight: THE MISNOMER OF MENTAL ILLNESS.
1. E. Fuller Torrey. *The Death of Psychiatry*. (Radnor: Chilton Book Company, 1974), p. 36.
2. Barbara Brown. *Supermind*. (New York: Harper & Row, Publishers, 1980), p. 6.
3. Arthur Custance. *The Mysterious Matter of Mind*. (Grand Rapids: Zondervan Publishing House, 1980), p. 9.
4. Torrey, *op. cit.*, p. 40.
5. Thomas Szasz. *The Myth of Psychotherapy*. (Garden City: Doubleday/Anchor Press, 1978), p. 7.
6. Thomas Szasz. *The Myth of Mental Illness*. (New York: Harper & Row, Publishers, 1974), p. 262.
7. Lois Timnick, "Psychiatry's Focus Turns to Biology," *Los Angeles Times*, 21 July 1980, part 1, p. 20.
8. Jonas Robitscher. *The Powers of Psychiatry*. (Boston: Houghton Mifflin Company, 1980), p. 9.
9. Ann Landers, *Santa Barbara News Press*, 3 April 1980, p. B-12.
10. Ann Landers, *Santa Barbara News Press*, 15 April 1986, p. B-5.
11. Torrey, *op. cit.*, pp. 43-44.

Chapter Nine: MENTAL ILLNESS BY BALLOT.
1. Jonas Robitscher. *The Powers of Psychiatry*. (Boston: Houghton Mifflin Company, 1980), p. 155.
2. Russ Pulliam, "Alcoholism: Sin or Sickness?" *Christianity Today*, 18 September 1981, p. 23.
3. "UCSB Professor Says Alcoholism Not Disease," *Santa Barbara News Press*, 10 June 1984, p. D-3.
4. Pulliam, *op. cit.*, pp. 23-24.
5. Bruce J. Ennis and Thomas R. Litwack, "Psychiatry and the Presumption of Expertise," *California Law Review*, May 1974, p. 741.
6. "AAPL and DSM-III," *Newsletter of the American Academy of Psychiatry and the Law*, Summer 1976, p. 11.
7. "Current DSM-III Outline," *Psychiatric News*, 17 November 1978, p. 17.
8. Alfred Freedman, Harold Kaplan, and Benjamin Sadock. *Modern Synopsis of Comprehensive Textbook of Psychiatry*, 2nd Ed. (Baltimore: Williams & Wilkins, 1976), p. 407.

Chapter Ten: DISEASE, DIAGNOSIS, AND PROGNOSIS.
1. Thomas Szasz. *The Myth of Psychotherapy*. (Garden City: Doubleday/Anchor Press, 1978), p. 25.
2. Jonas Robitscher. *The Powers of Psychiatry*. (Boston: Houghton Mifflin Company, 1980), p. 150
3. Leonard Kurland, "A New Wrinkle in a Colossal Rip-Off," *Los Angeles Times*, 5

September 1980, Part II, p. 7.

4. *Ibid.*, p. 7.

5. Robitscher, *op. cit.*, p. 161.

6. Mary Stewart Van Leeuwen, "A Christian Examination of Applied Behaviorism," *Journal of the American Scientific Affiliation*, September 1979, pp. 136-137.

7. Robitscher, *op. cit.*, p. 166.

8. George Albee, "The Answer Is Prevention," *Psychology Today*, February 1985, p. 61.

9. Walter Reich, "The Force of Diagnosis," *Harper's*, May 1980, p. 24.

10. Martin and Deidre Bobgan. *The Psychological Way/The Spiritual Way*. (Minneapolis: Bethany House Publishers, 1979), p. 60.

11. Hugh Drummond, "Dr. D. Is Mad As Hell," *Mother Jones*, December 1979, p. 52.

12. Bobgan, *op. cit.*, pp. 61-62.

13. Albee, *op. cit.*, p. 60.

14. David L. Rosenhan, "On Being Sane in Insane Places," *Science*, January 1973, p. 252.

15. Thomas Szasz. *The Manufacture of Madness*. (New York: Harper & Row, Publishers, 1970), p. 35.

16. Christopher Lasch. *Haven in a Heartless World*. (New York: Basic Books, Inc., 1977), p. 186.

17. Hillel J. Einhorn and Robin M Hogarth, "Confidence in Judgment: Persistence of the Illusion of Validity," *Psychological Review*, Vol. 85, No. 5, 1978, p. 395.

18. Bobgan, *op. cit.*, p. 46.

19. Robitscher, *op. cit.*, p. 196.

20. Ronald Schlensky quoted by Chet Holcombe, "Mental Health Fund Shift Seen," *Santa Barbara News Press*, 3 January 1980, p. C-8.

21. American Psychiatric Association, Amicus Curiae brief, Tarasoff v. Regents of University of California, 551 P. 2d 334 (Cal, 1976).

22. Jim Mann, "Psychiatry's Role in Court Challenged," *Los Angeles Times*, 9 November 1980, Part 1, p. 20.

23. Larry Stammer, "Two Professionals Urge Ban on Psychiatric Testimony," *Los Angeles Times*, 4 December 1981, Part 1, pp. 3, 8.

24. "Idaho Eliminates Insanity Defense," *Santa Barbara News Press*, 3 April 1982, p. A-6.

25. Thomas Szasz, "Nobody Should Decide Who Goes to the Mental Hospital," *Co-Evolution Quarterly*, Summer 1978, p. 65.

26. Harold Mavritte quoted by John Hurst, "State Mental Health Law," *Los Angeles Times*, 16 June 1980, Part II, p. 8.

27. Howard Kissel, "Putting Psychiatry on the Witness Stand," *Women's Wear Daily*, 10 July 1984, p. 18.

Chapter Eleven: THE LABELING GAME.

1. Jonas Robitscher. *The Powers of Psychiatry*. (Boston: Houghton Mifflin Company, 1980) p. 151.

2. E. Fuller Torrey. *The Death of Psychiatry*. (Radnor: Chilton Book Company, 1974), p. 64.

3. Hugh Drummond, "Dr. D. Is Mad as Hell," *Mother Jones*, December 1979, p. 56.

4. O. R. Gursslin, R. G. Hunt, and J. L. Roach, "Social Class and the Mental Health Movement," *Mental Health of the Poor*, F. Riessman, J. Cohen, and A. Pearl, eds. (New York: The Free Press, 1964), p. 63.

5. "The Children of Pavlov," *Time*, 23 June 1980, p. 65.

6. Christopher Lasch. *Haven in a Heartless World*. (New York: Basic Books, Inc.,

1977), p. 189.

7. David L. Rosenhan, "On Being Sane in Insane Places," *Science*, January 1973, p. 253.

8. Walter Reich, "The Force of Diagnosis," *Harper's*, May 1980, p. 29.

9. "'Labeling' Causes Observers to See Commonplace Behavior as Neurotic," *Brain/Mind Bulletin*, 17 March 1980, p. 2.

10. Drummond, *op. cit.*, p. 56.

11. Reich, *op. cit.*, p. 32.

12. *Ibid.*, pp. 29, 32.

13. Martin and Deidre Bobgan. *The Psychological Way/The Spiritual Way*. (Bethany House Publishers, 1979), pp. 38-41.

Chapter 12: MENTAL ILLNESS OR IRRESPONSIBILITY.

1. Henry Fairlie. *The Seven Deadly Sins Today*. (Washington: New Republic Books, 1978), p. 58.

2. David Einstein, "Results of Sanity Trials Show Weakness in System," *Santa Barbara News Press*, 26 February 1981, p. B-4.

3. Nils Bolduan, "Helpless Souls Who Wander City Streets," *Santa Barbara News Press*, 12 April 1981, p. A-14.

4. Rousas Rushdoony, "The Chalcedon Report," *Chalcedon*, January 1981, p. 1.

5. Rousas Rushdoony, "The Cult of Victimization," Position Paper No. 71, *Chalcedon*, P. O. Box 158, Vallecito, CA 95251.

6. Rousas Rushdoony, "Loyalties, Position Paper No. 62, *Chalcedon*.

7. Eleanor Harris Howard, "Q & A Nancy Reagan on the White House, Marriage and Kids," *Los Angeles Herald Examiner*, 27 August 1981, p. A-9.

8. Vernon Scott, "Sid Caesar Kicks 'Legal' Drug Habit," *Santa Barbara News Press*, 21 November 1980, p. C-15.

9. Jonas Robitscher. *The Powers of Psychiatry*. (Boston: Houghton Mifflin Company, 1980), pp. 162-163.

10. Peter Breggin, "Misuse of Psychiatric Drugs—East and West," *Esalen Catalog*, September 1985-February 1986, p. 7.

11. Larry Thomas, "Alcoholism Is Not a Disease," *Christianity Today*, 4 October 1985, p. 15.

Part Four: PSYCHOQUACKERY.

1. Morris B. Parloff, "Psychotherapy and Research: Anaclitic Depression," *Psychiatry*, November 1980, p. 282.

Chapter Thirteen: IS PSYCHOTHERAPY A PANACEA?

1. Alan Stone quoted by Lois Timnick, "Psychiatry's Focus Turns to Biology," *Los Angeles Times*, 21 July 1980, Part I, p. 21.

2. Hans J. Eysenck, "The Effects of Psychotherapy: An Evaluation," *Journal of Consulting Psychology*, Vol. 16, 1952, p. 322.

3. *Ibid.*, pp. 322-323.

4. Hans J. Eysenck, "Psychotherapy, Behavior Therapy, and the Outcome Problem," BMA Audio Cassette / T-308 (New York: Guilford Publications, Inc., 1979).

5. Hans J. Eysenck, letter to editor, *American Psychologist*, January 1980, p. 114.

6. Hans J. Eysenck, "The Effectiveness of Psychotherapy: The Specter at the Feast," *The Behavioral and Brain Sciences*, June 1983, p. 290.

7. Sol Garfield, "Psychotherapy: Efficacy, Generality, and Specificity," *Psychotherapy Research: Where Are We and Where Should We Go?* Janet B. W. Williams and Robert L. Spitzer, eds. (New York: The Guilford Press, 1983), p. 296.

8. *Ibid.*, p. 295.
9. *Ibid.*, p. 303.
10. S. J. Rachman and G. T. Wilson. *The Effects of Psychological Therapy*, 2nd Enlarged Ed. (New York: Pergamon Press, 1980), p. 251.
11. Eysenck, "Psychotherapy, Behavior Therapy, and the Outcome Problem," *op. cit.*
12. P. London and G. L. Klerman, "Evaluating Psychotherapy," *American Journal of Psychiatry* 139: 709-17, 1982, p. 715.
13. Donald Klein statement in "Proposals to Expand Coverage of Mental Health under Medicare-Medicaid," Hearing before the Subcommitte on Health of the Committee on Finance, Nincty-Fifth Congress, Second Session, 18 August 1978, p. 45.
14. Jay B. Constantine letter, printed in Blue Sheet, Vol. 22 (50), 12 December 1979, pp. 8-9.
15. Nathan Epstein and Louis Vlok, "Research on the Results of Psychotherapy: A summary of Evidence," *American Journal of Psychiatry*, August 1981, p. 1033.
16. Michael Shepherd, "Psychotherapy Outcome Research and Parloff's Pony," *The Behavioral and Brain Sciences*, June 1983, p. 301.
17. Rachman and Wilson, *op. cit.*, p. 77.
18. *Ibid.*, p. 259.
19. Allen E. Bergin and Michael J. Lambert, "The Evaluation of Therapeutic Outcomes," *Handbook of Psychotherapy and Behavior Change*, 2nd Ed., Sol Garfield and Allen Bergin, eds. (New York: John Wiley & Sons, 1978), p. 145.
20. Jean Seligmann et al, "Getting Straight," *Newsweek*, 4 June 1984, p. 65.
21. Stanton Peele, "Out of the Habit Trap," *American Health*, September/October 1983, p. 42.
22. *Ibid.*, p. 47.
23. *Ibid.*, p. 42.
24. Andrew M. Mathews, Michael G. Gelder, and Derek W. Johnston. *Agoraphobia: Nature and Treatment*. (New York: The Guilford Press, 1981), p. 108.
25. Leonard Syme, "People Need People: Social Support and Health," *The Healing Brain* audio tape series, tape /12, Los Altos: Institute for the Study of Human Knowledge, 1981.
26. James Lynch, "Listen and Live," *American Health*, April 1985, p. 39.
27. J. M., "Crosstalk: Me and My Compeer," *Psychology Today*, January 1985, p. 73.
28. Annette Leavy quoted by Dick Robinson, "Pick a Therapist: Years and Years on the Wrong Couch," *American Health*, June 1985, p. 91.
29. *Brain/Mind Bulletin*, Vol. 11, No. 1, 18 November 1985, p. 1.
30. Lester Luborsky et al, "Therapist Success and Its Determinants," *Archives of General Psychiatry*, Vol. 42, June 1985, pp. 602-611.
31. Susan S. Lang, "The Mental State of the Union," *American Health*, November 1984, p. 62.
32. Hans Strupp, Suzanne Hadley, Beverly Gomes-Schwartz. *Psychotherapy for Better or Worse*. (New York: Jason Aronson, Inc., 1977), pp. 115-116.
33. Suzanne Hadley, National Institute of Mental Health, 6 March 1978, letter on file.
34. American Psychiatric Association Commission on Psychotherapies. *Psychotherapy Research: Methodological and Efficacy Issues*, 1982, p. 228.
35. "Ambiguity Pervades Research on Effectiveness of Psychotherapy," *Brain/Mind Bulletin*, 4 October 1982, p. 2.
36. Allen E. Bergin, "Therapist-Induced Deterioration in Psychotherapy," BMA Audio Cassette /T-302 (New York: Guilford Publishers, Inc., 1979).
37. R. Bruce Sloane et al. *Psychotherapy Versus Behavior Therapy*. (Cambridge: Harvard University Press, 1975), p. xv.
38. David Gelman and Mary Hager, "Psychotherapy in the '80's," *Newsweek*, 30

November 1981, p. 73.

39. Richard B. Stuart. *Trick or Treatment*. (Champaign: Research Press, 1970), p. i.

40. Strupp, Hadley, Gomes-Schwartz, *op. cit.*, pp. 51, 83.

41. Bergin and Lambert, *op. cit.*, p. 154.

42. Morris B. Parloff, "Psychotherapy and Research: An Anaclitic Depression," *Psychiatry*, November 1980, p. 284.

43. Carol Tavris, "You Are What You Do," *Prime Time*, November 1980, p. 47.

44. Bergin, "Therapist-Induced Deterioration in Psychotherapy," *op. cit.*

45. Michael Scriven quoted by Allen Bergin, "Psychotherapy Can Be Dangerous," *Psychology Today*, November 1975, p. 96.

46. Michael Scriven, letter on file.

47. Martin and Deidre Bobgan. *The Psychological Way/The Spiritual Way*. (Minneapolis: Bethany House Publishers, 1979), pp. 21-23.

48. Dorothy Tennov. *Psychotherapy: The Hazardous Cure*. (New York: Abelard-Schuman, 1975), p. 83.

49. Allen E. Bergin, "Negative Effects Revisited: A Reply," *Professional Psychology*, February 1980, p. 97.

50. "Skeptical Eye," *Discover*, December 1983, p. 8.

51. Robert Rosenthal. *Experimenter Effects in Behavioral Research*. (New York: Appleton-Century-Crofts, 1966), p. viii.

52. Bergin and Lambert, *op. cit.*, p. 180.

53. Bergin, "Therapist-Induced Deterioration in Psychotherapy," *op. cit.*

54. Truax and Mitchell quoted by Sol Garfield, "Psychotherapy Training and Outcome in Psychotherapy," BMA Audio Cassette /T-305 (New York: Guilford Publishers, Inc., 1979).

55. Bernie Zilbergeld. *The Shrinking of America*. (Boston: Little, Brown and Company, 1983), p. 190.

56. Ruth G. Matarazzo, "Research on the Teaching and Learning of Psychotherapeutic Skills," *Handbook of Psychotherapy and Behavior Change*, Allen Bergin and Sol Garfield, eds. (New York: John Wiley & Sons, 1971), p. 915.

57. Strupp, Hadley, Gomes-Schwartz, *op. cit.*, p. 66.

58. Richard L. Bednar and Jeffrey G. Shapiro, "Professional Research Commitment: A Sympton or a Syndrome," *Journal of Consulting and Clinical Psychology*, Vol. 34, 1970, pp. 323-326.

59. Arthur Shapiro, "Opening Comments," *Psychotherapy Research*, Janet B. W. Williams and Robert L. Spitzer, eds. (New York: The Guilford Press, 1984), p. 107.

60. J. Richard Greenwell, "Human Nature," *Science Digest*, April 1982, p. 42.

61. Morris Parloff quoted by Daniel Goleman, "Deadlines for Change," *Psychology Today*, August 1981, p. 69.

62. George Miller quoted by Elizabeth Hall, "Giving Away Psychology in the '80's," *Psychology Today*, January 1980, p. 46.

63. David Myers, "The Psychology of ESP," *Science Digest*, August 1981, p. 19.

64. David Myers. *The Inflated Self*. (New York: The Seabury Press, 1980), p. 136.

65. Allan Fromme interviewed by Elain Warren, "Most Neurotics Don't Need Therapy," *Los Angeles Herald Examiner*, 4 June 1981, p. C-6.

66. Myers, *The Inflated Self*, *op. cit.*, p. 136.

Chapter Fourteen: IS PSYCHOTHERAPY A PALLIATIVE?

1. Ruth Matarazzo, "Research on the Teaching and Learning of Psychotherapeutic Skills," *Handbook of Psychotherapy and Behavior Change*, Allen Bergin and Sol Garfield, eds. (New York: John Wiley & Sons, 1971) p. 911.

2. Ernest Havemann, "Alternatives to Analysis," *Playboy*, November 1969, p. 214.

3. Truax and Mitchell quoted by Sol Garfield, "Psychotherapy Training and Outcome in Psychotherapy," BMA Audio Cassette /T-305 (New York: Guilford Publishers, Inc., 1979).

4. Morris Parloff, "Psychotherapy and Research: An Anaclitic Depression," *Psychiatry*, November 1980, p. 288.

5. Joseph Durlak, "Comparative Effectiveness of Paraprofessional and Professional Helpers," *Psychological Bulletin* 86, 1979, pp. 80-92.

6. Jerome Frank, "Mental Health in a Fragmented Society: The Shattered Chrystal Ball," *American Journal of Orthopsychiatry*, July 1979, p. 406.

7. Hans H. Strupp and Suzanne W. Hadley, "Specific vs Nonspecific Factors in Psychotherapy," *Archives of General Psychiatry*, September 1979, p. 1126.

8. Allen E. Bergin and Michael J. Lambert, "The Evaluation of Therapeutic Outcomes," *Handbook of Psychotherapy and Behavior Change*, 2nd Ed., Sol Garfield and Allen Bergin, eds. (New York: John Wiley & Sons, 1978), p. 149.

9. Jerome Frank quoted by Bergin and Lambert, *ibid.*, p. 149.

10. Gurin et al quoted by Bergin and Lambert, *ibid.*, p. 149.

11. Bergin and Lambert, *ibid.*, p. 149.

12. Parloff, *op. cit.*, p. 287.

13. *Ibid.*, p. 288.

14. "Talk Is as Good as a Pill," *Time*, 26 May 1986, p. 60.

15. Sally Squires, "Should You Keep Your Therapist?" *American Health*, June 1986, p. 74.

16. Allen Bergin,"Psychotherapy and Religious Values," *Journal of Consulting and Clinical Psychology*, Vol 48, pp. 97-98.

17. M. L. Smith, G. V. Glass, and T. I. Miller. *The Benefits of Psychotherapy*. (Baltimore: Johns Hopkins University Press, 1980.)

18. Eugene Gendlin. *Focusing*. (New York: Everest House, 1978), p. 6.

19. Donald Klein, "Specificity and Strategy in Psychotherapy," *Psychotherapy Research*, Janet B. W. Williams and Robert L. Spitzer, eds. (New York: The Guilford Press, 1984), p. 308.

20. *Ibid.*, p. 313.

21. Joseph Wortis, "General Discussion," *Psychotherapy Research*, *op. cit.*, p. 394.

22. James W. Pennebaker quoted by Kimberly French, "Truth's Healthy Consequences," *New Age Journal*, November 1985, p. 60.

23. Robert Spitzer, "General Discussion," *Psychotherapy Research*, *op. cit.*, p 396.

24. E. Fuller Torrey, "The Case for the Indigenous Therapist," *Archives of General Psychiatry*, Vol. 20, March 1969, p. 367.

25. R. Bruce Sloane et al. *Psychotherapy Versus Behavior Therapy*. (Cambridge: Harvard University Press, 1975), p. 225.

26. Jerome Frank. *Persuasion and Healing*. (New York: Schocken Books, 1961, 1974 ed.), p. 167.

27. Bergin, "Psychotherapy and Religious Values," *op. cit.*, p. 98.

28. Lewis Thomas, "Medicine Without Science," *The Atlantic Monthly*, April 1981, p. 42.

29. James Fallows, "The Case Against Credentialism," *The Atlantic Monthly*, December 1985, p. 65.

30. Frank, "Mental Health in a Fragmented Society," *op. cit.*, p. 404.

31. Bergin and Lambert, *op. cit.*, p. 180.

32. Bryce Nelson, "Cultural Changes Impact on Course of Psychotherapy," *The Dallas Morning News*, 31 March 1983, p. 1C.

33. Jay Haley. *Strategies of Psychotherapy*. (New York: Grune & Stratton, Inc., 1963), p. 69.

34. Frank, *Persuasion and Healing*, *op. cit.*, p. 161.

35. Matarazzo, *op. cit.*, p. 960.

36. Hans J. Eysenck, "Psychotherapy, Behavior Therapy, and the Outcome Problem," BMA Audio Cassette /T-308 (New York: Guilford Publications, Inc., 1979).

37. E. Fuller Torrey. *Witchdoctors and Psychiatrists*. (New York: Harper & Row, Publishers, 1986), p. 198.

Chapter Fifteen: IS PSYCHOTHERAPY A PLACEBO?

1. Arthur Shapiro interview by Martin Gross. *The Psychological Society*. (New York: Random House, 1978), p. 230.

2. Hans Eysenck, "The Effectiveness of Psychotherapy: The Specter at the Feast," *The Behavioral and Brain Sciences*, June 1983, p. 290.

3. Lewis Thomas, "Medicine Without Science," *The Atlantic Monthly*, April 1981, p. 41.

4. William S. Kroger. *Clinical and Experimental Hypnosis*, 2nd Ed. (Philadelphia: J. B. Lippincott Company, 1977), p. 137.

5. *Ibid.*, p. 136.

6. Thomas Kiernan. *Shrinks, Etc.* (New York: Dial Press, 1974), p. 255.

7. Leonard White, Bernard Tursky, and Gary E. Schwartz. *Placebo: Theory, Research, and Mechanisms*. (New York: The Guilford Press, 1985), p. 204.

8. *Ibid.*, pp. 204-205.

9. V. Jane Knox et al, "Subject Expectancy and the Reduction of Cold Pressor Pain with Acupuncture and Placebo Acupuncture," *Psychosomatic Medicine*, October 1979, pp. 483, 485.

10. "False Feedback Eases Symptoms," *Brain/Mind Bulletin*, 16 June 1980, pp. 1-2.

11. "Biofeedback Helps by Deception," *Psychology Today*, April 1981, p. 30.

12. Christopher Cory,"Cooling by Deception," *Psychology Today*, June 1980, p. 20.

13. John S. Gillis, "The Therapist as Manipulator," *Psychology Today*, December 1974, p. 91.

14. *Ibid.*, p. 92.

15. Leslie Prioleau, Martha Murdock, and Nathan Brody, "An Analysis of Psychotherapy Versus Placebo Studies," *The Behavioral and Brain Sciences*, June 1983, p. 284.

16. Arthur Shapiro, "Opening Comments," *Psychotherapy Research*, Janet B. W. Williams and Robert L. Spitzer, eds. (New York: The Guilford Press, 1984), p. 106.

17. *Ibid.*, p. 107.

Chapter Sixteen: The Emperor's New Clothes.

1. Howard Kendler in *Autobiographies in Experimental Psychology*. Ronald Gandelman, ed. (Hillsdale, NJ: Lawrence Erlbaum, 1985), p. 46.

2. Allen E. Bergin and Michael J. Lambert, "The Evaluation of Therapeutic Outcomes," *Handbook of Psychotherapy and Behavior Change*, 2nd Ed. Sol Garfield and Allen Bergin, eds. (New York: John Wiley & Sons, 1978), p. 170.

3. Ursula Vils, "Professor Helps Play Bubble to the Surface," *Los Angeles Times*, 10 September 1981, Part V, pp. 1, 15.

4. Ronald L. Koteskey, "Abandoning the Psyche to Secular Treatment," *Christianity Today*, 29 June 1979, p. 20.

5. Anne Rosenfeld, "Depression: Dispelling Despair," *Psychology Today*, June 1985, p. 32.

6. Frances Adeney, "The Flowering of the Human Potential Movement," *Spiritual Counterfeits Project Journal*, Vol. 5, No. 1, Winter 1981-1982, p. 17.

7. Aristides, "What Is Vulgar?" *The American Scholar*, Winter 1981-1982, p. 21.

8. Alexander W. Astin, "The Functional Autonomy of Psychotherapy," *The Investigation of Psychotherapy: Commentaries and Readings*. Arnold P. Goldstein and Sanford J. Dean, eds. (New York: John Wiley, 1966), p. 62.
9. *Ibid.*, p. 65.
10. Bernie Zilbergeld, "Psychabuse." *Science 86*, June 1986, p. 52.
11. Dr. Lawrence LeShan. Association for Humanistic Psychology, October 1984, p. 4.
12. Hans Christian Andersen. *The Emperor's New Clothes*. (New York: Golden Press).
13. Thomas Szasz, "Nobody Should Decide Who Goes to the Mental Hospital," *Co-Evolution Quarterly*, Summer 1978, p. 60.

Part Five: THE PSYCHOLOGICAL WAY OR THE SPIRITUAL WAY?
1. Jay E. Adams. *The Use of the Scriptures in Counseling*. (Grand Rapids: Baker Book House, 1975), p. 15.

Chapter Eighteen: BEYOND COUNSELING.
1. Michael A. Wallach and Lise Wallach. *Psychology's Sanction for Selfishness*. (San Francisco: W. H. Freeman and Company, 1983) p. ix.
2. *Ibid.*, p. 11.
3. Edward E. Sampson, "Psychology and the American Ideal," *Journal of Personality and Social Psychology*, Vol. 35 (767-782), November 1977, p. 770.
4. Wallach, *op. cit.*, p. 14.
5. *Ibid.*, p. 14.
6. *Ibid.*, p. 31.
7. Karen Horney. *The Neurotic Personality of Our Time*. (New York: Norton, 1937), p. 92.
8. Carl Rogers. *On Becoming a Person* (Boston: Houghton Mifflin, 1961), p. 119.
9. Carl Rogers, "Toward a Modern Approach to Values: The Valuing Process in the Mature Person," *Person to Person: The Problem of Being Human*, C. Rogers and B. Stevens, eds. (New York: Pocket Books, 1971), p. 23.
10. Wallach, *op. cit.*, pp. 17-18.
11. Kenneth Vaux, "How Do I Love Me?" *Christianity Today*, 20 September 1985, p. 25.